Welcome to the EVERYTHING® series!

W9-AKQ-553

These handy, accessible books give you all you need to tackle a difficult project, gain a new hobby, comprehend a fascinating topic, prepare for an exam, or even brush up on something you learned back in school but have since forgotten.

You can read an *EVERYTHING*® book from cover to cover or just pick out the information you want from the five useful boxes in this book: e-facts, e-questions, e-profiles, verses and psalms, and quotes. We literally give you everything you need to know on the subject, but we throw in a lot of fun stuff along the way, too.

We now have well over 100 *EVERYTHING*® books in print, spanning such wide-ranging topics as weddings, pregnancy, wine, learning guitar, one-pot cooking, managing people, and so much more. When you're done reading them all, you can finally say you know *EVERYTHING*®!

E-FACTS

Important sound bytes of information

Provides the answers to questions you may have

Descriptions of important people in saints' lives

Excerpts of verses and psalms by and about saints

Quotes by and about saints

THE
EVERYTHING®

SAINTS BOOK

Discover the lives
of the saints
throughout history

Ruth Rejnis

Adams Media Corporation
Avon, Massachusetts

For Carolyn Janik, dear friend

Copyright ©2001, Adams Media Corporation.
All rights reserved. This book, or parts thereof, may not be reproduced
in any form without permission from the publisher; exceptions
are made for brief excerpts used in published reviews.

An Everything® Series Book.
Everything® is a registered trademark of Adams Media Corporation.

Published by Adams Media Corporation
57 Littlefield Street, Avon, MA 02322
www.adamsmedia.com

ISBN: 1-58062-534-7
Printed in the United States of America.

J I H G F E D C B A

Library of Congress Cataloging-in-Publication Data
The everything saints book
p.   cm.
ISBN 1-58062-534-7
1. Christian saints–Biography.
BX4655.2 .E94   2001
282'.092'2–dc21
[B]   2001022612

This publication is designed to provide accurate and authoritative information with regard to the subject
matter covered. It is sold with the understanding that the publisher is not engaged in rendering legal,
accounting, or other professional advice. If legal advice or other expert assistance is required, the services of a competent professional person should be sought.
—From a *Declaration of Principles* jointly adopted by a Committee of the
American Bar Association and a Committee of Publishers and Associations

Illustrations by Barry Littmann and Michelle Dorenkamp.

This book is available at quantity discounts for bulk purchases.
For information, call 1-800-872-5627.

Visit the entire Everything® series at everything.com

Contents

INTRODUCTION **Why We Need the Saints** . . IX

"Saints Alive!" v

The Saint Beside You x

Their Relevance Today x

Boring? Uh-Uh! xii

Taste and Temperament xiv

The Extras xvi

Enjoy! xviii

PART I
SOME BEST KNOWN AND LOVED SAINTS / 1

CHAPTER 1 **Mary, Mother of Jesus** 2

Early Days 3

Marian Devotion 4

Beliefs 5

Seeing Mary 6

CHAPTER 2 **St. Joseph** 8

Betrothed 8

A Worker's Household 9

A Rise in Devotion 11

CHAPTER 3 **Sts. Anne and Joachim** 12

A Grandparents' Garden 12

A Role for Today 13

CHAPTER 4 **St. Anthony of Padua** 14

The Case of the Missing Money 14

Why Lost Objects? 16

Becoming a Franciscan 16

CHAPTER 5 **St. Augustine of Hippo** 18

The World Stage 18

An Explorer 19

A Religious Life 22

The *Confessions* and Other Writings . 23

Legacy 24

Final Days 25

CHAPTER 6 **St. Catherine of Siena** 27

In a Secret Cell 27

A Public Role 29

CHAPTER 7 **St. Francis of Assisi** 32

A Bon Vivant 32

Starting Small 33

The Missionary 34

One with Nature 35

Approaching the End 36

CHAPTER 8 **St. Francis Xavier** 39

Among the First Jesuits 39

Man of the People 41

CHAPTER 9 **The Gospel Writers** 43

The Gospels 43

St. Matthew 44

St. Mark 45

St. Luke 46

St. John 47

CHAPTER 10 **St. Ignatius of Loyola** 49

In Spain 49

The Beginning 50

The *Exercises* 51
From "Older" Student to Missionary . 51
Obedience? 53
Staying Home 54

CHAPTER 11 **St. Joan of Arc** **56**
A Country at War 57
Visions and Voices 58
In Battle 59
The Tide Turns 61
The Transcript 62

CHAPTER 12 **St. John of the Cross** **63**
Holy Orders 64
Conflict from Within 64
Writings from the Soul 65

CHAPTER 13 **St. John the Baptist** **66**
The Baptism 66
The Martyr 67

CHAPTER 14 **St. Jude** **68**
Not Desperate, Just Impossible 69
Answered Prayers 70

CHAPTER 15 **St. Mary Magdalene** 72
Witness 73
Change in the Air 74

CHAPTER 16 **St. Nicholas of Myra** 75
A Pious Activist 75
A Popular Patron 77
Saint to Santa 77
True Gift Giving 78
Relics in Bari 79

CHAPTER 17 **St. Patrick** **80**
Saints Galore 80
The Farthest Reaches 81
Enslavement 82
Travels 83
Who *Was* Patrick? 86
About Those Snakes 86

CHAPTER 18 **St. Paul of Tarsus** **88**
The Missionary 89
Travels 90

CHAPTER 19 **St. Peter** **92**
Early Years 93
The Passion 94
The Early Church 95

CHAPTER 20 **St. Teresa of Ávila** **97**
Life as a Carmelite 98
Mystic and Writer 100
Tough Times 101

CHAPTER 21 **St. Thérèse of Lisieux** 103
Asked to Write 104

CHAPTER 22 **St. Thomas Aquinas** 107
Family Kidnapping 107
The Student 108
The Magnum Opus 108
Gentle Genius 110

CHAPTER 23 **St. Thomas More** 112
Utopia 114
The Problem 115
The Scaffold 115

CHAPTER 24 **St. Valentine** 118

    The Two Valentines 119

    Celebration 119

    Love Notes 120

CHAPTER 25 **St. Vincent de Paul** 121

    Upwardly Mobile 121

    Setting the Standard 122

    Founding Orders 123

PART II
AMERICAN SAINTS: GROWING IN NUMBERS / 125

CHAPTER 26 **St. Elizabeth Ann Seton** . . 126

    The Anglican Elizabeth 127

    Clouds on the Horizon 128

    An Answer 129

    Another Loss 130

    Serenity 131

CHAPTER 27 **St. John Nepomucene Neumann** 132

CHAPTER 28 **St. Frances Xavier Cabrini** . . 135

CHAPTER 29 **St. Rose Philippine Duchesne** 138

CHAPTER 30 **St. Katharine Drexel** 139

    The Heiress 139

    Katharine's Choice 140

    Making a Difference 142

    Special Acclaim 143

    Her Miracles 144

CHAPTER 31 **Bl. Damien of Molokai** 145

    European Roots 145

    The Outpost 146

    Damien Sets Sail 147

    Controversy 147

    Road to Sainthood 148

CHAPTER 32 **Bl. Junípero Serra** 150

    The Other California Missions 151

    In Question 152

CHAPTER 33 **Bl. Kateri Tekakwitha** 153

CHAPTER 34 **Bl. Theodore Guerin** 154

PART III
MARTYRS, MORE SAINTS, AND SHRINES / 155

CHAPTER 35 **The Horrible Fates of Early Martyrs** 156

    The Making of a Martyr 157

    Giving Their Lives 159

CHAPTER 36 **How the Veneration of Saints Grew** 166

    The Confessors 166

    Virgins and Ascetics 166

    Saint Who? 168

    Getting Organized 169

    Going Overboard 170

    Back to Reason, and Sensible Veneration 171

    The Rise of Patron Saints 171

CHAPTER 37 **Later Saints, Martyred and Otherwise** 173

St. Jerome 173
St. Simeon Stylites 176
St. Gregory I (the Great) 177
St. Hildegard of Bingen 178
St. Thomas à Becket 179
St. Elizabeth of Hungary 181
St. Francis de Sales 182
St. Isaac Jogues 185
St. Alphonsus Liguori 186

CHAPTER 38 **Shrines and Other Saintly Stops** 190

Shrines, Cathedrals, and Basilicas . 190
Shrines in the United States 191
Shrines in Canada 196
Shrines in Mexico 198
Shrines in Europe 199

PART IV
THE MAKING OF A SAINT / 207

CHAPTER 39 **How the Canonization Process Works** 208

Formalization 208
A Global Process 208
Advancing the Cause 209
The Slightly Faster Track 211
The Miracle Requirement 212
When a Cause Holds Up 213
Wanted: People Like Us 213

CHAPTER 40 **Waiting to Be Tapped for Sainthood** 216

Bl. Padre Pio 216
Mother Teresa of Calcutta 218
Pope John XXIII 220
Pope Pius XII 222
Dorothy Day 224
Archbishop Fulton J. Sheen 229

CHAPTER 41 **Disappearing Saints: Whatever Happened to . . . ?** . . 232

St. Barbara 232
St. Catherine of Alexandria 233
St. Christopher 234
St. Julian the Innkeeper 235
St. Philomena 237

APPENDIX A **Saintly Lives in Historical Context** 239

APPENDIX B **Doctors of the Church** 246

APPENDIX C **Calendar of Saints' Feast Days** . . 247

APPENDIX D **On the Job: Saints by Occupations** 251

APPENDIX E **Patriotic Saints: For Nations, Cities, and Regions** 264

GLOSSARY 272

INDEX 278

Why We Need the Saints

"Saints Alive!"

"She has the patience of a saint."

"Well, I'm no saint, but . . . "

"That guy has got to be the patron saint of hypochondriacs!"

How often have you heard those words, or voiced them yourself?

Or maybe over the years you briefly thought about particular saints—say when you were at Central High your archrival on the basketball court was St. Charles Borromeo High School across town. From time to time you might have wondered who Charles Borromeo was.

Or you may have been watching television the morning of May 23, 1994, to see coverage of the funeral for Jacqueline Kennedy Onassis at St. Ignatius Loyola Church on Park Avenue in Manhattan. In searching for words to fill their narrative for a couple of hours—since the cameras were not allowed inside the church—did any of the newscasters think to explain in a sentence or two who Ignatius of Loyola was? Too bad, you'd like to have known.

Mock all and sundry, but leave the saints alone.

—OLD ITALIAN SAYING

How about St. Patrick's Day? We think we know at least a little about that saint and the snakes and the shamrocks, and we're always eager to celebrate March 17. Do you have any idea who Patrick was, even as you toast him and wish "Happy St. Paddy's Day" to folks around you and wear green that day? Was he a king? A missionary? A chieftain? A landowner? You're not sure.

Over the years specific saints, and certainly the general concept of sainthood, have probably touched your life countless times in one context or another.

E-QUESTIONS?

What is a saint?
Saint comes from the Latin *sanctus,* which means "holy." St. Paul of Tarsus first used the term to mean all of the Christian faithful. According to the Roman Catholic Church, which conducts the **canonization** process, the saints occupy a hallowed place in heaven in the presence of the Beatific Vision. The church offers the saints to the faithful as models of virtue.

The Saint Beside You

Before exploring those canonized from the distant past and recent years, you should know—indeed maybe you're already aware—that living, breathing saints are all around us. And there are many saints who've died and will never be formally canonized. Qualities for sainthood are not common, true, but they are not that rare, either, as you will see in reading the pages that follow. No doubt there is someone in your life or in your community who seems to you a living saint, with many of the qualities of some of the canonized men and women coming up.

Their Relevance Today

We need these saints, even in the fast-paced, presumably sophisticated times we live in today. Or *especially* in these times.

We know what "being good" means, or we're pretty certain we do, but the saints have shown us. Most of us concede we'll never, ever lead a life *that* exemplary; but the more the saints have been through, the more their lives teach us courage in our own trials. Their stories tell of perseverance and faith, and they especially show us true charity, inspiring us to reach a little higher and lead fuller, richer lives.

On the one hand we must never imagine that our own unaided efforts can be relied on to carry us even through the next 24 hours as "decent" people. If He does not support us, not one of us is safe from some gross sin. On the other hand, no possible degree of holiness or heroism which has ever been recorded of the greatest saints is beyond what He is determined to produce in every one of us in the end. The job will not be completed in this life; but He means to get us as far as possible before death.
—C. S. LEWIS (1898–1963), *MERE CHRISTIANITY* (TOUCHSTONE, 1980)

We need the saints, too, because they define sanctity. Otherwise sanctity becomes an amorphous concept difficult to grasp. Attach it to a specific saint, though, and we nod and think "Ah, I see what you mean."

In the 1960s, Vatican Council II, a **conclave** in Rome of cardinals and other Roman Catholic Church dignitaries redefined saints and the way they affect the faithful. Vatican II said that the relationship between saints and the living was one of "communion and solidarity," and not of "supplicant and benefactor." Saints, the council added, offered an "example in their way of life, fellowship in their communion and aid by their intercession."

That "intercession" helps the rest of us enormously. Saints, exalted as they are, can still appear very human and, because of that, approachable with our prayers. The church says that's fine. However, we are cautioned to ask saints only to *intercede* for us with God, to more or less act as our agent. It is God who grants the favors, not the saints.

Those are the serious reasons we need saints. Here is a minor example of how they fit smoothly into the twenty-first century: St. Isidore of Seville is now considered the patron saint of Internet users, his cause having been promoted by Spanish computer buffs. Here is a man who lived in the sixth and seventh centuries. He would certainly be awestruck at today's technology. Can you imagine his delight sitting at a computer and seeing what it can do?

St. Isidore of Seville (ca. 560–636)

St. Isidore of Seville

Born to a noble family in Cartagena, Spain, Isidore succeeded his brother as bishop of Seville. He was considered the most learned man of his era, from antiquity to the Middle Ages.

His mission was to spread a uniform and literate Catholicism. In that regard—and here is what has made him patron saint of Internet users—he compiled a multivolume encyclopedia of all knowledge, including, of course, theology—a sort of Middle Ages database. He is responsible for other impressive works, including *History of the Kings of the Goths, Vandals and Sueves* (all Germanic tribes), still a source for the history of Spain, a book on astronomy, and a writing detailing the lives of every great man and woman mentioned in the Bible. Known also as "the Schoolmaster of the Middle Ages," Isidore founded schools throughout Spain.

Isidore loved to give to the poor. It is said that toward the end of his life it was impossible to get into his house, because it was so crowded with beggars and others in need. St. Isidore's feast day is April 4, and he is a Doctor of the Church.

E-FACTS

Some 33 saints have also been given the title **Doctor of the Church,** reserved for those whose life and works make them pre-eminent teachers of the faith. In the stories of specific saints' lives, we will note who carries this title. Appendix B lists all of the Doctors of the Church.

Boring? Uh-Uh!

Okay, you may say, they're good people and they're relevant. But with all that praying and good works, the saints must be, well, a bit on the dull side, right?

Wrong. The canonized are an absolutely fascinating assortment of men and women—with the accent on *assortment.* No two are the same, just as it is with the rest of us. All that these men and women seem to have in common is their canonization and probably their strong faith.

Many led exciting, even dangerous lives. They battled evil people, corrupt governments, bureaucratic processes, savage seas, and persecution. Sometimes, they died for their belief. Some knew what it was to be alone in a foreign, at times inhospitable, country. A few were what we might today call dissidents, which made life even harder for them. Some committed crimes—Moses the Ethiopian, for one, organized a band of thieves—before they saw the light. None of their missteps mattered, however, to the church that ultimately canonized them. Their assets far outweighed their debits.

> It is easier to make a saint out of a libertine than out of a prig.
> —GEORGE SANTAYANA, *THE LIFE OF REASON: REASON IN RELIGION*, 1905

Saints can be tall like Teresa of Ávila, or short like John of the Cross, who was about 5 feet 2 inches in height, or Ignatius Loyola who was about the same.

They can have white, black, brown, yellow, red, or olive skin.

Some were born aristocrats; a few were kings. The rest fall mostly into what today would be called the middle-income range, although there were those who lived at the poverty level, too.

What is a plaster saint?
A **plaster saint** is a person without human feelings or failings.

True, most were single and belonged to religious orders, but Elizabeth Ann Seton, the first American-born saint, was married and had five children. St. Bridget of Sweden had eight (which might have been enough to canonize her right there).

Intriguing Differences

Heaven knows saints can be offbeat, too. Benedict, who went on to found a major religious order, lived in an underground cave for several years, and Anthony of Egypt called a cemetery home for a while. When

St. Benedict

it comes to giving up things for Lent, the twelfth-century Morand would probably beat the rest of us: he lived through that 40 days eating nothing more than a bunch of grapes.

But the prize for bizarre must go to Simeon Stylites, a hermit *who lived on top of a pillar for 37 years!* It was just six feet in diameter. He was a holy and respected man, with people, even noblemen, coming from miles to hear him preach. (Men only, though. Women were not allowed into his enclosure.)

Some saints spent a lifetime no farther away from home than a local convent or monastery. Others—Francis Xavier, for example—were missionaries who traveled great distances, to places that had sometimes been unknown to them and their countrymen. A few, like Isaac Jogues, were martyred for their faith far from home.

Did the saints walk about praying all the time, eyes in a missal or gazing heavenward? A few were contemplatives and spent their days in prayer and physical labor around the monastery or convent. But most of the holy people you will read about here went out into the world to change it for the better. Many of them also wrote books and essays, gospels and epistles, that are still read and discussed today. Incidentally, a few were functionally illiterate and dictated their words to be put on paper.

E-QUESTIONS?

What is a hagiography?
A **hagiography** is a biography of a saint, sometimes an idealizing one.

Taste and Temperament

In that they also loved the good things in life, saints were very human. Francis of Assisi had a serious sweet tooth; Jerome played the fiddle; Joan of Arc loved horses; Vincent de Paul was a ventriloquist, John Bosco an acrobat, and Charles Borromeo a top chess player. It is said Thomas Aquinas usually had an open bag of peanuts by his side.

Saints had their physical frailties just like us. Teresa of Avilá suffered from headaches. Thérèse of Lisieux, the "Little Flower," endured

St. Camillus de Lellis

tuberculosis for much of her short life. Ignatius of Loyola and Camillus de Lellis limped. The Venerable Bede had asthma.

In their youth some caused their parents no amount of grief, just like some kids today. When her mother and father said no to her wish to enter a convent, the beautiful Catherine of Siena cut off her long blond hair and her parents placed her under house arrest.

Francis of Assisi's father called him a madman to everyone in town when Francis began to strip himself of his worldly goods to help the poor and sick.

It's a good thing being good-natured, or at least serene, is not a requirement for **canonization**. In his own words, Vincent de Paul considered himself "of a bilious temperament and frequently subject to anger." Paul of Tarsus seemed to have difficulty getting along with some people some of the time. And the fiddle-playing Jerome was what might politely be called feisty, always ready to get into a fight for what he considered a righteous cause.

E-FACTS

There are more than 10,000 saints of the Roman Catholic Church. The exact number cannot be calculated, one reason being that some saints were named as part of a group, for example, as in the case of early Christian martyrs. Individual names were not noted or were unknown.

Thérèse of Lisieux was, however, a sweet soul who made it a point to get along with everyone. Once a nun praying next to her was rattling her rosary beads enough to annoy even the already saintly Thérèse. But would she say what we probably would?—"Pssst, do you *mind!*" No, in her head she put the racket to music, letting it serve as a backdrop to her prayers.

All of the saints showed charity and mercy to those they served—the poor, the sick, prisoners, and so on. The unfortunate and needy did not have to suffer ill humor from those ministering to them. In fact, the saints were surprisingly cheerful, given all that many of them had to endure.

As the witty Teresa of Avilá put it back in the sixteenth century: "From silly devotions and from sour-faced saints, good Lord, deliver us."

> There is a kind of reticence about the saints, like the reticence of the Lord himself, and it is this that makes them able to do God's work and to speak his word, without making people feel threatened or "got at" by them, without crushing the bruised reed or extinguishing the smouldering wick.
> —SIMON TUGWELL, BRITISH MEMBER OF THE DOMINICAN ORDER

There are saints who died tragically young, and others who lived to be over 100. Some died of illness or accident; far too many died horrible deaths as martyrs.

So in many ways the saints were just like us (aside from the martyrdom). They would have to be like us, if you think about it. Otherwise, what's the point? If we are to learn from them and their lives—and we are supposed to—we have to be able to identify with their foibles, lapses, and uncertainties, even if their piety seems several notches above our own.

The Extras

Yet if the saints were such a mixed bag in the sense of their life's work, disposition, and so on, what exactly qualified them for sainthood?

Chapter 39 explains the path to canonization. Suffice it to say here that what made them different was their strong faith and love of God. Even when buffeted by bad fortune, illness, imprisonment, misunderstanding, fatigue, and all of the other life problems that drain the rest of us, they remained steadfast, not questioning God but continuing to praise him. If they did have a pang of "Why me, Lord?" it passed quickly. To the saints, the bad days would end in God's good time, and they sought only to go on loving and serving him, whatever his will for them.

While the saints were alike in important areas, a few did have elements, you might say, in their lives that made them quite different from us.

Take **mysticism**. This is the belief that personal communication or a union with God is achieved through intuition, faith, or a sudden insight, rather than through plain old rational thought or reasoning. Several of the saints you will read about in the pages that follow were mystics—John of the Cross and Hildegard of Bingen, just to mention two—and left behind a body of work in print that endures today.

Some saints experienced **ecstasy**, which can be defined in this context as an overwhelming emotion, of being in a state of rapture. They may have experienced visions, too. While in states of ecstasy, saints have levitated—lifted off the ground for a short time, often in full view of others.

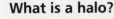

What is a halo?
A **halo** is a ring or circle of light around the head of a holy person in an artistic depiction. The Greeks and Romans used halos to depict association with the gods. Early Christians took up the practice, with the halo meaning light and used for Jesus Christ. Around the fifth century, the halo's use in art extended to Jesus' mother, Mary, and to the saints.

After coming out of those trances, some wrote of their experiences. Today we might call those writings, and many of the prayers to God by both men and women, a bit over the top. But centuries ago florid prose by the educated, especially members of religious orders, was common. They took their faith seriously, especially worship and penance for sins real or, it may seem to us, imagined. Wearing a hair shirt, which Thomas More did as recently as the sixteenth century, and practicing the most severe austerities was not unknown. As we move back in time to the centuries just after the Crucifixion, all of this becomes even more common among the pious, who were closer in time to the life of Jesus and eager to emulate him, if not by crucifixion then by other severe means.

A very, very small number of saints have experienced **stigmata**. That is, bodily marks resembling those Jesus suffered on the cross— nails in each hand, in the crossed feet, and a wound in the side from being pierced with a spear. Sometimes the marks were not visible to the public, but a person did feel pain in those areas. Padre Pio, a modern-day Italian priest who is on the road to canonization (and whom you will read more about in Chapter 40), endured the stigmata for years and sometimes took to wearing gloves with the fingers cut out to hide the wounds on his hands. (The church rarely accepts the stigmata as authentic and makes no attempt to explain its origin, so individuals and institutions can define it any way they want, in physical, psychological, or religious terms.)

E-FACTS

Padre Pio carries the title "Blessed," which is given to those who are just a step away from canonization. The abbreviation "Bl." will be used in these pages to denote those with that standing.

Enjoy!

If you're new to saint watching, you're likely to find the rest of this book particularly engrossing. Even if you're somewhat knowledgeable about these holy people, you are bound to find some new ingredient in the lives of your favorites, or learn about saints you never heard of before.

This book is certainly not a work of theology or of scholarship. It is instead an introduction to several dozen saints and a look at their life and times. They were real people who have affected and will continue to affect many lives, including, perhaps, your own. One or two of them will maybe catch your fancy, to become favorites you can turn to for the rest of your life. You don't have to be of any particular religion, or of any faith at all for that matter, to pray to the saints. They're equal opportunity listeners!

Here, then, are saints of the Roman Catholic Church, although Eastern Orthodox Christians and several Protestant denominations recognize some of these holy people as well.

At the end of the chapters that follow, books or videos will occasionally be mentioned that will tell more about a particular man or woman or about the broad topic of saints. Where applicable, there will also be a Web site with information you can use. Here are some suggestions that go along with this chapter.

Suggested Additional Reading:

The HarperCollins Encyclopedia of Catholicism edited by Richard P. McBrien, 1995. This is a 1,300-plus-page illustrated guide to everything Catholic, including some saints' biographies.

"The New Dictionary of Your Favorite Saints," "Saints You Can Count On," "Saints We Need Every Day," and "Saints Who Worked Miracles" are 28-page booklets available for $1 apiece, plus a stamped self-addressed envelope, from *Catholic Digest*, Dept. XS-1, St. Paul Square, P. O. Box 64090, St. Paul, Minnesota 55164.

Saint Watching by Phyllis McGinley (Viking, 1969). A Pulitzer Prize–winning poet discusses some saints who intrigue her in an insightful and amusing manner. This marvelous book is out of print, but you might try a used-book store or perhaps your public library. It's worth the digging.

If you're online, here are some Web addresses for additional reading:

- *Catholic Online Saints and Angels* (*http://saints.catholic.org*) offers short biographies of several hundred saints.
- *Catholic Pages* features more information about saints, as well as any other topic about the church. The address is *www.catholic-pages.com*.

PART I

Some Best Known and Loved Saints

CHAPTER 1

Mary, Mother of Jesus
(First Century)

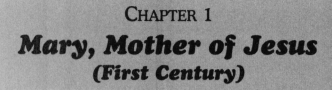

Mary is of course a saint. But we more often hear of "Saint" Mary with a few words following—St. Mary of the Lake, for example, in the name of a church or school, or Our Lady of Grace. In addition, hundreds of schools, churches, and other institutions do not carry her name specifically but rather are named after one of the events that defined her life: the Immaculate Conception or the Assumption.

Mary could be called the most important woman in history. She has certainly been the most honored and she is pre-eminent among the saints. Still, there is astonishingly little known about her life, and only a few words attributed to her (and of those, as you will see later, some were not truly her own expression).

E-FACTS

The flagship of Columbus's flotilla to the New World was the *Santa María*.

Early Days

Mary may have been the daughter of Anne and Joachim (see Chapter 3) and was betrothed to the carpenter Joseph in her teenage years. She was visited by the **archangel** Gabriel who, according to the gospel of Luke, said to her, "Hail, O favored one, the Lord is with you!" (An archangel is an angel of the highest order.) After calming her fears, he went on to tell her she would conceive and bear a son named Jesus, who would be called "the Son of the Most High."

Gabriel explained that she would conceive by the power of the Holy Spirit. With great faith Mary responded, "Let it be done to me according to your word."

"The Magnificat"

My soul magnifies the Lord and my spirit rejoices in God my Savior, because he has acknowledged his servant's humility. From now on all generations will call me blessed because the Almighty One has done great things for me! His mercy falls on every generation that fears him. With his powerful arm he has routed the proud of heart. He has pulled the princes from their thrones and exalted the humble. He has filled the hungry with good things and sent the rich away empty. He has come to help his servant Israel, remembering his mercy, in accordance with the promise he made to our fathers—to Abraham and his seed forever.

When she visited her cousin Elizabeth, who was pregnant at what the Bible says was an old age with her son who would be John the Baptist, Mary tells Elizabeth her news and goes on to offer the exultant prayer of praise known as "The Magnificat," which still holds an important place in church liturgy.

It is now believed that Mary did not create the Magnificat, which on reflection is far too sophisticated for a 15-year-old to have composed. It was probably written by St. Luke in his gospel or perhaps had its beginnings in a song composed by early Christians.

We hear little about or from Mary as Jesus grows up, even after he undertakes his public life at age 30. In upcoming chapters, you will read about those few brief references. But she is in evidence at the end of his life. Mary is at the foot of the cross at the Crucifixion, and Jesus asks his apostle John to look after her.

Knowing virtually nothing about an important historic figure allows each age to imbue him or her with the qualities and traits that are needed or admired at that time. It has been that way with Mary. In years past it was her apparent meekness and remove from her son's public life that was found to be appealing and right.

In later years, however, small details of her life have been interpreted in a new light. For example, after Jesus' ascension into heaven Mary was in Jerusalem where, with the rest of the small band of Christians, she waited for the coming of the Holy Spirit and the beginning of carrying Christ's message to the world. Now it is believed that Mary was part of the nucleus of the new community of believers and did not take a backseat in the movement of the new religion.

The wish to pray is a prayer in itself.
—GEORGE BERNANOS, *THE DIARY OF A COUNTRY PRIEST* (1936)

Marian Devotion

If little was said about the mother of Jesus during her lifetime, the millennia have since propelled her to a position right behind Jesus in interest, study, devotion, and the publication of millions of words. No other saint has had so much written about him or her, a compelling fact given that so little is known about Mary.

Written works keep evolving, with contemporary themes such as "how the Blessed Virgin applies to our lives today" and, as in the "upper room" example, "how women of today can identify with Mary."

Art has also contributed to the continuing interest in Mary, with hundreds of paintings and sculptures done by masters as well as by unknown artists. In churches and museums, these works have been widely reprinted for the public in books and magazines and also appear on television and the Internet.

Special Marian exercises—reciting the rosary, for one—also keep Mary prominent in church liturgy, as the faithful often ask her to intercede for them with Jesus in the hope that he will not deny his mother what she asks of him.

E-QUESTIONS?

What is a marian?
Marian is an adjective used to denote special reverence for Mary, in devotions and feasts. A Marian year, for example, is a 12-month period periodically set aside by popes as a time of renewed devotion to the Blessed Virgin. Marian feasts—the Assumption and the Immaculate Conception—honor Mary.

Beliefs

The church holds to four principal doctrines about the Blessed Mother. From the ancient world there is her virginity before, during, and after the birth of Christ, and her divine maternity that made her the mother of God. The Roman Catholic Church says it is important to realize that Mary does perform the miracles that constitute her doctrines, but not by her own power. She channels the power that comes from God.

Dating as recently as the nineteenth century is the third doctrine: the Immaculate Conception, which states that Mary was conceived without original sin. (The Immaculate Conception has often mistakenly been thought to refer to Jesus.) Finally, there is the Assumption, which was officially declared in the twentieth century. Here Mary was taken, body and soul, into heaven at the end of her years on Earth.

Special Days

Where and when Mary died is uncertain, although there has been a good deal of speculation. The apostle John is believed to have cared for her after the Crucifixion, but here too there is no agreement by religious scholars as to exactly how or where that occurred.

Several days commemorate Mary throughout the church year. Solemn occasions are January 1 for Mary, the Mother of God; the Annunciation on March 25; the Assumption on August 15; and the Immaculate Conception on December 8. A special feast day is the day of her birth, which is celebrated on September 8.

Under a variety of titles the Blessed Mother is patron saint for many nations (discussed in Appendix E).

Seeing Mary

Mary's name will crop up in the next few hundred pages in the context of those saints who have a special devotion to her and those who claim to have seen her in an apparition. Over the centuries these visions have also served to keep Mary alive in the minds and hearts of the faithful and have led writers to fill even more reams of paper about her.

What is an apparition?
An **apparition** is the inexplicable appearance of someone, usually an individual who is deceased.

There have been more apparitions of Mary than of any other saint, and even, if one keeps score, more than there have been of Jesus. According to some sources there have been around 20,000 appearances of Mary from the year A.D. 40 to the present. Few of them are sanctioned by the church.

In most apparitions the Virgin is a young woman with dark hair wearing a white garment trimmed in blue or gold or silver. In some visions she says nothing; in others she exhorts the faithful to pray for a particular cause.

Usually she is seen by just one person or a handful of people. Even if many gather to await a second apparition, she is visible only to the initial person or persons who saw the apparition. But if they don't actually see Mary, crowds have several times witnessed phenomena that serve as proof of her appearance. One such occasion was 70,000 people witnessing a whirling sun at Fatima, Portugal, that accompanied a Marian appearance to three children (see page 201).

Sometimes the apparition isn't a moving, speaking figure, but something that appears to be . . . Well, no one knows quite what to make of it. Statues of the Virgin are said to weep. A couple of years ago in Clearwater, Florida, the tinted windows of an office building seemed to be forming a mosaic of the Blessed Mother, attracting believers and the curious. Special parking areas near the building were roped off for the "viewing."

Whether scientists can explain those phenomena, the devout are willing—eager—to believe that a link exists between them and Jesus in the form of his mother, Mary, as she visits the faithful on earth, bringing directives from him and taking back their prayers and adoration.

E-QUESTIONS?

What is hyperdulia?
Hyperdulia is the term for the special reverence rendered to Mary. Both it and the veneration paid to the saints differ from "worship," which is accorded God.

Suggested Additional Reading:

In Search of Mary: The Woman and the Symbol by Sally Cunneen (Ballantine Books, 1996). The author of two other books on religious topics looks at the latest findings about Mary by historians, anthropologists, and religious scholars. The Virgin in art is also explored.

If you'd like to know more about Marian apparitions (several are discussed in Chapter 38), two writers have explored that topic in books that are informative and balanced, for both the skeptic and the believer.

The Great Apparitions of Mary: An Examination of Twenty-Two Supranormal Appearances by Ingo Swann (Crossroad Publishing, 1996). The author, a scientist and artist, hopscotches around the world investigating the best known spots of Marian apparitions. His investigations are made with the eye of the scientist.

Searching for Mary: An Exploration of Marian Apparitions Across the U.S. by Mark Garvey (Plume, 1998). The author travels highways and back roads visiting Marian apparition sites from Bayside in Queens, New York, to Belleville, Illinois, to California City in California. An evenhanded and compassionate work.

CHAPTER 2

St. Joseph
(First Century)

When we think of Joseph, it is usually as a figure in the Nativity scene standing next to Mary and watching over the infant Jesus in the manger. Here is a good man far overshadowed through history by his wife and the Marian devotion accorded her. He has certainly been overshadowed by her son.

Not much is known about Joseph's life. He left no words behind for hagiographers to study. And he apparently died before the Crucifixion because he was not at Calvary with Mary.

Still, to this day, he continues to attract in a quiet way the faithful, some to churches bearing his name, who are devoted to him for his fidelity to family and home. In fact, it is said that next to Mary, he and St. Jude (Chapter 14) are the most popular in terms of prayers and devotions by the faithful for special favors.

Betrothed

The gospel authors Matthew and Luke, whose words are the only ones we have about Joseph, agree that Mary and Joseph were to be married at the time Mary discovered that she was pregnant.

Mary is informed that her pregnancy is divine, but Joseph does not know about that part of it. He is, quite understandably, aghast at the news, since the two had not lived together. He decides he will "set her aside" and not marry her, certainly a kind alternative to having her stoned to death, a common custom at the time with errant girls.

But then an angel appears to him in his sleep and says, "Joseph, son of David, do not fear to take Mary to be your wife, for that which is conceived in her is of the Holy Spirit; she will bear a son, and you shall call his name Jesus, for he will save his people from their sins." Joseph wakens satisfied, and decides to marry Mary.

> I don't recall up to this day ever having petitioned him for anything that he failed to grant. It is an amazing thing the great many favors God has granted me through the mediation of this blessed saint, the dangers I was freed from both of body and soul. For with other saints it seems the Lord has given them grace to be of help in one need, whereas with this glorious saint I have experience that he helps in all our needs.
>
> —St. Teresa of Ávila, on praying to St. Joseph

Since Mary and Joseph had planned to be married anyway, it is conceivable that Joseph was a young or reasonably young man. When we see paintings of Joseph, or when he is portrayed in films, he is often presented as much older than she. On the other hand, the hypothesis that he was no longer living at the time of the Passion of Christ could lend some credence to his having been many years Mary's senior.

A Worker's Household

Joseph was probably not a poor man, but he was not a prosperous one, either. Though he was linked to the house of King David, at the time of the Annunciation he was, and remained, a carpenter in a small town.

E-FACTS

Those busy revisionists have been at it again. It is thought now that Joseph might have been a *tekton,* a Greek word for a skilled craftsman. Biblical references use that word for him. A tekton works with metal of all kinds and with stone, although Joseph might have been a carpenter, too. Also, small-town Nazareth was within sight of Sepphoris, a large Palestinian city second in size only to Jerusalem. Sepphoris, destroyed by military action around the time of Jesus' birth, was then under reconstruction, providing plenty of work for artisans like Joseph and Jesus.

Whatever his income, when he and Mary brought their infant to the temple on the occasion of Mary's purification after Jesus' birth and the baby's presentation, the couple took with them only two turtledoves as an offering, nothing grander. Doves were gifts of the working class.

A short time after Jesus' birth, Joseph was warned in a dream to take the baby into exile in Egypt because King Herod had called for the slaying of male children under two years of age. Herod had heard that a "king" had been born and wanted no such person eventually threatening him.

E-FACTS

The babies who were slain under Herod's edict because of their link with Jesus have been called the Holy Innocents. They are commemorated as martyrs on their feast day, December 28.

So Joseph left. After the death of Herod he brought his little family back to Nazareth and then—well, little else is noted about this saint. When Jesus was about 12, Joseph and Mary took him to Jerusalem, lost him, and found him talking with the learned men at the temple.

In those times sons worked alongside their fathers, so Joseph taught carpentry (and possibly metalwork) to Jesus. He was known to be a fair and just man and did not stand in Jesus' way when his foster son began a public life at age 30.

Joseph is mentioned later in the Bible when Jesus is scorned for his humble beginnings: "Is this not Jesus, the carpenter's son?"

A Rise in Devotion

Joseph enjoyed veneration in the East from the fourth to the seventh centuries. Devotion to the saint in the West rose dramatically when his feast day was introduced to the Roman calendar in 1459. Various saints claimed a special interest in him, too, mentioning him in their writings, which further publicized his name and his life. Two of his more notable "fans" were St. Teresa of Ávila and St. Francis de Sales.

Joseph served his role well and became an example for fathers of families. In 1870 Pope Pius IX declared him Patron of the Universal Church. Pope Leo XIII placed him next to the Blessed Mother among all saints.

E-FACTS

A curious trend surfaced during the economic recession of the late 1980s. Those having trouble selling their homes would "plant" a statue of St. Joseph on the property, head down, and then pray to the saint for success with their venture. The practice continues today with hard-to-sell properties. The church considers this a superstition.

Some folks bury a statue of this saint on their property when they move *into* a home, sort of asking for his blessing while they live there. The statue is buried rightside up, and then turned over when the owners decide to sell.

Should the statue be on (or, more accurately, *in*) the front lawn or the backyard? It's your choice. Have a birdbath, or plant a butterfly garden and add a bench. It can be comforting to ask the saint's protection for your home, especially if you're going away for a long time.

This saint has two feast days: on March 19, and another on May 1, which was named the feast of St. Joseph the Worker by Pope Pius XII. He is the patron saint of carpenters, manual workers, all workers (May 1), fatherhood and families, a holy death, social justice, Belgium, Canada, China, Korea, and Peru. Also, priests, brothers, and nuns turn to St. Joseph in particular when praying over financial problems in their communities.

You can read more about devotion to St. Joseph in Chapter 38, about special shrines, basilicas, and cathedrals to saints around the world.

CHAPTER 3

Sts. Anne and Joachim
(First Century)

What was Anne like? Impossible to say. The mother of Mary is a little-documented saint, though her influence belies her vague history. Churches, shrines, and feast day celebrations attest to our continuing interest in this holy woman.

Her husband, Joachim, is just as little known. Anne might have been born in Nazareth, the daughter of a nomad. Actually, even her name is uncertain. That is true of Joachim, too, and he also could have been a Nazarene.

Anne was about 20 when she married Joachim; his age then is unknown. The couple was desolate when they had no children; and when publicly taken to task for that lack, Joachim went into the desert and fasted for 40 days.

Then, one day while Anne was praying, an angel appeared and told her she would have a child. Anne, who was 40 by then, promised to dedicate the child to God's service. That baby was, of course, Mary. Joachim is said to have died about 16 years later, just after the birth of Jesus.

A Grandparents' Garden

At least one church named after Saint Anne has created a spot on its grounds honoring both Anne and Joachim, which it called a grandparents' garden.

St. Ann's Church in Lawrenceville, New Jersey, wanted to have a statue of the saint on the premises. She is usually pictured with Mary, seldom with Joachim. "Today, more than ever we need concrete reminders of spousal love," the church said, announcing that it would capture the couple's devotion in two life-size statues.

The church noted that grandparents are strong connectors to the complex family system of which we are all a part. The garden is a place where anyone can come to remember their grandparents. Also, grandparents might also come to the statues to pray for their children and grandchildren. In the base of each statue are names of hundreds of grandparents submitted by parishioners.

E-FACTS

A procession to celebrate the feast of St. Anne (sometimes spelled Ann) is not uncommon in some ethnic, especially Italian, neighborhoods in this country. Selected faithful carry a 500- to 600-pound statue of the saint through the streets of the community. Often a festival at night closes the day's events.

A Role for Today

Joachim has a feast day, and churches have been named after him— or what we have taken to be his name.

What has kept Anne a major player among saint watchers and the devoted has been prayers by those pleading for her intercession. She is the patron saint of Canada, of cabinetmakers, grandmothers, homemakers, pregnancy, and women in labor. In some countries, Anne is prayed to with special fervor by women who want a child.

This couple were Jesus' grandparents, and the mother and father of Mary, and were obviously good and pious people. Praying to them is likely to hit its mark no matter what their true names may be, or whatever the details of their lives.

St. Anne and St. Joachim share the feast day of July 26. For more relating to devotion to Anne, turn to Chapter 38, about basilicas, shrines, and cathedrals bearing saints' names.

CHAPTER 4
St. Anthony of Padua
(1195–1231)

Dear St. Anthony, come around
Something is lost and can't be found.

How many millions of parochial school children have, over the years, earnestly murmured that little prayer when they could not find a missing schoolbook or special toy or any item important to them? St. Anthony is, after all, the finder of lost objects.

And how many grownups, far from school age, still recite those words, or a brief prayer of their own creation, when they've lost the car keys or a wallet and are having palpitations as they scramble around searching?

The Case of the Missing Money

Does the prayer work? There are many, many St. Anthony believers.
To take one example, a midwestern woman named Carol has often asked that scholar's help. In her early sixties and no more forgetful than the rest of us, she recalls a particular plea of a few years ago when houses near her neighborhood were ruined by flooding. Carol had the habit of placing a bit of cash under the dining room carpet, "just in case," as she put it. During

the flood, even though her home was in no immediate danger, she removed the money, added some bills to it, and hid it on the second floor of the house where, she reasoned, floodwaters were not likely to reach.

Two years passed. Now having a bit of a cash-flow squeeze, Carol remembered the $500. She would use some of it for a graduation gift for a favorite godchild. She went upstairs to the bedroom bureau, which had a narrow slot along the side of a top drawer that she had often used for hiding things. The money was not there.

Then where was it? "I had no idea," she recalled (or should we say, *couldn't* recall). "I started to panic, and picked up the edges of all the carpeting upstairs. It wasn't there. I was upset at the time I hid the money and just didn't remember *where* I put it."

A Prayer of St. Anthony

Lord Jesus, bind us to you and to our neighbor with love.

May our hearts not be turned away from you.

May our souls not be deceived nor our talents or minds enticed by allurements of error, so that we may never distance ourselves from your love.

Thus may we love our neighbor as ourselves with strength, wisdom, and gentleness. With your help, you who are blessed throughout all ages.

Carol, who had worshiped at St. Anthony's Church in her community for nearly 30 years, whispered a fervent prayer to her church's namesake. "I was confident about St. Anthony's help," she says, "but still edgy over the missing money, so I thought for a few minutes and then decided while I was upstairs I'd do some cleaning to calm down. I figured I'd straighten out the medicine cabinet and then the linen closet."

While arranging the closet, she came to a shelf that held, among other items, a plastic guest towel holder she had received as a gift. It was filled with three packages of unopened paper guest towels. As she moved the holder, she saw a tip of green poking out from beneath the bottom packet of towels. It was the money!

Don't tell Carol that St. Anthony did not steer her to the linen closet. She still does not remember putting the bills there, although she reasons that during those upsetting days she might have thought that hiding it on a high shelf was safer than keeping it on or near the floor if there should be another flood.

Why Lost Objects?

How did it come about that St. Anthony would be linked with lost objects? Perhaps it has been handed down from a particular incident in his life. A **novice** (one who is in the probationary stage of being admitted to a religious order) had carried off a book that Anthony needed. He prayed for its return and the novice, suddenly motivated by an unknown force, brought it back to him.

However, consider this when you think of St. Anthony. Although he is one of the most popular of the canonized, with a constant stream of prayers directed to his attention, he is more than a finder of money, key chains, term papers, sneakers, and theater tickets. He was an exceptional teacher and is one of the few (there are only 33) Doctors of the Church.

E-FACTS

The monthly publication of the Franciscan friars is not named after their founder, Francis of Assisi, but instead is called the *St. Anthony Messenger.* For information about the magazine, call ✆(800) 488-0488; e-mail *StAnthony@AmericanCatholic.org;* or check out ✐*www.AmericanCatholic.org.*

Becoming a Franciscan

Anthony was born in Lisbon, Portugal, and first entered religious life in Coimbra, in northern Italy. Here his life crossed with that of Francis of Assisi. He met a group of visiting Franciscans who were on their way to Morocco, and they impressed him with their missionary zeal. Tragically, the missionaries were martyred in Africa. Their remains were brought through Anthony's part of Italy on the way back to final interment at the monastery.

Anthony was moved to enter the Franciscan **order** and later was posted to Morocco to preach the gospel. He became ill, however, and was forced to return home, disappointed in what seemed like the end of his dream of becoming a missionary. Back in Italy he took on a number of small assignments and was considered a fairly typical, nothing-out-of-the-ordinary young brother. Then one day, in what in modern times—and perhaps even then—would have been considered either the opportunity of a lifetime or a moment of sheer terror, Anthony was asked to fill in as a preacher at an important religious event.

The young man stunned the audience with his eloquence and the learning that lay behind his words. His fame spread and soon he received a letter from Francis himself authorizing Anthony to preach and also to teach theology to the Franciscan friars.

E-QUESTIONS?

What is St. Anthony's bread?
Alms or donations given for the intercession of this saint are known as **St. Anthony's bread**.

Anthony preached all over Italy and into France. He was as affecting a speaker as the most dynamic evangelist, addressing himself not only to the laity but to recalcitrant clergy as well. His continual exhortation to give to the needy earned him the title "Friend of the Poor." The saint was so dynamic he often preached outdoors because the crowds who came to hear him were too large for the nearby church.

Anthony did not live to old age and never became the missionary to foreign places he had dreamed of earlier. He was only 36 when he died in Padua, not far from the Dolomite Alps, where he had spent his later years. He is buried there.

He was canonized just one year after his death and was made a Doctor of the Church by Pope Pius XII in 1946.

St. Anthony's feast day is June 13. He is the patron saint of Portugal, infertility, lost objects, the poor, and travelers.

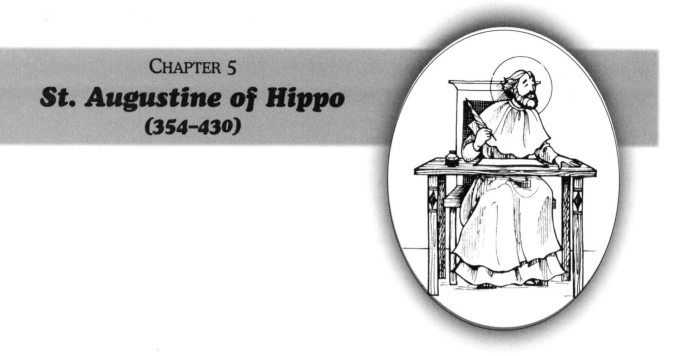

CHAPTER 5

St. Augustine of Hippo
(354–430)

Late have I loved Thee, Beauty, at once so ancient and so new!
Late have I loved Thee! You were within me, and I was in the world
outside myself. . . . You were with me, but I was not with Thee.

Even casual saint observers may recognize these words as those of a
major figure of the early days of Christianity. Over recent years the quote
has been updated and "Thee" changed to "You."

Augustine did indeed come late from the good life of the senses,
making his way fitfully toward God. Tracing his journey can aid anyone
engaged in a similar difficult quest. But alongside Augustine's personal
odyssey is his impact on all of Western thought. Here is a truly remarkable
man of formidable intellect—complex, and quite human within it.

The World Stage

You will see as you read on through this book that many saints are far
larger than the small town where they grew up or spent their adult years,
which was often in a convent or monastery. St. Francis of Assisi, for
instance, is universal; you cannot confine him to one small town in Italy.

The mind of Thomas of Aquino (St. Thomas Aquinas) leaped far past, and his acclaim far beyond, the dot on the map where he was born. It is that way with Augustine as well. Though he lived in his fair share of villages and traveled around North Africa and well into Italy, over time his words would be played and reinterpreted in every corner of the earth for well over a thousand years.

He was born Aurelius Augustinus in the North African town of Tagaste (a village that is now Souk Ahras in eastern Algeria, near the border of Tunisia), then part of the Carthaginian empire. His father, Patricius, was a pagan landowner, and his mother, Monica, was a good Christian who would for years pray for her wayward son to become one, too.

St. Monica (331–387)

This holy woman seems to have spent her life crying, coping, and praying. She prayed for her pagan, apparently hot-tempered husband to be converted to Christianity. He did convert, and one hopes a better disposition came along with his new faith. She coped with a difficult mother-in-law, and no doubt asked God's intercession in that difficult situation as well.

St. Monica

But Monica's principal energy was directed toward her prodigal offspring. Here is a mother who followed her son many miles to an unknown (to her) country to see him repent of his sins. This was an annoyance to Augustine, although he never spoke unkindly of her.

At one point, after years of prayerful entreaties, she had a vision in which God assured her that Augustine would indeed find salvation.

An Explorer

Augustine was an excellent student, and after finishing school he led the life of a young man with few worries and ample money. He would say later that it was all nothing but a desert of sin, pride, and sensuality.

He did study law for a while, but dropped it to take up writing, where his true talent lay. He also took up a mistress, a relationship that was to last 15 years and see him, at the age of 18, become father to a son, Addeodatus.

Intellectually curious, Augustine was particularly intrigued by the mystery of evil. He began to be influenced by the Manichaeans, a cult that espoused **dualism**: a doctrine that holds that the universe is under the dominion of two opposing principles; one good and the other evil.

Augustine embraced Manichaeism for a while, but ultimately found it unrewarding and discarded it.

My second year at Oxford was an attempt to reinforce my intellectual instincts with systematic study of Christian ethics. Back to basics. I wanted to build a better foundation for my political views. . . . I knew a lot about the "how" and "what" of politics. Now I wanted to think more about the "why." So I read Augustine and Aquinas, Martin Luther and Reinhold Niebuhr . . .

—GEORGE STEPHANOPOULOS, FORMER AIDE TO FORMER PRESIDENT CLINTON, IN *ALL TOO HUMAN* (Little, Brown, 1999)

To Italy

Eventually, Augustine left Africa for Rome to study and teach rhetoric. His mother, Monica, by now widowed and undaunted in her attempts to bring religion to her son, elected to go along with him. As you can imagine, Augustine wasn't too happy about that. In fact, he tricked her, telling her his boat was sailing at a later time than it did and leaving her without even saying good-bye! His mistress and son went with him.

Eventually he left Rome and headed north to Milan, the administrative seat of the Roman Empire. Who should he find there but . . . Monica. Her reward: Augustine weakened in his no-religion-please resolve. He listened to the words of St. Ambrose, bishop of that northern Italian city and quite a match for Augustine intellectually. Ambrose baptized Augustine and his son in 387. That is quite a tribute to Ambrose. And probably to Monica, too. Augustine was 33 at the time.

St. Ambrose (340–397)

Born in western Germany, Ambrose was a high-ranking Roman official living in Milan, then capital of the Roman Empire. When the bishop of Milan died, leaving warring factions, Ambrose, to his horror, was voted into the post by acclamation. He was not even baptized, let alone a priest. But no matter. Within a week, all of that was taken care of: baptism, confirmation, holy orders, and consecration as bishop of Milan.

He did well in the position. He was a pious man, looked after the poor, preached often and well, and even gave away all of his property. One man affected by his holiness and intellectual ability was St. Augustine.

Ambrose wrote prodigiously but is mainly remembered for his administrative talents in keeping the peace during turbulent times: heresies, civic upheaval, and political power plays. On the subject of ruling, he said, "An emperor should not abolish liberty, even in the case of those who owe him a military obedience. The difference between good and bad rulers is that the good love freedom, the bad slavery."

St. Ambrose's feast day is December 7. He is a Doctor of the Church and the patron saint of learning.

What about his mistress in all of this? (She was never given a name in his writings.) She went along to Italy with him. Of the woman he had lived with for so long, he writes that she was "torn from my side." However, it seems that in reality it was Augustine's decision to have her return to North Africa. He sent her packing, you might say.

Angel is the name of their office, not their nature. If you seek the name of their nature, it is spirit; if you seek the name of their office, it is angel; from what they are, spirit, from what they do, angel.

—St. Augustine

A Religious Life

After baptism, Augustine lived a communal life of prayer for a few months with his mother, brother, and a few others. He and Monica then set out to return to North Africa. They stopped at Ostia, awaiting their ship. Augustine wrote that the two talked most of the day, about faith and of the afterlife. He said that "for one fleeting instant" the two of them seemed to touch the heaven for which they both longed. Monica told Augustine she was satisfied now, happy to see her son living a Christian life. Within days she fell ill and died at Ostia.

Augustine was devastated by her death. Augustine wrote of his mother (in words he would dare not use today!), "She had a woman's weak body, but a man's strong faith." He remembered all she had suffered because of him, and he wrote, addressing God, "This was the mother, now dead and hidden awhile from my sight, who had wept over me for many years so that I might live in your sight." He added, "Let him not mock at me, but weep himself, if his charity is great. Let him weep for my sins to you, the Father of all the brothers of your Christ."

St. Monica is interred in Rome at the church of Sant'Agostino. Her feast day is August 27, one day before her son's. She is the patron saint of married women and mothers.

Augustine returned to Tagaste alone, since Monica died en route. Once home he founded what could loosely be called a monastery (for one thing, Augustine was not ordained). His son died around this time, too, in 389.

Alone now, Augustine was ordained within two years in Hippo. While living in his monastery, he began to venture out to preach. Augustine was very popular like Anthony of Padua, who was such a compelling evangelist that to accommodate everyone who wanted to hear him he had to preach in a public square rather than in a church.

In 395 Augustine was named coadjutor to the bishop of Hippo and became bishop himself the following year. Augustine rose to a leadership position in church affairs in North Africa, but that is not why he and his life are still of interest today.

The *Confessions* and Other Writings

Augustine fascinates people because he had been a sinner, repented, and went on to think, preach, and—especially—write about the God he found. It was a constant struggle, he wrote, to give up his life of carnal indulgence—that is, concupiscence.

What is concupiscence?
Concupiscence is a strong, especially sexual, desire.

When he cries, "Oh, God, make me chaste, but not yet," it makes this towering mind seem all too human. Indeed, how many of us can see ourselves in Augustine: soon, very soon, *but not yet.*

Augustine touches on every area of life in his writings, from abortion to telling the truth to capital punishment (he is against it). He wrote more about marriage than any other early theologian and believed sexual relations were sinful and anyone who engaged in them committed sin. Marriage was essential for the human race, he wrote, but sex was an explosive force that could ruin society. (Ah, those reformed sinners!) That thinking did not, of course, last very long. The church went on to make marriage a sacrament and a source of grace.

Augustine wrote, too, of original sin and free will and predestination, adding to all of it his own feelings and life experiences.

There are some who read Augustine and grumble, "Hey, he had his wild times and now wants to make sure none of us do." They see him as a sour grinch finding sin here, there, and everywhere.

No one said Augustine was easy!

During the period from 397 to 400, he wrote *Confessions.* That was followed in 416 by *On the Trinity,* and from the years 413 to 426 he wrote *City of God. Confessions* remains his most renowned work.

Is not the life of man on earth all trial? Who wishes for troubles and difficulties? Thou commandest them to be endured, not to be loved. No man loves what he endures, though he loves to endure. For though he rejoices that he endures, he had rather there were nothing for him to endure. In adversity I long for prosperity, in prosperity I fear adversity. What middle place is there betwixt these two, where the life of man is not all trial? Woe to the prosperities of the world, once and again, through fear of adversity, and corruption of joy! Woe to the adversities of the world, once and again, and the third time, from the longing for prosperity, and because adversity itself is a hard thing, and lest it shatter endurance. Is not the life of man upon earth all trial: without any interval?

And all my hope is no where but in Thy exceeding great mercy.

—St. Augustine, *The Confessions of Saint Augustine,*
(Modern Library/Random House, 1999)

Legacy

In all, Augustine wrote more than 90 books, several hundred sermons, and hundreds of letters. As a writer, he was a beautiful and brilliant stylist and was responsible for permanently affecting Western Christianity with his thought and words. Indeed, some scholars debate whether he or St. Thomas Aquinas left the heavier imprint on Christian thought and doctrine.

His thinking about the beginning of the world is conceded today to be the likely scenario: As early as the fifth century, Augustine cautioned that accepting God as literally creating the earth in six days was erroneous. In *The Literal Meaning of Genesis,* he states his belief that the days of creation were not successive and certainly not limited to six.

Instead, Augustine believed that God "made all things together, disposing them in an order based not on intervals of time but on causal connections." To his reasoning, some things were made in fully developed form and others were in "potential form," which developed over time to become the condition we find today.

An example of the enduring attraction to the mind of this saint came in 1999, when Pulitzer Prize–winning author Gary Wills published *Saint Augustine,* which addressed aspects of Augustine's life from a different perspective. Wills, whom some consider the country's most visible Catholic intellectual, sees Augustine's mother, Monica, as less domineering than others have depicted her. Wills retitles Augustine's *Confessions* and calls it *The Testimony.* To him the word *confession* has a bad connotation, having to do with admitting to a crime. Augustine is not doing that, rather he is owning up to his sins and praising his Creator—all of it, says Wills, a testimony to God and faith. The bottom line: Though overall an ardent admirer of Augustine, Wills does not agree with all of the bishop of Hippo's thinking, particularly as it applies to present times.

Final Days

Augustine served as bishop of Hippo for 35 years, until his death at the age of 75 in 430, during the siege of Hippo by the Vandals. This man, who for so long had a restless soul, wrote to God in words that are also familiar to many of us: "You have made us for Yourself, and our hearts are restless until they rest in You."

St. Augustine is a Doctor of the Church. His feast day is August 28. He is the patron saint of theologians, printers, and England.

Suggested Additional Reading:
The Confessions of St. Augustine, translated by B. Pusey, D.D. (Modern Library/Random House, 1999).

The Confessions of St. Augustine, translated and with an introduction by John K. Ryan (Doubleday Image, 1960).

St. Augustine in 90 Minutes, by Paul Strathern (Ivan R. Dee, 1997). If you haven't got the time to plow through Augustine readings, this 85-page book in the "90 Minutes" series, covering philosophers, saints, and other great thinkers, can give you an overview of Augustine's ideas and a look at the times in which he lived.

Bookstore shelves are full of good works on St. Augustine and his writings. Because of his prominence and the interesting life he led, many scholars and others have wanted to write about this saint. You should have no trouble finding a good book about him or a translation of one of his own works.

A Town, Hotel, Two Saints

Although the saint's name is pronounced Au-GUS-tin, the name of the oldest European settlement in America, in northeast Florida, is known as St. AU-gus-teen. First visited by Ponce de León in 1513, this small city of 20,000 is named for the saint. In 1888 the Casa Monica Hotel opened there, named after Augustine's mother. The Moorish revival–style building was soon sold to Henry Flagler, the noted developer of so much of the east coast of Florida. He changed its name to the Cordova.

The hotel closed during the Depression, and was largely unoccupied until 1962, when it became the county courthouse. When a new courthouse was built in the early 1990s, the building was acquired by a Florida developer and art lover who opened Casa Monica again in late 1999, the oldest hotel in the oldest city in the United States.

CHAPTER 6

St. Catherine of Siena
(1347–1380)

In life, Catherine possessed two traits not usually found at the same time in saints: she was one of the great mystics of the church, and yet she was also a worker among the people.

With no formal education (she could not read or write), Catherine is one of the most imposing saints. She is one of only three women to carry the title Doctor of the Church (the other two are St. Teresa of Ávila and St. Thérèse of Lisieux). You could also say that Catherine was one of the few important women in all of Europe at the time. Yet she lived only 33 years.

In a Secret Cell

Catherine was born in Siena, near Florence, the 24th of 25 children—yes, that number is correct—and the daughter of a prosperous fabric dyer. When she was 15, the appropriate age at the time, her family hoped for a suitable marriage for her. Catherine shocked them by insisting there would be no ordinary marriage for her; she was to be married to Christ. To emphasize the point she cut off her long golden hair.

Her parents were shocked and punished their daughter. However, with Catherine's already considerable inner resources—she began having visions when she was six—she was able to create what she called a "secret cell," where in her mind she would retreat from the drudgery her life had become. Eventually her father saw her point, although he may have been helped along by the sight of a dove hovering over Catherine's head as she prayed.

Now free to do more or less as she chose, Catherine elected not to join a formal religious order and instead became a Dominican tertiary.

What is a tertiary?
Tertiaries belong to the third order, that is, they are lay persons who remain "in the world" but follow regulations that do not include taking vows (poverty, chastity, and obedience).

She was pelted with doubts and demonic visions and taunting voices, but she dispelled them with laughter. Jesus appeared to her after one of those episodes. "And where were you when all this was happening?" she asked. His reply: "I was in your heart." From then on Catherine received daily visitations from Jesus.

Catherine's words and actions have survived through some 400 letters; a collection of her mystical experiences, published as *The Dialogue;* and the work of her confessor, disciple, and later biographer, Blessed Raymond of Capua. Since she was illiterate (as were many women of the time), she dictated her words.

Bl. Raymond of Capua (1330–1399)
Raymond, a Dominican prior, was serving as a lector in Florence and Siena when he met Catherine. He became her spiritual adviser and a close confidant throughout her life. He claims he was cured of the plague by Catherine's prayers. With her, he worked toward meeting with the pope, then living in Avignon, and urging him to return to Rome. Later he was sent to France by Pope Urban VI to win the support of King Charles V, but the trip was unsuccessful. After Catherine's death, he was elected master general of the Dominicans. He went on to work hard to reform the order, establishing several new houses. Raymond was beatified in 1899.

Catherine is responsible for several miracles, including one within her own family. Raymond, who claimed she cured him of the plague, tells the story of how Catherine's widowed mother, Lapa, was seriously ill. After her daughter's prayers to God came this message: It would be better for Lapa to die than to face the terrible trials that lie ahead. But Lapa did not want to die and refused a deathbed confession, so Catherine continued to pray for her recovery.

Nonetheless, one day while her daughter was at church Lapa died. "Lord, my God," said Catherine, in tears, "are these the promises You made me? That none of my house should go to hell? . . . As long as there is life in my body I shall not move from here until my mother is restored." Lapa moved, and she was revived. She lived to be nearly ninety, but her long life was indeed filled with sorrows.

A Public Role

After those three years at home, Catherine went out into the world, ministering to the ill in hospitals and taking care of those particularly shunned by society, such as prisoners and patients stricken by leprosy and plague. She was, she said, following Christ's bidding to her: "The service you cannot do me you must render your neighbors."

Catherine truly had supernatural gifts, and though she had many followers during those early years, a few doubted her abilities and stirred up trouble. At one point she was brought before the Dominicans in Florence, but the accusations against her were dismissed. In Siena, she was so acclaimed for her work with the sick and the needy that she began to attract disciples.

QUESTIONS?

What is a disciple, and what is an apostle?
A **disciple** is one who believes in, follows, and may even imitate a master. An **apostle,** in the context of Christianity, is a person (or a group) sent out by God to spread a message. One can be both a disciple and an apostle: the Twelve Apostles, for example.

They called her, with affection, "Mama," although she was at this time still in her twenties and almost all of her followers were many years older.

Catherine had another religious experience, in 1374, when Christ commanded her to go out into the world beyond Siena—to France. She complied and became a more public figure. She wrote to popes and magistrates, counseling them on their roles and how to perform their duties. And this from a woman—and a very young one at that. It is a tribute to Catherine's intelligence and perseverance that her advice was so often heeded.

With a larger stage now than the small-town feuds of Siena, Catherine stepped into the issue of the **Avignon**-based papacy. She traveled to meet with the two sides in the conflict over where the papal seat should be based and was met with enthusiastic crowds along the way. Meeting with Pope Gregory XI in Avignon, France, and giving him the respect due a pontiff, she nevertheless was quite frank in telling him he ought to return to Rome. The court in Avignon was mired in sin, she said. The pope belonged in Rome, the cradle of Christianity.

How did the pope react to her bluntness? He returned to Rome. Unfortunately, he died soon after and was succeeded by Urban VI, a man considered so power-hungry that the College of Cardinals did the unthinkable: they reconvened and elected a second pope.

E-QUESTIONS?

What is the College of Cardinals?
The **College of Cardinals** is composed of all who hold the rank of cardinal in the church and who meet as a unit to discuss and/or vote on an issue or take part in an election, such as for a pope. A cardinal must be younger than 80 years of age to vote for a pope.

But Urban would not abdicate—if they thought him power-mad, did they really think he would give it all up? Thus the church had two rivals, eventually warring rivals for decades. This was not an admirable era in the papacy.

In her great mystical work, *The Dialogue*, Catherine of Siena writes of God speaking to her of virtues, such as love of neighbor:

These and other virtues I give differently to different souls, and the soul is most at ease with that virtue which has been made primary for her. . . .

The same is true of many of my gifts and graces, virtue and other spiritual gifts, and those things necessary for the body and human life. I have distributed them all in such a way that no one has all of them. Thus have I given you reason—necessity in fact—to practice mutual charity. . . . Whether you will it or not, you cannot escape the exercise of charity! Yet, unless you do it for love of me, it is worth nothing to you in the realm of grace.

—*THE DIALOGUE*, TRANSLATED BY SUZANNE NOFKE (PAULIST PRESS, 1980)

Catherine was not impressed by Urban but thought he had, after all, been officially chosen by the college and was the true pope. She was greatly distressed by the whole quarrelsome business and, feeling it was a profound wound to the church that could be healed only by great sacrifice, she experienced her last vision. She felt that the church, with all its weight, had literally been placed on her back, and she dropped to the ground in terrible pain and in paralysis, dying several weeks later. Upon her death the marks of the stigmata appeared on her body in plain view. (She had received the stigmata earlier, but at her prayerful request it had been seen only by her.)

In Chapter 36 you will read how relics, which sometimes include body parts, of the saints end up in several places. Catherine of Siena is an example. Her head is on display in the Church of Santa Domenico in Siena; her body is in Rome, at the Church of Santa Maria sopra Minerva.

Catherine was named a Doctor of the Church in 1970. Her feast day is April 29, the day of her death. She is the patron saint of nurses and nursing services, nursing homes, Italy, Siena, and fire prevention.

Suggested Additional Reading:

The Dialogue by Catherine of Siena (Classics of Western Spirituality, Paulist Press, 1980). The saint's own account of her mystical experiences.

CHAPTER 7
St. Francis of Assisi
(1181–1226)

St. Francis is one of the most beloved saints. Whether for his love of the simple life or his interest in animals—indeed in all of creation—Francis of Assisi is venerated by the faithful who know their saints from A to Z, as well as by those who know little or nothing about them.

If you are asked to close your eyes and envision St. Francis, you would probably come up with pretty much the same description as everyone else: clad in Franciscan habit, in bare feet or simple sandals, one hand holding a bird and, oh, maybe a fawn at his feet. We might not know his facial features; but the overall image is clear, just as the image of Joan of Arc in a suit of armor and shorn hair is an immediate evocation of that saint.

For such a simple man, Francis of Assisi led a hearty life. He missed little, and what he experienced he felt with passion.

A Bon Vivant

Francis was born in Assisi, in the Umbrian region of Italy, to a wealthy fabric merchant and his wife. His father was away on business in France when his mother had him christened Giovanni, but when

Pietro di Bernardone returned home he insisted, because of his love for France, that the infant's name be changed to Francesco.

The youth grew up taking full advantage of his fortunate circumstances. He traveled, spent money freely, and generally lived quite a self-indulgent life. He was said to be charming, charismatic—and generous.

Even war did not tame his spirits. He went off to fight in a conflict and was taken prisoner. He spent a year in jail and then succumbed to a serious illness. His recovery was slow. Both experiences brought about a spiritual crisis.

E-FACTS

Many legends about St. Francis of Assisi tell of his ability to communicate with birds and beasts. Among them is this story:

During the time Francis was praying and fasting for 50 days in his solitary cell on Mount Alverna, the devil tried to plague and distract him by sending hundreds of mice. The mice were nibbling at his feet, chewing at his clothes. Francis was about to give up and chase the mice away when suddenly a cat jumped out of the long, loose sleeve of his robe. The miracle happened so quickly that only two mice escaped.

Legend has it that the descendants of this miraculous cat still sit motionless in front of holes and crevices, waiting to catch the mice that got away.

Francis gave serious thought to the way he had been living, going so far as to make a **pilgrimage** to Rome in 1206.

Starting Small

A different Francis returned home from Rome. Now was the time, he had decided, to devote his life to serving the poor and the sick.

His father thought he was insane. In fact, Pietro di Bernardone not only publicly denounced his son, he also disinherited him.

No matter, Francis continued his work. And then came an event in his life that makes him seem so like the rest of us. He misunderstood a directive—though his was from God. One day, after his decision to work with the poor, he was praying in a church just outside Assisi. The crucifix lit up and a voice spoke, telling him, "Francis, repair my church, which has fallen into disrepair, as you can see." So the saint went out and returned with the thirteenth century equivalent of a tool kit and began to repair that particular church, which had indeed seen better times. Only later did Francis realize he was to repair *the* Church, and bring it back to simplicity and devotion to the poor.

Francis retreated to a small **chapel**, the Portiuncula, to devote his life to preaching and to the needy. He soon began attracting disciples, who were at first curious about the rich boy who had given it all away to work with the needy. Among those interested in the saint's work were several prominent citizens of Assisi. With all of those willing workers in mind, Francis founded the Franciscan order in 1209. It would be dedicated to absolute poverty, humility, and the love of all created things.

E-FACTS

It is believed that neither Francis of Assisi nor any other St. Francis wrote the prayer beginning: "Lord, make me an instrument of your peace/where there is hatred, let me sow love. . . ." Saint scholars now attribute those words to an Anglican clergyman.

The Missionary

Francis was not to remain in Assisi long. With an unaccountable desire to preach to the Mohammedans, he left home for Syria in 1212 but was shipwrecked along the way. Rescued, he tried to become a missionary again, but this time he became ill in Spain and was forced to return to Italy.

By now there were a great many men (and one woman, St. Clare) who had become attracted to his simple life.

St. Clare (1194–1253)

Clare was a surprising follower of Francis. The beautiful Assisi-born daughter of a nobleman, the 12-year-old Clare would not marry the man chosen for her. Instead, after hearing a sermon by St. Francis, she joined his friars. Francis had no convent yet, and so he sent her to live with nearby nuns. She was joined by her 15-year-old sister, Agnes.

Eventually, Clare moved to a house with her small group of nuns, a **convent** she was to supervise for 40 years. Interestingly, the Poor Clares, as the order became known, was soon joined by Clare's mother and another sister.

This was an extremely austere religious order that took a vow of strict poverty. Throughout her life Clare fought hard to maintain that ruling. She became extremely influential over the years and is credited, next to St. Francis, with being most responsible for the growth of the Franciscans.

She was canonized just two years after her death. Her feast day is August 11. She is the patron saint of television and television writers.

Francis sent his first missionaries to Tunis and Morocco in 1219. Then this religious vagabond finally realized his missionary dream when he along with 12 of his friars reached Egypt to evangelize the Mohammedans in Palestine and Egypt. His work was for the most part unsuccessful, but in any event trouble was brewing at home, so Francis was forced to return to Italy. A movement was under way in his order to stray from his original rule of simplicity; Francis was successful in holding back the dissenters.

One with Nature

Besides Francis's preaching, and of course his outreach to the poor and to outcasts such as prisoners and lepers, what appeals to us is his overall dedication to leading the simple life, especially the extraordinary sense he had of being one with nature. He felt a union with all things created by

MONROE COUNTY LIBRARY SYSTEM
MONROE MICHIGAN 48161

God, living and inanimate. All people were his brothers and sisters. Indeed, he spoke of Sister Water and Brother Fire (see his poem "The Canticle of the Sun").

He spoke to flowers newly in bloom. Paintings and statues that show the saint with a few animals or birds around him (the way we envisioned him at the beginning of this chapter) are accurate. At times he actually preached to animals. Looking beyond skin, fur, and feathers, he would communicate with them simply as one soul speaking to another.

And they understood. Hunted animals would seek refuge alongside him. Fish refused to die in his hands. When he walked, birds followed him.

E-FACTS

It has become popular for churches to hold a blessing of the animals. Often that is St. Francis's feast day, and his blessing is invoked as parishioners bring along the expected dogs and cats, but also horses, pet toads, gerbils, snakes.

Francis is responsible for a worldwide custom that endures to this day: the Christmas **crèche**. In his time he naturally filled it with live animals. (In the last few years in contemporary life, using living creatures in a Nativity scene has come back in style.)

His friars and other believers said that whenever Francis walked there was a ray of light about him, and sometimes he was even lifted above the ground in a silver cloud.

He was interested in music, playing the fiddle occasionally, and he really loved sweets. On one occasion when he was speaking before a crowd he told them, "You see before you a sinner, one who has eaten cakes made with lard during Lent."

Approaching the End

Francis eventually retired from most of the activities of his order. One day, while praying in his cell, he received the stigmata, witnessed by three of his friars.

The Canticle of the Sun
(Written by St. Francis shortly before his death)

Most high, omnipotent, good Lord,
Praise, glory, honor and benediction—all are yours.
To you alone do they belong, Most High,
And there is no one fit to mention you.

Praise be to you, my Lord, with all your creatures,
Especially to my worshipful Brother Sun,
Who lights up the day, and through him do you give brightness;
And beautiful is he and radiant with great splendor;
Most High, he represents you to us.

Praised be my Lord, for Sister Moon and for the stars,
In heaven you have formed them clear and precious and fair.

Praised be my Lord, for Brother Wind
and for the air and clouds and fair and every kind of weather,
By whom you give your creatures nourishment.
Praised be my Lord for Sister Water,
Who is greatly helpful and humble and precious and pure.

Praised be my Lord for Brother Fire,
By whom you light up the dark,
And fair is he and gay and mighty and strong.

Praised be my Lord for our sister, Mother Earth,
Who sustains and keeps us
And brings forth diverse fruits with grass and flowers bright.

Praised be my Lord for those who for your love forgive
And bear weakness and tribulation.
Blessed those who shall in peace endure,
For by you, Most High, shall they be crowned.

*Praised be my Lord for our Sister, the Bodily Death,
From whom no living person can flee.
Woe to them who die in mortal sin;
Blessed those who shall find themselves in your most holy will,
For the second death shall do them no ill.

Praise you and bless you my Lord, and give him thanks,
And be subject unto him with great humility.

—*The Writings of Saint Francis of Assisi*,
Translated by Father P. Robinson (Dolphin Press, 1906)

In great pain during his final illness, Francis called out "Welcome, Sister Death." He died in Assisi on October 3, 1226. At the moment of his death a light shone from his body, and the church bells at San Stefano pealed with no assistance from a bell ringer. Giving his blessing to the friars who had gathered around him, he told them, "I have done my part. May Christ teach you to do yours."

Francis was canonized in 1228. His feast day is October 4, and he is the patron saint of ecologists and ecology, merchants, and Italy.

E-PROFILE

Basilica Restored

A 1997 earthquake in the central hills of Italy killed 10 people, made thousands homeless—and cracked many priceless and irreplaceable medieval and Renaissance sites. One of those was the thirteenth century Basilica of St. Francis, begun soon after the saint's death and where his bones are interred. You may have seen pictures on television news programs at the time showing the destruction to this church. Four people were killed inside the basilica.

In November 1999, the Franciscan brothers celebrated the end of the first stage of restoration work and the reopening of the basilica, with the Italian president attending ceremonies and an electronic hookup with Pope John Paul II in Rome.

To get an idea of the damage caused by the seismic event, rated 5.5 on the Richter scale, believed to be the 22nd earthquake of that strength or greater to have struck the basilica in its seven centuries: the basilica shattered into 500,000 fragments from the tremors; frescoes by Cimabue and Giotto crashed into pieces. One fresco that has been restored—or at least 80 percent of it—was pieced together from 3,000 fragments. The restoration has so far cost $17 million, and is expected to take another two years.

Now, seismologists say, the basilica should be able to withstand a similar earthquake because it would roll with tremors.

CHAPTER 8

St. Francis Xavier
(1506–1552)

There are more than a few men called "Frank" whose first and middle names are "Francis Xavier" (and at least one woman, as you will see later in this chapter). "Francis X. Jones" or "F. X. Smith" are likely to be Francis Xaviers.

Why give a child both names of this saint?

This was a special holy man, an explorer and missionary, a visionary whose travels took him as far as Japan, then pretty much unknown to Westerners. Indeed he is responsible for hundreds of thousands of conversions in Asia.

Among the First Jesuits

Francis was born on April 7 near Pamplona, Spain (where the famous running of the bulls takes place every year), in the Basque area of that country. He studied at the University of Paris, and while there he met Ignatius of Loyola (read more about him in Chapter 10). He did not agree with all of Ignatius's ideas—Francis was, shall we say, more than a bit fun loving—but he did see eye to eye with him on important religious issues, and eventually elected to join Ignatius in his missionary life. When

Ignatius founded the Society of Jesus (the Jesuits), Francis became one of the order's first seven priests, along with Ignatius and six of his university friends.

Francis took his vows at Montmartre in 1534. A few years later, after the pope formally approved the Society of Jesus, Francis and another priest were sent as the first Jesuit missionaries to the East Indies. Before leaving for the Orient, the pope appointed him apostolic nuncio to the Indies. For Francis, that journey would become an 11-year odyssey from which he would not return.

E-QUESTIONS?

What is a nuncio?
A **nuncio** is a papal delegate of the highest rank, accredited to a civil government.

Setting Sail

It took five months to get around the Cape of Good Hope, then, hugging the coast of Africa and making a few stops, the ship reached India and Goa, which was then a Portuguese colony. Onboard ship Francis ministered to all, physically and spiritually.

Francis spent several months preaching at Goa. He did not actually bring Christianity to that region. It had been introduced by the Portuguese, but the church had fallen into a sorry state there. Francis also ministered to the sick and taught children.

He was to travel widely in Southeast Asia and the South Pacific, visiting Malacca in Malaya, the small islands near New Guinea, and Morotai, close to the Philippines. Finally, hearing about Japan, he traveled to that remote and isolated country. The Japanese culture impressed him, and he stayed for two years.

He wrote of the people: "The Japanese are in all matters naturally curious, eager to learn as much as possible; and so they never cease to ply us with one question or another, and to inquire further about our answers. Especially they seek most eagerly to hear what is new about religion."

E-FACTS

Today most of the population of Japan are members of either the Shinto or Buddhist faiths. A very small percentage is Christian.

Japan changed his thinking about his method of proselytizing. He decided he would take into account the existing culture of the countries he visited and link that culture with the word he was preaching, instead of essentially disregarding a country's unique composition.

Always interested in moving on, Francis thought about his next port of call: China. However, this was a country closed to foreigners. Wouldn't it be quite a coup, though, if he could bring Christianity to even a bit of that sprawling nation? China was not that far away from Japan, but his dream was not to be realized. Francis fell ill while on a ship heading for China and had to disembark on the small island of Sancian near the China coast. He died there on December 3 at age 46, tantalizingly close to his goal.

O my Lord Jesus! Teach me to be generous; teach me to serve you as you deserve; to give and not to count the cost; to fight and not to heed the wounds; to toil and not to ask for rest; to labor, seeking no reward, save that of knowing that I do your will. Amen.

—St. Francis Xavier

Man of the People

Francis Xavier is considered by many to be the greatest Christian missionary since St. Paul. He traveled thousands of miles in underdeveloped, sometimes nearly impassable lands spreading the word of God, but also ministering to the sick and imprisoned, teaching children, and in general trying to make temporal life easier for the people. Here was a man who lived with the people in each land he visited, able to reach them only through an interpreter—and through the example of his own life.

He is credited with many miracles. One occurred in Ceylon, now Sri Lanka, where Francis found himself preaching to a roomful of skeptics.

He prayed to God to make his listeners more open to his message. Then he turned to two men in the room and asked them to bring to him a man who had been buried just the day before, right next to the church. The men went and dug up the corpse. Francis knelt by the body, prayed, and then ordered the dead man to rise in God's name. The man stood up, alive, and yes, the congregation was converted. Not bad for a man who, like Augustine, took some heavenly coaxing to trade an enjoyable worldly life for one of service to God.

Some descendants of Francis Xavier's early converts are still paying tribute to the man who was known as "the Apostle of the Indies" and "the Apostle of Japan."

E-FACTS

St. Francis Xavier is held in particularly high regard by the residents of Kagoshima, at the southern tip of Japan's main island.

While he was in what is now Malaysia, Francis met a Japanese man named Yajiro, who spoke so glowingly of his country that the missionary was moved to see it for himself. He and two fellow Jesuits, along with Yajiro, who acted as translator, arrived at Kagoshima on August 15, 1549. Francis preached there and compiled a catechism.

In 1999 a memorial mass was celebrated in Kagoshima, with an envoy from the Vatican attending. The city unveiled its third statue of St. Francis Xavier in 1999 also. When you consider that today only 0.5 percent of that city's 1.8 million people are Catholic, that's quite a tribute.

Francis Xavier is buried in the Church of the Good Jesus in Goa, India. At his death—and this certainly makes one shudder, no matter what its ultimate aim—his right arm was ordered severed from his body by the Jesuit SuperioGeneral and returned to Rome, where it now reposes in the Church of the Gesu. Apparently the symbolism was that Francis Xavier was the church's right arm in Asia.

The missionary was canonized in 1622 by Pope Gregory XV and in 1927. His feast day is December 3. He is the patron saint of Borneo, the East Indies, Japan, foreign missions, and of tourists.

CHAPTER 9

The Gospel Writers
(Sts. Matthew, Mark, Luke, and John)

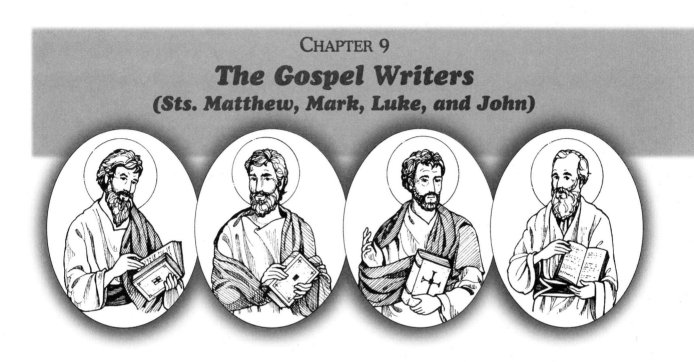

We know them as the four men who wrote the Gospels of the New Testament. Two names we might recognize as apostles, but what about the other two? Who were these four whose work has endured for millennia as God's message to the faithful?

E-FACTS

> The word **gospel** comes from the old English *godspel* meaning "good news."

Perhaps the first question here should be: What are the Gospels?

The Gospels

Four books make up the Gospels. With the inspiration of the Holy Spirit, four men put on paper the life of Jesus, his teachings, miracles, and, most important, his Crucifixion and Resurrection and the message he wanted to impart. They drew on their own knowledge of time and events, the oral tradition of stories, especially those told by Jesus' apostles and others who followed him. They each wrote at different times and in different places.

Jesus never wrote anything in his public life, except for once drawing in the sand to illustrate a point while preaching.

E-FACTS

A book that can help you understand the Gospels and, for that matter, the Bible, is the *International Bible Commentary,* edited by William R. Farmer and published by the Liturgical Press in 1998. Written by several scholars from around the world with the aim of making the Bible more approachable for the average reader, it can be found in religious bookstores.

St. Matthew

Matthew was one of the Twelve Apostles. He was a tax collector before he left that work at Jesus' directive.

Matthew wrote his gospel, probably somewhere in Syria, for a community of Christians who had been Jewish. He stressed how Jesus came to the Jews as a new Moses and thereby fulfilled the Old Testament prophetic texts. He also emphasized Christians growing together in faith, in a community of love.

Interestingly, many scholars debate whether the first gospel as we know it today is in fact Matthew's original work. It is now believed it was written by Matthew in Hebrew, and then translated into Greek by a well educated Grecian Jew knowledgeable in rabbinic scholarship.

Matthew's feast day is September 21. He is the patron saint of accountants and bankers.

Ask, and it will be given to you; seek, and you will find; knock, and it will be opened to you.

—MATTHEW 7:7

St. Mark

Mark was not one of the original apostles, although he probably was a disciple of Jesus. Mark's is said to be the clearest and the shortest of the four Gospels. Written somewhere around A.D. 65–70, it contains more miracles and less teaching than the others. Broadly speaking, Mark's gospel emphasizes Christianity in times of persecution (which was true of Rome in the year 64) amid feelings of abandonment. Mark notes the words of Jesus on the cross: "My God, my God, why have you forsaken me?" Mark tells readers how patterning their lives after Jesus', especially his self-sacrificing love, is what it takes to be a Christian, and that this is where hope lies.

> Above all, it's the gospels that occupy my mind when I'm at prayer. My poor soul has so many needs, and yet this is the one thing needful. I'm always finding fresh lights there, hidden and enthralling meanings.
>
> —ST. THÉRÈSE OF LISIEUX

Mark's gospel was probably written in Rome. Because he often explains phrases in **Aramaic** (a Semitic language), it is believed that his readers were Gentile pagans who converted to Christianity. Since they did not understand Aramaic, they were obviously not Jewish.

Mark is said to have been the first to bring Christianity to Egypt, taking along the gospel he had written and establishing churches in Alexandria.

E-FACTS

> Christians in Egypt—known as Copts—now compose around 10 percent of that country's 64 million people.

His feast day is April 25, and he is the patron saint of Egypt and of notaries.

St. Luke

Saint watchers, and even many who are not, are likely to know Luke's profession immediately: he was a physician.

He was not one of the apostles. In fact, Luke never met Jesus. He was from Antioch (although some say Greece), and wrote the Third Gospel there around the year 85.

Luke's gospel was directed at Christians who had been pagans. The work was marked by its concern for those who needed good words the most and were most often left out: women, the poor, and so on. It is Luke who gives an account of the Nativity, stressing how humble Jesus' birth was.

Because he wrote for those in the Hellenic world, with their ideals of Greek humanism, Luke endeavored to show those people that the ideal for the people's lives now was not the heroes of Greek culture, but Jesus. He tells them that Jesus is the one who heals and forgives and that without him they are alone.

Not having known Jesus, Luke was able to maintain a certain distance from the Passion and Resurrection, taking a long view of Christianity and its impact. His gospel goes beyond the Resurrection and Pentecost.

E-QUESTIONS?

What is pentecost?
Pentecost, which comes from the Greek for "the fiftieth day," is the liturgical feast held 50 days after Easter, commemorating the point from which the apostles began to carry the message of Christ to the world. It is less commonly known as Whitsunday.

A companion of St. Paul's, Luke went along with him on his second and third missionary journeys to Macedonia and Greece, on his final journey to Jerusalem, and then on with him to Rome. In one of Paul's letters to the Colossians, he calls this gospel writer "Luke, the beloved physician," which seems to confirm Luke's profession.

After Paul's death, Luke is said to have gone to Greece, where he lived to be 84 years of age. It is uncertain where and when he wrote his gospel, but it is thought to have been written either in Greece or what is now Ephesus, Turkey, A.D. 70–85.

His feast day is October 18, and he is the patron saint of doctors, artists, butchers, and notaries.

E-FACTS

The Book of Kells is a lavishly illustrated, opulent version of the four Gospels. It can be found at Dublin's Trinity College library, and it is one of the most remarkable documents in existence.

Written in Latin circa the 700s and comprising 680 pages of calf-vellum parchment, the book today can be viewed in four volumes approximating the four Gospels rather than the original single tome. The text, and especially the remarkable, meticulous illustrations, took years to complete. In the 1700s, a bookbinder trimmed the pages, cutting off some of the irreplaceable illustrations in the decorative borders. For more about this and other subjects, you might want to read *How the Irish Saved Civilization* by Thomas Cahill (Doubleday, 1995), which has enjoyed a long run on bestseller lists.

St. John

John often carries appellations to his name: St. John the Evangelist or St. John the Divine (for his theological brilliance). His was the last gospel, written around the year 95, although it may have been as late as the first decade of the second century.

John was one of Jesus' Twelve Apostles. Born in Galilee, he was the brother of James the Greater, another apostle. John was a fisherman until, like James and Matthew and the others, he was called by Jesus to follow him.

One of the three apostles closest to Jesus (the others were James and Peter), John was, along with Peter, the first apostle at the tomb after the Resurrection. John was the only apostle at the Crucifixion, and it was there that Jesus placed his mother, Mary, into John's care.

E-FACTS

The Gospels of Matthew, Mark, and Luke contain many similarities and so are called the **synoptic Gospels**—having a common viewpoint. The Gospel of John was written much later and has a style of its own. In art, the gospel writers have these emblems: Matthew's is a man; Mark's, a lion; Luke's, an ox; and John's an eagle.

John is thought to have gone to Rome during the reign of the Emperor Domitian, and barely escaped being martyred there. In Ephesus (a sizable Greek city and prominent center of early Christianity, now part of modern Turkey), after the death of Domitian, he wrote the Fourth Gospel and three epistles. John is also the author of the Book of Revelation, which opens with, "In the beginning was the Word . . . ."

John's gospel was directed at a Christian community around Ephesus. It contains only a bit in common with the **synoptic Gospels**. What stands out in John's words is how few miracles by Jesus are mentioned. Highlighted is Jesus' claims to divinity, but John also stresses Jesus' humanity, such as when he weeps over the death of his friend Lazarus.

John died in Ephesus, the only apostle who was not martyred.

John's feast day is December 27. He is the patron saint of Asia Minor (the Near East).

CHAPTER 10

St. Ignatius of Loyola
(1491–1556)

To saint watchers, the name St. Ignatius equals "Jesuits." And that religious order, which he founded, is equated in many minds with education and learning. Jesuits are also known for missionary work that spans the globe.

Oddly, Ignatius did not have too much interest in school when he was young. But then wasn't Einstein said to have done poorly? Didn't he even flunk a subject or two?

In Spain

Ignatius was born in Spain in a castle at Azpeita, in the Basque province of Guipúzcoa, of a noble family. The youngest of 13 children, he was christened Iñigo López de Loyola.

As a youth Ignatius became a court page and then went into the military. At 30 he was seriously wounded when a cannonball shattered his leg during the siege of Pamplona, when Spain was at war with the French. One day, during a lengthy convalescence at the home of his brother and sister-in-law, Ignatius was looking for something to read. Not finding the romantic adventures he preferred, he picked up a book about the saints. As he read, it seemed to him that the saints led truly heroic lives. When Ignatius's leg finally healed it was slightly shorter than his other leg, and had a raised bump on it. Ignatius later said in his autobiography, which he wrote in the third person: "Because he was determined to make a way for himself in the world, he could not tolerate such ugliness and thought it marred his appearance." Ignatius told the surgeons to remove the bump, a terribly painful operation performed at that time without anesthesia.

With the inspiration he gathered from reading about the saints, Ignatius decided that when he was healed he would become a soldier again, but this time for Christ.

E-FACTS

The Jesuits' missionary endeavors have sometimes led to martyrdom, as you will read in other places in this book. In November 1989, six Jesuits were killed at Central American University in El Salvador.

The Beginning

By the time he turned 31, Ignatius was feeling well enough to start his new life. He left his brother's castle for a pilgrimage to the Catalonian shrine of Our Lady of Monserrat. There he traded in his expensive-looking clothes for a beggar's, and laid his sword and dagger from military service at the shrine's altar of Our Lady.

Next, he walked to the nearby town of Manresa and began to beg for food. He allowed his hair to grow wild in atonement for the former pride he had taken in it.

Ignatius followed a path similar to other men you will read about in these pages, turning away from a life of wealth and pleasure. Most seem to have first spent time in prayer, as hermits or in a **monastery** (a dwelling place of monks), before entering the second phase of their life—service to God in the outside world. Manresa served the purpose of a hideaway for Ignatius, although he was certainly not cloistered there.

Unlike other saints in the beginning of their spiritual development, Ignatius received a number of mystical visions. In one, a strong ray of light emanated from the Eucharist on the altar while he prayed.

The *Exercises*

It is said Ignatius wrote most of his *Spiritual Exercises* in Manresa. This was the guide to prayer for which he is most noted—besides founding the Jesuits—although it was not published until much later, in 1548.

The insights and systems relating to God and prayer that he put down on paper became the *Exercises*. One insight he kept coming back to centered on how to discern God's will. For example, if you are faced with two choices that seem equally good, the *Exercises* will lead you, through prayer, to know which choice would be for the greater glory of God.

Ignatius left Manresa in 1523, on his way to Africa. He begged for all that he needed en route. But it was not a successful missionary journey, and he was forced to return to Barcelona.

From "Older" Student to Missionary

Now, the once-wayward student elected to fill another void in his life: education. Realizing how much he needed to know for the life he aspired to, Ignatius returned to school. Picture it: a man in his thirties, learning Latin grammar alongside students who were nine to 13 years of age. Imagine the taunts from those boys! No matter. He studied and learned and in two years was ready to move on.

Ignatius enrolled at the University of Paris for more study and became friends with six men who would work with him for the rest of their lives: Blessed Peter Favre, St. Francis Xavier (Chapter 8), Diego Lainez, Alfonso Salmerón, Nicholas Bobadilla, and Simón Rodríguez.

E-PROFILE

Bl. Peter Favre (1506–1546) et al.

The French Peter Favre (or Fabre or Lefevre) was born into a farming family at Savot. While studying in Paris, he became friends with Francis Xavier and Ignatius of Loyola.

Peter was ordained in 1534 and was sent as an emissary by Pope Paul III to settle religious differences in European countries.

He often lectured on the *Spiritual Exercises* of Ignatius and was quite popular in Germany, France, and Iberia. He attracted Francis Borgia and Peter Canisius to the Jesuits, both of whom are saints. St. Francis Borgia's feast day is October 10. He is sometimes known as the Jesuit Order's second founder. St. Peter Canisus's feast day is December 21; he is a Doctor of the Church and a patron saint of Germany. (Note that even though Peter helped add two saints to the roster, he's still only "Blessed"!). Peter's feast day is August 11. He is best known for his *Catechism*, a book that was printed in 15 languages and is still in use today in parochial schools.

All six men listened to Ignatius's religious insights and plans for future missionary work and earnestly wanted to join him, although Francis Xavier, who was initially more interested in a good time, took a bit longer to come around. This small group would form the nucleus of the Jesuit order.

Around this time, too, Ignatius began to attract followers based on his *Spiritual Exercises* and gained another type of attention. Because his teaching was a new and different concept, he was dragged in by the Inquisition and even put in prison for a short time. But there was nothing heretical about the *Exercises*, so Ignatius was exonerated.

Ignatius graduated from the university at 43 with a master of arts degree. He and his band of six relied on the *Exercises* as their guide. On August 15, 1534, the Feast of the Assumption, they went to Paris, to the chapel of St. Denis in Montmartre to make their vows of poverty and chastity. Their third vow—they saw themselves as missionaries—was to go to Jerusalem to convert the Muslims. If for some reason that could not be accomplished, they agreed they would offer their services to the pope and he could direct them to where he thought they would be most useful.

E-FACTS

In 1231 Pope Gregory IX set up the Inquisition as a system for removing heresy from the church in various parts of Europe and for punishing those considered heretics. Besides Ignatius of Loyola a few other saints ran afoul of this tribunal.

It's the *Spanish* Inquisition, which was most powerful in the late sixteenth century, we hear about most. It was inaugurated by the Spanish monarchs Ferdinand and Isabella in 1479 to deal with heresy but also to dig out converted Jews and Muslims who were practicing their original religion underground. The Spanish Inquisition was only abolished in 1834 by decree of the monarch.

The group reached Jerusalem, but Ignatius became ill and was forced to return to Spain to recover. He would meet the others later in Venice, he told them.

We must adapt the Society [of Jesus] to the times, not the times to the Society.

—IGNATIUS OF LOYOLA

When they all met again, their number had grown to 10; another three men had listened to Ignatius's message and joined him. They were ordained to the priesthood, although they were still not a formal religious order.

By this time a threat of war in Jerusalem kept the missionaries from returning there. The group separated and went their different ways, volunteering in hospitals and teaching the *Exercises* in various Italian cities. Months went by, and when conditions still did not look good for travel to Jerusalem, Ignatius called everyone back to meet in Rome.

Obedience?

The group agreed to stand by the decision made in Montmartre: to offer their services to the pope. But should they become a formal religious order, which would mean taking a vow of obedience to the Vatican, along with vows of poverty and chastity? The group prayed over the issue and then agreed that they would swear obedience. They unanimously elected Ignatius as the head of the order. On September 27, 1540, Pope Paul III signed a document establishing the Society of Jesus, who became known as the Jesuits. The pope immediately ordered some of the men to leave for missionary work in foreign countries, which was just what they had hoped for.

Staying Home

Ignatius remained in Italy, putting together the constitution for the Jesuit order and handling the other responsibilities of a Superior General. He was a patient man, it is said, and a charitable one, and kind to the men in his order. He was also particularly good at taking down a peg or two the pompous and conceited who flaunted their education. There's no need to wonder why that particular posturing irked him.

In 1550, Ignatius was given funds toward building the Roman College for the Jesuits, which became the model for all of his other schools of learning.

E-FACTS

Among the Jesuit schools in this country are Georgetown University in Washington, D.C., Loyola University in Chicago, Loyola College in Baltimore, and Loyola Marymount University in Los Angeles.

These were interesting times in western Europe, times that affected Ignatius and his ventures. Martin Luther had initiated an important component of the Protestant Reformation. Ships were sailing from Spain and Portugal to explore the world (Columbus's flotilla reached the New World the year after Ignatius was born). These new events seemed to call for more and more missionaries and more uses for the *Exercises,* so it was a busy time for the Jesuits.

A Prayer of St. Ignatius of Loyola

Here I am, O supreme King and Lord of all things, I, so unworthy, but still confiding in your grace and help, I offer myself entirely to you and submit all that is mine to your will. In the presence of your infinite goodness, and under the sight of your glorious Virgin Mother and of the whole heavenly court, I declare that this is my intention, my desire, and my firm decision: Provided it will be for your greatest praise and for my best obedience to you, to follow you as nearly as possible, and to imitate you in bearing injustices and adversities, with true poverty, of spirit and things as well. . . . If it pleases your holiest Majesty to elect to accept me for such a state of life.

Ignatius had been ill so many times over the years that when he took to his bed again in July 1556, there was no special alarm. However, this turned out to be his last illness. When the saint died on July 31 at the age of 65, he had seen the Jesuits grow in 15 years from 10 men to more than 1,000 in nine countries and in Europe, Brazil, and India. Today there are more than 22,000 members of the Society of Jesus, and his *Spiritual Exercises* is a classic, still read after more than 400 years.

Ignatius's feast day is July 31. He was canonized in 1622. During the proceedings leading to his being declared a saint, more than 200 miracles were attributed to him. "For the greater glory of God" was St. Ignatius's motto, both for himself and for the Jesuits. St. Ignatius Loyola is the patron saint of retreats and spiritual exercises.

Suggested Additional Reading:

The Spiritual Exercises of St. Ignatius, translated and with commentary by Pierre Wolff (Triumph, 1997). A teacher of Ignatian spirituality interprets and evaluates this noted work for the reader.

CHAPTER 11

St. Joan of Arc
(1412–1431)

What is it about Joan of Arc that has made her one of the best known saints, one whose short life is replayed over and over on the stage and in film?

Is it the idea of a young, illiterate peasant girl leading troops into battle that fascinates us? Is it her horrifying death by fire?

And what of Joan herself? Did she really hear God speaking to her, or was she simply a confused, troubled girl? Was the Maid of Orleans, as she came to be known, a national heroine? An instrument of God? Saint or sorceress?

We are given much to think about every time a director comes out with a new version of the Joan of Arc story. Creative license shifts Joan's story this way and that, and she emerges appearing however Otto or Luc or any other director sees her. Did you take the quiz in the Introduction on movies about saints? There are many more "Joan" movies than mentioned there, around 50 of them—17 in 1909 alone, the year she was beatified. The A&E cable program *Biography* airs Joan of Arc's story frequently due to its popularity. In the music world, there have been operas about this saint.

Let's get down to what is known about Joan's life, minus what has been added for audience interest by a director's or composer's dramatic license.

Sarah Bernhardt portrayed the saint onstage in 1890, and a silent film about Joan was released by Cecil B. DeMille in 1906.

E-FACTS

A Country at War

Jeanne d'Arc was born on January 6 in Domrémy, in northeastern France, about 200 miles east of Paris. It will help you visualize the towns in Joan's story if you draw a circle extending out from Paris about 200 miles in all directions. Within that circle are the places of importance you will read about here.

Joan's father, Jacques d'Arc, was a farmer and reportedly a disciplinarian. Her mother, it is said, was a pious woman. Joan had two brothers, and it is believed neither she nor her siblings could read or write.

The times were turbulent. Little more than 50 years earlier, the Black Plague had swept across France, killing an astonishing one-third to one-half of the population. Now, during Joan's early years, battles that would become known as the Hundred Years War were raging. The English, under the house of the Plantagenets, were fighting the French Valois to become rulers of France. At about this time the English had reached the Loire River in France. The land south of the Loire was held by the Valois, under the leadership of Charles, the uncrowned dauphin, oldest son (some say illegitimate) of the mad Charles VI.

The English, with the help of their Burgundian allies, held the land north of the Loire. Domrémy remained loyal to the French. When the Anglo-Burgundians marched into the town, the women and children fled to the nearby hills.

E-FACTS

Mark Twain wrote a book about Joan of Arc. It took him more than a dozen years to complete, and he considered it his masterwork. It was not well received, however, perhaps because it was not what readers expected from a humorist.

Visions and Voices

Not long after the attack on Domrémy 13-year-old Joan began hearing voices. She described what she saw as a bright light, accompanied by the voices of God and of several saints. She was a good girl, they said, and it was to be her mission to unite France under Charles VII.

Were the voices real? Subsequent events and startling happenings that focused on Joan seem to confirm them. Some skeptics, however, would say that Joan, perhaps having a difficult adolescence and enduring the trauma of war so close to her, was merely hysterical. She imagined the voices, either to draw attention to herself or to get out of Domrémy and away from its dangers (although wanting to go into battle is hardly seeking a safe haven).

About this time her father had a dream in which he saw Joan riding away from home with men. The only women who did that were prostitutes. Jacques d'Arc told one of his sons he would rather drown his daughter than see her leave in this way! He quickly arranged a marriage for her with a young man from the region. But Joan told the young man she would never marry. The disappointed suitor was so angry at her response he took her to civil court. Showing a determination and courage that would stand her well in future, more serious battles, Joan said she would have no part of her father trying to marry her off: she was not bound by her father's promises.

Joan was determined to listen to her voices and take on the job of saving France. When she was 16, and had only once been outside of her village, she asked her uncle to accompany her to a nearby town. She told the magistrate there that God wanted him to go with her to where the dauphin lived.

The war was keeping the young son of the king from taking his place on the throne after his father's death. The 26-year-old dauphin is often portrayed on stage and screen as possessing a variety of not-too-sterling qualities, among them weakness, cunning, vacillation, detachment, great ambition, and excessive love of pleasure. In some works he is a simpering fool, in others a calculating demon in the ways he used Joan.

Joan next went to Robert di Boudricourt, the French commandant, who, quite understandably, laughed at her and her offer to help. His smile disappeared, however, when some of her prophecies came true: for one, the French were defeated in a specific battle she predicted would happen just outside Orleans.

In Battle

Di Boudricourt sent Joan to Chinon to see the dauphin, who had her interrogated by theologians. They declared her free of heresy. Indeed, one of her inquisitors was chilled to hear Joan tell him something about himself no one else knew.

By now Joan had donned a suit of armor and had closely cropped her hair. To her, the look was more a matter of efficiency than of deterring unwanted attention from young men.

The French troops were dispirited from frequent losses, so the dauphin gave serious consideration to the youthful would-be warrior. This was almost a no-lose situation for him. If he allowed Joan into war and she failed, it would be her fault. If she succeeded, it would be his success. Sequestered with her at one point, he emerged beaming. Joan had told him a secret, too, something no one else knew. He allowed the young girl to lead an expedition that would relieve Orleans, which was being hammered by the British.

Joan dictated this letter to the king of England before she left for battle in Orleans. The message is simple and direct. Given her youth and lack of education she has a limited vocabulary, but her words are strong, though certainly free of abstractions or nuance.

> King of England and you, Duke of Bedford, who call yourself Regent of the realm of France, and you, William de la Pole, Earl of Suffolk, John Lord Talbot, and you, Thomas Lord Scales, who call yourselves lieutenants of the Duke of Bedford, hand back to the Maid, who is sent by God, the King of Heaven, the keys of all the fine towns of France you have taken and ravaged. She is ready to make peace if you return to France all you have stolen from her. And you, archers and soldiers, noble or not, who are before the city of Orleans, go in God's name back to your own country. If you stay, await news of the Maid, who will very soon come upon you to your very great hurt. King of England, if you do not do what I ask, I will force your men to depart wherever I meet them in France; if they do not, I shall have them all slain. God, the King of Heaven, has sent me to drive them out of France, but I will show them mercy if they obey me. Do not believe that it is from God that you will hold the kingdom of France, for it is King Charles, the true heir, who will so hold it. That is the will of God . . . If you will not do what is right, there will be a greater uproar than France has known for a thousand years. You can be very sure that God will give such powers to the Maid and her good soldiers that you will find them invincible, and battle will show to whom God gives the better right.

Joan won a brilliant victory for the French and rode on to capture Troyes, to the north and east of Orleans, soon after. The troops' morale was high; the people warmly embraced her.

On July 17, 1429, the dauphin was crowned King Charles VII at Rheims, and Joan was right there with him. Strangely, though, by the following month her winning streak had ended. She failed to capture

Paris. The following spring, waging a new campaign, she was captured near Compiègne and turned over to the British.

The Tide Turns

Now Joan met with nothing but misfortune. Both Charles's and Joan's enemies at court said they feared her losses were the result of her falling from favor with God. She was charged with heresy and witchcraft before the court of Bishop Pierre Cauchon, which declared her visions were the work of the devil. Sometimes there were as many as 70 judging her, mostly ecclesiastics and lawyers. Charles made no effort to intervene on her behalf. Perhaps he found her popularity with the people threatening and was not unhappy at her arrest.

Exhausted by the questioning, surviving on meager rations, and deprived of sleep, Joan was tricked at the Anglo-Burgundian trial into signing a form that admitted the charges against her. As part of her "apology," she was to stop wearing armor and wear women's clothes. Still, a few days later she appears to have regretted signing that paper. There seems to have been evidence to suggest that Joan was raped during this time. In any event, after those few days, she defiantly donned armor again. Now her fate was sealed. Cardinal Cauchon came to her cell and pronounced her death sentence, condemning her as a heretic.

To the end Joan was not sure if she would be executed. Screaming, and crying to Jesus to save her, she was led barefoot to the stake at the marketplace in Rouen and burned to death. Her ashes were thrown into the Seine. She was 19 years old.

Twenty-five years later, in 1456, after continuing attempts by her family, the charge of heresy was lifted. Joan was canonized almost 500 years later, in 1920.

Was the Maid of Orleans a martyr for her faith, or was her death politically motivated? A question remains to this day: Why would God and the saints she said had spoken to her have any interest in France's victory over England? Still, there were those occasions when Joan looked into the future, or told someone a "secret" only he knew.

The Transcript

The trial of Joan of Arc survives in several versions. In 1841 a scholar named Jules Quicherat dug out the trial proceedings and the transcript of the hearing 25 years after her death that rescinded the charges against her. He published them in 1841 in five volumes.

Now it was possible to know Joan better. For instance, a touching note that emerged, having nothing to do with battles or her trial, was how impressed the young warrior was by Charles's court. She remarked on the more than 50 lighted torches in that room, something that could be expected to attract the attention and even awe of a young country girl.

Her spirit comes through in the testimony. Here was a teenager—and a female—who was the equivalent of a general, directing men into battle. Being anointed by the dauphin certainly helped Joan with troops who were commanded to follow where she led, but she was also firm, focused, and quite practical in war. Her values went with her. She required of her troops that they not gamble, or womanize, or help themselves to the spoils of war.

Even at the most dire moments of her trial, Joan did not ask God to punish her tormentors. She had no particular theological message to impart. She did no preaching, either at her trial or before. She simply did the job God had directed her to do, and she did it the best way she knew how. She did not know, of course, how her obedience and steadfastness were to end.

Joan of Arc's feast day is May 30. She is the patron saint of France and of the military.

Suggested Additional Reading:

Joan of Arc by Mary Gordon (Lipper/Viking, 2000). This noted writer offers her impressions of Joan as part of the Penguin Lives series.

Joan of Arc: The Image of Female Heroism by Marina Warner (University of California Press, 1981). The British author of several books on religious topics offers a fascinating, readable—and balanced—look at the Maid of Orleans.

CHAPTER 12

St. John of the Cross
(1542–1591)

Among a handful of saints who could be considered the greatest mystics of all time, and one of the greatest Spanish poets as well, is St. John. Have you heard the expression "dark night of the soul"? John is the author of the spiritual classic with that title *(The Dark Night)*, as well as several other works.

He led a harsh, often criminally rough, life, suffering persecution by his own church, indeed from his own religious order. Yet he remained, it is said, a cheerful soul.

An instant of pure love is more precious to God and the soul, and more profitable to the church, than all other good works together, though it may seem as if nothing were done.

—JOHN OF THE CROSS

Holy Orders

John was born Juan de Yepes y Álvarez in Fontiveros, Old Castile, Spain. His father died soon after his birth, and Juan grew up in poverty. He became a Carmelite friar at the age of 21, taking the name Juan de Santa María. Dedicated to prayer and solitude, it had become somewhat complacent, even lax, about its mission the Carmelite order by the time John joined.

In Chapter 4 you read how St. Anthony of Padua crossed paths with St. Francis of Assisi, and Chapter 7 mentions St. Clare's listening to the preaching of St. Francis of Assisi. John's story is another instance where one saint influenced another. When he was 25, John was introduced to Teresa of Ávila, who at 52 was the leader of a Carmelite reform movement and one of the most important religious personalities of her time. She later would be named a Doctor of the Church. (Teresa is discussed in Chapter 20.)

Teresa and John were of like minds. They both sought to retain the Carmelites' original simplicity, which they considered to be a dedication to prayer. John was in fact considering joining another order, so dissatisfied was he with the Carmelites. The two joined forces. John began a parallel reform for men to Teresa's Discalced Carmelites movement for women.

What does discalced mean?
Discalced means barefoot, unshod.

John became prior of the first community of discalced **friars**, taking the name Juan de la Cruz—John of the Cross. Later, when Teresa became prioress of a **convent** in Ávila, she asked John to be its spiritual director.

Conflict from Within

Differences between the reform movement and the traditionalists plagued the Carmelite order. When he was 35, John was kidnapped and taken to a Carmelite monastery opposed to reform in Toledo, where he was held for nine months, surviving only on bread and water and subjected to regular beatings.

After his release he made his way back to his community, where he was eventually elected to several offices as **prior** and provincial in different parts of Spain and established several houses for the order. In 1582 Teresa died. In 1590 conflict among the Discalced broke out, and one year later the Madrid general chapter took away all of John's titles and offices because of his support for the moderates in the order.

Now a mere monk, John was sent to a monastery in Andalusia, where he contracted a fever and died on December 14. He died alone and almost forgotten in the very congregation he had helped to found.

Writings from the Soul

But what a body of work John of the Cross left! No doubt strengthened in thought and work by such a severe life, the powerful mystic was able to explain and analyze what he called "the dark night of the soul," when God cannot be seen and the soul suffers the desolation of abandonment. In John's view, that suffering, if courageously borne, can lead a soul to its splendid union with God. John carefully discusses how stripping away our imperfections, especially ego, can lead us closer to God and his love.

John's best-known work is *The Dark Night of the Soul,* which is derived from a poem he wrote while a prisoner in Toledo. He also wrote *The Spiritual Canticle* and *The Living Flame of Love.*

He was canonized in 1726. John of the Cross is a Doctor of the Church; his feast day is December 14. He is the patron saint of poets.

Suggested Additional Reading:

Dark Night of the Soul by St. John of the Cross, translated and edited and with an introduction by E. Allison Peters (Doubleday Image, 1990). Besides the saint's writings, this book includes trenchant comments on his life and work.

St. John of the Cross: His Life and Poetry by Gerald Brenan (Cambridge University Press, 1973) contains a biography of the saint, along with several of his works.

CHAPTER 13
St. John the Baptist
(First Century)

John's father was Zachary, a priest of the temple of Jerusalem. The angel Gabriel appeared to him and told him that his wife, Elizabeth, would bear a child, even though at the time she was an old woman ("old" being open to interpretation as we look back at those days). The child was John. Elizabeth and Mary were cousins, and so too were their sons, John and Jesus.

The Baptism

John led a solitary life as a hermit in the desert of Judea until he was about 30 years old. He emerged wearing clothing made of camel hair, tied with a leather belt around his waist, and began preaching along the river Jordan about the evils of the time. Calling for atonement of one's sins and for baptism, he also spoke of the "strong one" who was to come.

John attracted large crowds, although it is said he was a hellfire and brimstone type of preacher, not given to much levity in his talks or as a person. Contrasting his preaching with Jesus', you could say Jesus was more lenient. John remained very much the ascetic as well; Jesus certainly did not, enjoying food and wine and friendships.

One day Christ visited his cousin along with the crowds of the poor seeking baptism. John acknowledged him as the Messiah and baptized him, although he is reported to have said, "It is I who need baptism from you."

John did not follow Jesus but instead stayed in the Jordan Valley. He was a powerful draw with the people, to the point where Herod Antipas, the tetrarch of Perea and Galilee, and son of Herod the Great, arrested him when John rebuked Herod for his adulterous and incestuous marriage to Herodias, the wife of his half brother.

While in prison, John sent a message to Jesus asking, "Are you he who is to come, or shall we look for another?" Jesus replied, "Go and tell John what you hear and see: the blind receive their sight and the lame walk, lepers are cleansed and the deaf hear, the dead are raised up and the poor have good news preached to them. And blessed is he who takes no offense at me."

One of John's best qualities was his humility. Although the masses to whom he preached wanted to consider him the Messiah, or at least have him denounce Jesus as savior, he would hear none of it and was quick to proclaim Christ the chosen one.

"No one can lay hold of anything unless it is given to him from on high," John explained. "You are yourselves witness to the fact that I said: 'I am not the Messiah; I am sent before him.' It is the groom who has the bride. The groom's best man waits there listening for him and overjoyed to hear his voice. That is my joy, and it is complete. He must increase, while I must decrease."

The Martyr

Familiar to many of us is the next episode in John's life. Herod promised his stepdaughter, Salomé, any prize for her dancing. Her mother, Herodias, told Salomé to ask for the head of John the Baptist on a platter. The request gave Herod the excuse he needed to rid himself of the prophet who was popular with the people and inspired them, and therefore was a threat.

On John's death, Jesus said: "I tell you, among those born of women none is greater than John; yet he who is least in the kingdom of God is greater than he."

John the Baptist's feast day is June 24. He is the patron saint of monks.

CHAPTER 14
St. Jude
(First Century)

Jude was one of the original Twelve Apostles. For the reason you will learn as you read on, his name and fame endure far more than the other 11, most of whom remain fairly unknown today, without much mention outside of church liturgy.

E-FACTS

St. Jude is sometimes confused with Judas Iscariot, the apostle who betrayed Christ.

Actually, not that much is known about Jude Thaddeus. It is believed he might have been one of four brothers who were Jesus' first cousins. The truth is, though, that this is speculation—albeit educated speculation by scholars and hagiographers. With all the studying of Jude's background, the course of his life with Jesus and after the Crucifixion, little has been passed on that cannot be debated.

Jude is mentioned in the Gospel of John: When Jesus was speaking at the Last Supper, Jude interrupted him, asking, "Lord, how is it that you will manifest yourself to us, and not to the world?" Jesus answered, "If a man loves me, he will keep my word, and my Father will love him, and we will come to him and make our home with him. He who does not love me does not keep my words; and the word which you hear is not mine but the Father's who sent me."

This apostle is also said to have written a short book of the New Testament, the Letter of Jude, in which he warned against false prophets. He is thought to have been martyred in Persia.

Why then, when this holy and devoted disciple is pretty much cloaked in anonymity, is his name well known today? It is because he is the patron saint of lost causes and desperate situations. It is not known how Jude came by this patronage, but many pray to him when things appear hopeless. They pray to find work when they have been unemployed for many months, to cure a relative with a serious addiction, to cure themselves of severe illness, or to get assistance with any number of other problems that seem to have no solution, or at least not an obvious one.

E-FACTS

At a fund-raising event at St. Jude Children's Hospital in Memphis, Tennessee, in October 1999, actress Marlo Thomas told how in 1962 her father, the comedian Danny Thomas, came to found the haven for children suffering from cancer and other catastrophic illnesses. In the early days of his career he made a promise to the saint: "Show me my way in life, and I will build you a shrine." Danny Thomas's career prospered; two decades after his appeal to St. Jude, the hospital opened.

Not Desperate, Just Impossible

In *A Book of Saints: True Stories of How They Touch Our Lives* (Bantam Books, 1994), author Anne Gordon tells her favorite St. Jude story. The supplicant was not in desperate straits, rather her plea was more like an impossible request—although "impossible" certainly seems difficult enough. The woman was 36 years old, and she and her husband had three sons. Her spouse wanted a daughter very much, but the woman's doctor had told her that childbearing was now impossible for her. She prayed to Jude anyway.

A Prayer to St. Jude

Most holy apostle St. Jude, faithful servant and friend of Jesus, the name of the traitor who delivered your beloved Master into the hands of the enemies has caused you to be forgotten by many, but the church honors and invokes you universally as the patron of hopeless cases and of things despaired of. Pray for me, I am so helpless and alone. Make use, I implore you, of that particular privilege accorded to you to bring visible and speedy help where help is almost despaired. Come to my assistance in this great need that I may receive the consolations and help of heaven in all my necessities, tribulations, and sufferings, particularly [make your request here], and that I may praise God with you and all the elect throughout eternity. I promise you, O blessed Jude, to be ever mindful of this great favor, and I will never cease to honor you as my special and powerful patron and do all in my power to encourage devotion to you. Amen.

One night in a dream her deceased grandmother appeared to her. She said, "I told you if you would pray to Saint Jude he would help you, didn't I?" The woman woke from the dream somewhat confused because she *had* been praying to that saint. She did not know at the time that she was two months pregnant. It seemed her grandmother had appeared simply to tell her that her dream had come true. The couple named their daughter Mary.

Superstitions? No, it's having faith. There is a difference.

Answered Prayers

Many churches hold an annual novena to St. Jude, so this is a busy saint, no doubt hearing as many pleas for hopeless causes as St. Anthony does for lost objects.

E-QUESTIONS?

What is a novena?
A **novena** is a series of prayers for a particular purpose, spread over nine days or nine weeks, and sometimes even ongoing.

It is a tradition that if St. Jude answers your prayers, you formally thank him. That can take the form of a special trip to a church or a shrine that carries his name, or some other fitting acknowledgment of your appreciation. Many place notices in the classified columns of daily and weekly newspapers that read something like "Thank you, St. Jude, for a favor received." No name goes with the advertisement, although there are sometimes initials at the end of the item. If you look in your paper, you can probably find notices like this from time to time.

St. Jude's feast day is October 28. You can read about a particular shrine to him on page 192.

E-FACTS

The color associated with St. Jude is green—the color of hope.

Suggested Additional Reading:

Jude: A Pilgrimage to the Saint of Last Resort by Liz Trotta (HarperSanFrancisco, 1998). A noted journalist investigates this saint, traveling to Rome and Turkey, but spending most of her time in the United States visiting churches and shrines. You might be thinking, what prayer of hers did St. Jude answer that she wrote a book about him in thanks? But Trotta says there was no desperate situation in her case. Her mother always prayed to the saint, and since Trotta sort of grew up with Jude, she wanted to know more about him and the strong devotion he fosters.

CHAPTER 15
St. Mary Magdalene
(First Century)

Yes, this famous "sinner" is a saint, and there are parish churches that indeed carry her name.

Mary Magdalene, whose image as a prostitute has been handed down to us through the history of Christianity, was actually a disciple of Jesus. She was one of several women who believed in him and followed him as he preached. The women did not get as much "press" as the Twelve Apostles, but they were just as faithful and supportive. The other women remain nameless, but Mary Magdalene is prominent in this gathering.

Yet little is known about her. All four gospels name Mary Magdalene as being among the women who followed Jesus to Calvary, where he was crucified. Then they went to his tomb, hoping to anoint his body, and found it empty. An angel guarding the tomb announced the unbelievable news that Jesus had risen.

E-FACTS

Mary Magdalene is a harlot who loves Jesus in the 1960s rock musical *Jesus Christ Superstar*, and she is portrayed as a prostitute in love with Jesus in the controversial 1988 film *The Last Temptation of Christ.*

E-PROFILE

St. Joseph of Arimathea (First Century)

Joseph of Arimathea, who was fairly well-to-do and a clandestine follower of Jesus, was present at the Crucifixion and persuaded Pontius Pilate to let him have Jesus' body. He wrapped it in the finest linens and herbs and laid it inside a tomb that was carved from rock on the side of a hill. Joseph either paid for this tomb for Jesus or placed him in his own family's resting place.

Little else is known about this Saint Joseph. He is supposed to have gone on to Gaul (France) as a missionary. He is also said to have inherited the chalice used at the Last Supper. Both tales may be legend. His feast day is real, however: March 17. He is the patron saint of funeral directors and undertakers.

Witness

The angel instructed the women to tell the apostles to meet Jesus back in Galilee and mentioned Peter by name. Two of the gospels tell of Mary Magdalene actually seeing the risen Jesus. Mary was weeping outside the tomb when suddenly she saw Jesus, but she did not recognize him. Mary then said to the man she believed to be a stranger, "Sir, if you have carried him away, tell me where you have laid him, and I will take him away." Jesus answered her with one word: "Mary." She recognized him and cried "Rabboni!" (Teacher). He instructed her, "Go to my brethren and say to them, I am ascending to my Father and your Father, to my God and your God." Mary went to the apostles and told them she had seen Jesus. (John was the only apostle present at the Crucifixion; see page 47.)

Mary Magdalene was characterized in the early church as "a woman from whom seven demons had gone out," but scholars in later years debate the interpretation of that statement and whether it referred to prostitution. She is thought to have been the unnamed repentant "sinner" in the New Testament, who washed Jesus' feet with her tears and hair during the early days of his ministry. The act prompted Jesus to say, "Her sins, which are many, are forgiven, for she loved much." Through the years the definition of Mary Magdalene as a sinner has persisted.

Some religious historians believe that Mary Magdalene is the "Mary" of the two women in the Book of Luke: Martha and Mary. Martha tended to household tasks while Jesus preached. Mary, on the other hand, set work aside to sit at his feet and listen to his words. For Mary's choice, Jesus said, "She has chosen the good part and it will not be taken from her." There is no proof, of course, that Mary and Mary Magdalene are the same person.

Change in the Air

Revisionism over the millennia has been a bit kinder to Mary Magdalene; she is no longer automatically cast as a sinner. In 1998 a movement began to repair her reputation, or at least look for a more positive message the faithful could take from her life.

More than 100 groups of lay Christians have met in homes, churches, and on college campuses to celebrate Mary Magdalene's life. This is in addition to official liturgical observances.

FutureChurch, the Cincinnati, Ohio–based group that launched the national program, is interested in elevating Mary Magdalene to the prominent role she played as a disciple of Jesus. There are, the group notes, too few women in leadership positions in the early church. They add, as later historians have acknowledged, that Jesus welcomed women into his circle, and they traveled with him as he preached. Mary Magdalene was an important witness in church history and should be given her due.

Today's women, says FutureChurch, ought to be able to take biblical women as role models and can easier see themselves in the gospels as they read about those women's lives.

Because she proclaimed the good news of the Resurrection to the other disciples, Mary Magdalene has been called "Apostle to the Apostles." Her feast day is July 22. She is a patron saint of hair stylists, repentant sinners, and repentant prostitutes.

"Jolly old St. Nich-o-las . . ." is a portion of the lyrics to a Christmas song and just about all most of us know about this saint from the early days of Christianity. That and the poem we know as "The Night Before Christmas," which is actually "A Visit from St. Nicholas," written by Clement C. Moore in 1823.

We might also wonder whether St. Nicholas serves as "Santa Claus" in some European countries. But what was it that made Nicholas worthy of sainthood and the fame he enjoys today?

A Pious Activist

If the public knows little about Nicholas, that is because saint scholars are largely in the dark about the man's history. There was little to pass along over the millennia. It is believed he was born in Asia Minor, in what is now part of Turkey, and that his parents were probably well off.

What was Asia Minor?
At this time **Asia Minor** was roughly the size of today's Turkey. It was the site of some of the earliest Christian communities— Smyrna and Ephesus, for example. The churches of Asia Minor began to fade in importance in the fourth century, giving way to Antioch, Constantinople, and Alexandria.

Nicholas became a priest, rising to become bishop of Myra, a rather lowly diocese in that region. He was known for his piety, hard work, and his miracles.

During the persecution of the Christians under the Emperor Diocletian, he was imprisoned. Nicholas was at the Council of Nicea, where he denounced Arianism, and he reportedly died at Myra.

What is arianism?
Arianism constituted doctrines of the ancient Greek theologian Arius, who claimed that Jesus Christ was the highest created being on earth, but was not divine. His argument was declared heresy by the church.

Several miracles have been attributed to this saint. For example, when he was a young priest sailing on a boat to Jerusalem, Nicholas warned the sailors of a severe storm approaching. But he added, "Don't be afraid. Trust in God because He will protect you from death." The storm came, and one sailor fell overboard. His body was recovered, but the sailor was dead. What had happened to Nicholas's promise to the crew? The saint prayed to God to calm the stormy waters, and the water did become smooth and glassy. Then he blessed the dead sailor, who suddenly awoke, suffering no injuries at all from the incident.

A Popular Patron

Considering so little is known about this saint, it is intriguing that devotion to him remains strong. He has been a particular favorite with Eastern Christians, who introduced Nicholas to Germany around 980. From there his fame spread throughout western Europe, where many churches are named after him; in England alone a few hundred churches bore his name before the Reformation. Celebrations of his December 6 feast day took place in many parts of the world. In the ninth century the first pope to bear his name dedicated a basilica to St. Nicholas.

To this day, Nicholas is particularly venerated in Russia, where he is a patron saint.

Saint to Santa

But what about Santa Claus? How did a bishop evolve into the jolly creature who delivers gifts to children?

Saints fell out of favor during the Reformation in Europe, except in Holland. It is thought the name Santa Claus came from English-speaking Dutch children who arrived in New Amsterdam (New York). They called the saint "Sinter Klaas" or "Sint Klaus," a shortening of Saint Nicholas. The name later evolved to our present-day Santa Claus.

Today, America's Santa and Sinter Klaas in the Netherlands are far apart in style, although their mission is the same: entering a home and distributing gifts. In Holland, the event takes place on the night of December 5 and 6, just before St. Nicholas's feast day, and Sinter Klaas is quite the pious bishop, not the rosy-cheeked Santa we know. He arrives on a horse, and not by sleigh.

The way Santa Claus looks is spun from the description of the good-natured gift giver in the poem "A Visit from St. Nicholas" and from the cartoons of American artist Thomas Nast that appeared in *Harper's Illustrated Weekly* in 1863 and again in the 1880s. Nast substituted a furry cap for the broad-brimmed hat that illustrates Moore's poem.

European countries celebrate Christmas with their own version of Santa Claus.

- In France, he is Père Noel, visiting on the night of December 24.
- In Germany, he is Nikolaus (St. Nikolaus in Catholic areas of the country), who comes at night on December 5 and 6 with small gifts for children. Major gift giving occurs on Christmas Eve and Christmas Day, with no sign of Nikolaus (or Santa).
- In England, Father Christmas used to bring holiday gifts, but now that country has pretty much adopted Santa Claus, as have Ireland, Canada, and Australia.
- In Holland, Sinter Klaas calls with gifts the night of December 5 and 6.
- In Sweden, goodies are brought by Tomten, who wears a white beard and a red suit, and visits during the night of Christmas Eve.
- Austrian consumers are said to be mourning the loss of Christkindl, a holy child who traditionally delivered presents to children, to the American-style Santa Claus.

True Gift Giving

An endearing story about golden balls also equated this saint with gifts. In Nicholas's diocese a nobleman with three young daughters had lost all his money. At that time and place, being without a dowry meant the young women could not be married, which meant there was nothing ahead but a life of prostitution.

Nicholas decided he would give them their dowry. Each girl would receive a golden ball. But he wanted no fuss, so he tossed the balls into the window of their room while the girls slept. One of the gifts was said to have landed in a stocking hanging by the hearth to dry. That off-target pitch evolved into our present-day custom of hanging Christmas stockings by the fire to be filled with small gifts and other goodies.

Nicholas's present to the three girls is considered perfect giving—it takes into account the needs and wants of the recipient, offers the gift without the expectation of being acknowledged and thanked, and the reward is simply the fact that the giver made someone happy. Paintings of St. Nicholas will often show him holding three bags of gold (sometimes bags of gold are substituted in the story for the golden balls).

Another tale that has endured is that this saint restored to life three children who were killed by an evil innkeeper who had cut up their bodies and pickled them in brine.

Both these stories have contributed to Nicholas's reputation as a protector of children.

Relics in Bari

The exact year of Nicholas's death is not known, along with so many other details of his life. However, in the eleventh century, Italian soldiers are said to have stolen his body, probably from Turkey, and moved it to Bari, Italy, where his relics remain.

St. Nicholas is said to be the only saint equally venerated by all Christian denominations. He is quite a busy patron saint, too: of Greece, Russia, brides, children, merchants, dockworkers, travelers, bakers, brewers, prisoners, sailors, and pawnbrokers.

Pawnbrokers? What hangs over the door of a pawnbroker's shop? Three golden balls. According to some sources, the three balls became a symbol for moneylenders in Renaissance Florence. They did in fact appear on the coat of arms of the Medici family, the richest merchants of that time.

CHAPTER 17
St. Patrick
(389–461)

Hmm, is it a coincidence that the chapter about St. Patrick is number 17?

But quickly now, what do you know about this enormously popular saint? That he killed the snakes in Ireland? Well . . . we'll see. That he introduced Christianity to that island? Yes and no.

You are likely to be surprised as you read on that Patrick led an interesting, diverse, and even complex life, and is probably not at all what you've thought about him. For one thing, he was not Irish, at least not by birth. Also, he spent a number of years in slavery on that emerald isle.

Saints Galore

Ireland is a religious country. It is hard to walk or drive there without coming upon a church or the remains of one, or a graveyard or other evidence of its holy men and women.

John Matthews, in *Drinking from the Sacred Well* (more on this book at the end of this chapter), says that the names of more than 10,000 Celtic saints have survived: "Some of them recorded only in the land, as place names that summon up long-forgotten events, legends, and miracles that have vanished, along with their owners, back into the mists from which they came."

Celtic saints can also be found in Wales and Scotland. When it comes to Ireland, Patrick is one of the most notable of the canonized (to us, he is the most popular). However, there is not much known about him, and what is known has been debated over the years.

Fortunately for saint scholars, Patrick left two written works to pore over and analyze: the *Confession,* written as he was close to death and which serves as the chief source of biographical data, and *Letter to the Soldiers of Coroticus*, in which he denounced the killing of a group of Irish Christians by marauding Christian Welshmen. Regardless of how much or how little of this holy man's life is known, its major points seem to be agreed upon by hagiographers.

The Farthest Reaches

Imagine if you can the Western world in the fourth century. Spain, Gaul (France), and Britain formed the western border of the Roman Empire. Missionaries spreading the word of Christianity had been successful in these regions. Ireland, however, was largely unexplored. Since there were not that many miles between Ireland and Britain, it is likely there was some trade between the two countries, along Ireland's eastern coast. However, the island was wild country; it did not in the least resemble the Ireland of today, with its patchwork shades of shimmering greens delineated by stone walls. It was heavily forested and travel was extremely difficult.

The country was governed by kings and tribal chieftains. Some of its people still worshiped the sun; in other areas the Druids, an ancient Celtic priesthood, practiced their rites. Druids appear in Irish and Welsh literature and history as magicians and wizards. Their rituals involved oak and mistletoe, belief in immortality and reincarnation—and, it is thought, human sacrifice.

A few missionaries had journeyed to Ireland, establishing small pockets of Christianity, so Patrick did not convert all of Ireland. Still, before his coming, the country remained just about the only part of the Celtic world that had not been completely converted to the religion of Rome, and Patrick did bring Christianity to many new parts of the island.

Patrick was born along the west coast of Roman Britain (although a few scholars believe he was born in Gaul). His father, Calpurnius, was a Roman citizen, a free subject, a deacon, and, what today would be called, middle class. His mother, Concessa, gave their child the Latin name Patricius. Being the son of a deacon, Patrick was brought up a Christian, with the sense that Rome was the spiritual and cultural center of the universe.

E-FACTS

During Patrick's time barbarous peoples were invading parts of western Europe. One group was the Vandals—a Germanic people dwelling south of the Baltic between the Vistula and Oder Rivers— who overran Spain, Gaul, and North Africa and, in 455, Rome. From their name comes the English word *vandal*.

Enslavement

When Patrick was 16 an event occurred that was to set the course for his adult life. A fleet of raiders came ashore near his home, destroying property, killing residents, and taking many captives. For some reason, Patrick's parents were absent at the time. Patrick was taken, along with others, mostly servants. He was sold into slavery in Ireland "to the ultimate places of the earth," he says. (Remember, Patrick considered himself tied to Rome; to his west, though only a handful of miles from his home, lay darkness.)

If Patrick considered the eastern shore of Ireland a no man's land, he must have been appalled as he traveled across the country, probably to Connaught in the west, where he was held in bondage. His master was kind, however, and Patrick worked for him some six years.

During that time he experienced a profound spiritual change. (Eventually he would consider these years of slavery crucial to his spiritual growth.) At this time he was only about 22 and quite naturally yearned for home and family in Britain. He tells of a voice in his sleep that told him, "Thou doest well to fast; thou shalt soon return to thy native land." Patrick believed the voice, taking the words to mean he was indeed going home. He began planning his escape.

He made his way safely across the country to the east coast town of Wicklow, 30 miles or so south of Dublin. Trading vessels were about to set sail; so with the thought of working his way home, Patrick approached one and was taken aboard as a crewman.

Neither the nationality nor race of the crew is known, but Patrick says they were heathen. Of course, he did a bit of proselytizing onboard. After sailing for three days, the ship landed along the shore of a country that also has not been named. Patrick said they then made their way on foot through a "desert" for nearly a month.

During that trek the crew eventually ran out of food. One of the men remarked to Patrick that they were likely to starve, and what was Patrick's God going to do about that? Patrick replied, "Nothing is impossible to the Lord my God. Turn to him truly, that he may send you food in your path this day till ye are filled, for he has plenty in all places." Soon a drove of pigs appeared on the road, and the hungry crewmen killed enough of them to eat for days. Patrick's worth rose several notches in their eyes.

The saint also seemed surprised at what appeared to be a certain miracle. Patrick performed many miracles over the course of his life, making him seem to have powers equal to those of the **Druids**, who were supposed to be his adversaries.

E-FACTS

St. Patrick's Day festivities in New York City are widely known, with their focal point as St. Patrick's Cathedral. But Savannah, Georgia, has a huge celebration on March 17, too. The year 2000 saw that city's 176th annual St. Patrick's Day parade draw some 500,000 revelers viewing some 250 parade entries. There are quite a few Irish social and religious groups in the area, where many immigrants headed on arrival in this country.

Travels

Where exactly *were* Patrick and the ship's crew? Scholars believe the boat made land along the southwest coast of Gaul, perhaps at what is now Bordeaux. Why it took them so long to get from there to Italy, their goal, and why they were in danger of starvation in a region that was not a wilderness is not known. The group supposedly traversed Gaul, then headed into Italy.

E-PROFILE

There are saints in Ireland as important to the Irish as St. Patrick. Here are four of them:

- **St. Brendan of Clonfert (ca. 484–577).** According to legend, Brendan was born in Kerry and ordained around 512. He founded numerous monasteries, the most famous located in Clonfert, the center of what is now the Irish Republic. He made many sea voyages as a missionary, including one to "The Land of Promise," which he wrote about in his *Navigatio Sancti Brendani Abbatis*. The work became very popular in the Middle Ages, and scholars believe Brendan may actually have reached Iceland, Greenland, and even Newfoundland. His feast day is May 16, and he is the patron saint of whales.
- **St. Brigid (or Bridget or Brighid) of Kildare (ca. 450–525).** Known as "Mary of the Gael," Brigid was believed to have been converted to Christianity by St. Patrick. She did good works for the poor and is credited with many miracles. Brigid became a nun and then abbess of the first Irish convent called, in Irish, Cill Dara, now known as Kildare. While explaining the Passion to a dying pagan, St. Brigid picked up some rushes strewn about the floor and wove them into a cross. The St. Brigid's cross, put together from rushes, is still made in Ireland. It is often placed in homes, especially on the saint's feast day, as a protection against evil and want. Her feast day is February 1, and she is the patron saint of Ireland, dairy workers, scholars, and fugitives.
- **St. Columba of Iona (ca. 521–597).** Also of royal descent, Columba was ordained and spent several years preaching and founding monasteries across Ireland. A man with a fiery temper, he became embroiled in a feud that led to the deaths of some 3,000 men in battle—with just one man killed on his side. The penitent Columba vowed to leave Ireland and never return, to do penance and convert a like number of pagans as the number of men slain (some say he did not volunteer to leave, but was asked). His great legacy was his evangelization of Scotland and northern England, and the many monks who left Columba's monastery in Iona to work all over Europe. His feast day is June 9, and he is a patron saint of Ireland, Scotland, and poets.
- **St. Kevin of Glendalough (died ca. 618).** Also known as "Coemgen," Kevin was born of royalty. He was ordained and lived for 17 years as a hermit in Glendalough, at the foot of the Wicklow Mountains, a few miles south of Dublin. He was, he said, following the direction of "a Shining One" who came to him in a dream. He then founded a monastery back at Glendalough. Many miracles are attributed to this saint, who was reputedly 120 years old at his death. His feast day is June 3.

It was probably in Italy that Patrick freed himself from the crew. He wanted to return home to Britain and though it certainly took awhile, he did find his way back. Along the way he spent several years at a cloister that appealed to him. When he did reach home he was greeted warmly, although it is not known if his immediate family was still alive or if the welcome was from other relatives and from friends.

He studied at a monastery in Britain (or Gaul) and was ordained around 417—although some scholars say Patrick never became an "officially" ordained priest.

About 10 years after his ordination, he was thought to have been consecrated as a bishop and sent to Ireland. Why return to the land of his enslavement? In a series of dreams, Irish youths came to him imploring him to go back, so Patrick acquiesced.

He traveled all over Ireland, preaching and deflecting opposition from hostile chieftains and Druids. Most of his work was in the northern part of the country. It is said he did not make his way south often, perhaps never. Still, he considered himself bishop of all Ireland.

He established a cathedral at Armagh, which was to become the center of the church's activities in Ireland. Indeed, Patrick is often known as Patrick of Armagh. Armagh is in Ulster, 50 or so miles inland from the east coast. He is thought to have chosen that spot because it was near a king who was favorably inclined toward Patrick and his work.

Patrick spent 30 fruitful years in Ireland. Besides effecting many conversions, he established a network of churches and monasteries throughout the country, all with native clergy, so there was no longer a need for missionaries. He worked to raise the standards of learning and in general to bring Ireland in line with other "progressive" countries that were allied with Rome.

E-FACTS

On the island of Inishmore, one of the Aran Islands, is the nearly sunken Church of St. Enda, where more than 120 Irish saints are said to be buried, including St. Enda himself. The church dates to the seventh or eighth century.

Who *Was* Patrick?

It is certainly difficult—more like impossible—to nail down the personality and temperament of one who lived so long ago, even if the person has left writings behind. Yet Patrick's *Confession* and the *Letter* have given students of the saint an insight into the man who took up such a huge missionary task.

In his book *The Life of St. Patrick and His Place in History* (see "Suggested Reading" at the end of this chapter), J. B. Bury writes:

> (He) had strength of will, energy in action, resolution without overconfidence, and the capacity for resisting pressure from without. It might be inferred, too, that he was affectionate and sensitive; subtle analysis might disclose other traits. But it is probable that few readers will escape the impression that he possessed besides enthusiasm the practical qualities most essential for carrying through the task which he undertook in the belief that he had been divinely inspired to fulfill it. A rueful consciousness of the deficiencies of his education weighed upon him throughout his career; we can feel this in his almost wearisome insistence upon his rusticitas. Nor has he exaggerated the defects of his culture; he writes in the style of an ill-educated man. His Latin is as "rustic" as the Greek of St. Mark and St. Matthew.

It is curious in this interesting analysis that Patrick appears so deficient in learning. His father held a reasonably high position in the community and was probably himself at least a moderately well educated citizen. Patrick's lack in erudition is no doubt due to his education being interrupted at a young age by enslavement.

About Those Snakes

All right, you might be thinking about now, what's the story with those snakes?

Patrick is supposed to have driven all the snakes from Ireland, but the story appears to be apocryphal—there is no historic record of such a feat. Still, here's a point to ponder: There are no snakes in Ireland.

Another attribution to this saint, that of using the shamrock to explain the Holy Trinity, is also likely to be legend. Or, as they say in this field, "pious fiction."

Where Patrick died and where he is buried are also not definitively known. His feast day is, of course, March 17, when everyone is Irish.

Suggested Additional Reading:

Drinking from the Sacred Well: Personal Voyages of Discovery with the Celtic Saints by John Matthews (HarperSanFrancisco, 1998). This book details, as far as it is possible, the lives of a dozen Celtic saints and also suggests points of meditation for the reader.

The Life of St. Patrick and His Place in History by J. B. Bury (Book-of-the-Month Club, 1998). A scholarly though eminently readable look at the saint by an author who is not above qualifying the murky facts with "we must suppose" and "Patrick may have . . ."

An Irish Toast

St. Patrick was a gentleman
Who through strategy and stealth
Drove all the snakes from Ireland,
Here's a toasting to his health;
But not too many toastings
Lest you lose yourself and then
Forget the good St. Patrick
And see all those snakes again.

—*Irish Toasts* (Chronicle Books, 1987)

CHAPTER 18
St. Paul of Tarsus
(Died ca. 64)

Like Augustine, Paul led an interesting life, shall we say, before his conversion, and afterward had a major and enduring effect on Christianity. He was born Saul, in Tarsus, Asia Minor, of Jewish parents. He described that city as a rather cosmopolitan capital of the Roman province of Cilicia, a crossroads for Asians and Europeans, Greeks and Jews to meet.

Probably holding Roman citizenship, Saul received both a Greek and a Jewish education, and then went into the trade of tent maker. He described himself as a **Pharisee** and as such became a serious persecutor of Christians. Paul was present at the stoning of St. Stephen, the first martyr. Although Paul was part of the crowd of onlookers, it is said he was in agreement with the stoning. After Stephen's death, Saul went into houses in the area looking for Christians and dragging them off to prison.

But Saul was to have an epiphany, as did so many others. He went to the high priest in Jerusalem asking for permission to seize the Christians of Damascus and bring them back to Jerusalem for punishment. On his way to Damascus he had a vision of Christ, and a flash of light threw him from his horse to the ground. A voice asked, "Saul, Saul, why do you persecute me?"

The Missionary

When Saul asked who spoke, the answer came back, "I am Jesus whom you are persecuting." Blinded at the time of the incident, Saul had to be led into Damascus. He spent several days there, unable to eat or drink. Then he met Ananias, a disciple of Jesus' who seemed to know the enormous task Saul would be taking on. Ananias laid his hands on him and his eyesight was immediately restored and he felt new strength surge through his body.

Saul had now experienced two miracles: a vision and then a cure. Not unsurprisingly, he asked to be baptized and set about preaching Christianity with the same passion he had brought to persecuting those of that faith.

He headed first to Jerusalem to meet with the apostles. It took some convincing for them to believe that their persecutor was now their ally, but eventually they accepted him, directing him to join the apostle Barnabas in three missionary journeys.

When entering a new community Paul—he had now taken the Hellenic Paul in place of Saul—tried a strategy of first making contact with the local synagogue. They would have nothing to do with him as a Christian who had been Jewish, which saddened him. So he turned to the Gentile community, which was more receptive. In fact over the years Paul became known as "the apostle to the Gentiles."

He was apparently not too skilled in social graces. He was intense and did not always work well with whoever was sent to accompany him on his travels, sending that man back where he came from. Yet he got along with the apostle Luke, who was an educated, sophisticated man. And with Peter as well, perhaps because Peter had known Jesus and been appointed head of the new church. Actually, Peter and Paul rather complemented each other. Peter was a large, rather easygoing man who meant well but was unschooled and not great on follow-through. Paul was smaller and angular and well educated.

I have been crucified with Christ; it is no longer I who live, but Christ who lives in me.

—St. Paul

Travels

Paul's missionary endeavors did not always run smoothly. He was often met with hostility and imprisonment, and was even stoned. He endured shipwreck and hunger. He was not well some of the time, suffering from what might have been migraines or perhaps sinusitis.

His travels were long. Though sometimes Paul had other missionaries accompanying him, he was alone much of the time. He sent letter after letter back to the Christian communities he had established and the friends he had made. These epistles—to the Thessalonians, Galatians, Corinthians, Philippians, Philemon, and Romans are read in churches to this day. His letters covered problems of the new Christians, interpreting the faith and observing Mosaic law (the law of the Jews attributed to Moses). The letters covered a period from about A.D. 50 to 65 and are the earliest of the New Testament writings.

Paul established Christian communities around the eastern Mediterranean. The aim for his second missionary journey was Corinth in Greece, and the third took him to Ephesus in Asia Minor.

Back in Jerusalem sometime around A.D. 50, Paul, with Peter supporting him, convinced other apostles that Gentile Christians did not need to be circumcised and have Jewish law forced upon them. That important decision ensured the universality of Christianity.

Eventually, around the year 57, Paul returned to Jerusalem, where he was arrested as a Christian and spent the next two years in prison. Exercising his right as a Roman citizen to appeal his case to Caesar, he was sent to Rome and was held under arrest there for about two years. Finally, he was beheaded, at the same time that St. Peter was crucified there.

On his way to Rome to what he knew would be his death, Paul was still writing to the communities he had visited and converted. At the end, he said, "I have fought the good fight, I have finished the race, I have kept the faith."

He is buried in Rome, in the major basilica St. Paul's Outside the Walls.

If I speak in the tongue of men and of angels, but have not love, I am a noisy gong or a clanging cymbal. If I deliver my body to be burned but have not love, I gain nothing.

—ST. PAUL

Overall, Paul was the greatest missionary in the history of the church; his writing became the basis for the foundation of Christianity. In fact, he has been called "the second founder of Christianity."

Paul's feast day is June 29, which he shares with St. Peter. He is the patron saint of Malta.

Suggested Additional Reading:

Liberating Paul: The Justice of God and the Politics of the Apostle by Neil Elliot (Orbis, 1994). Another look at a saint who has inspired a number of analytical works, in the same way Augustine has.

Paul: The Mind of the Apostle by A. N. Wilson (W. W. Norton, 1998). The author of acclaimed biographies of Tolstoy and C. S. Lewis tackles Paul, looking into what drove the saint and how he transformed the Christianity that he found into a broader religion.

The Writings of St. Paul edited by Wayne A. Meeks (W. W. Norton, 1972). A selection of critical writings on the saint and his influence by some of the foremost religious minds, it was edited by a professor of biblical literature at Yale University.

CHAPTER 19
St. Peter
(Died ca. 64)

In Roman Catholic teaching, Peter was the first pope, appointed by Jesus. Yet he also denied his master and was not to be found near the Crucifixion.

Peter was not a particularly saintly saint, as the gospel writers and religious scholars do not hesitate to tell us. He is also described as uneducated; yet once Peter came to believe in Jesus, he spent the remainder of his years preaching, advancing the cause of Christianity, and establishing the new church.

He was said to be a large man, bold and sometimes speaking without thinking, yet in other instances fearful. He seemed to spend his years stumbling over one mistake or another, then getting up, tripping again, dusting himself off and trying once more. Sound like someone you know? Maybe any one of us?

E-FACTS

"Saint Peter at the pearly gates" is an expression that conjures a warm and comforting image. It might be that Peter is at the pearly gates of heaven because he was the first pope, but more likely, it is because he reminds us of our often difficult struggle in life—and its ultimate reward.

Early Years

Peter was born in a small village near Lake Tiberias and was called Simon. He lived and worked as a fisherman on Lake Genesareth, alongside his brother, who was the apostle Andrew.

St. Andrew (First Century)

Andrew was the brother of Simon Peter, and worked with him as a fisherman. Andrew (Greek for "manly") was one of the Twelve Apostles, and he was also a disciple of John the Baptist. Andrew was the apostle who most remained in the background.

In the Bible story of the fishes and the loaves, it is Andrew who notes that the large crowd gathered to hear Jesus speak had nothing to eat. He mentions that a boy nearby had five loaves of bread and two fish, but that certainly wouldn't be enough. As the famous story goes, soon the contents of the boy's basket was feeding that mass of people.

Andrew is said to have traveled and preached after the Resurrection and performed miracles in Greece and Asia Minor. He was crucified in Greece on a cross that was planted in the shape of an X, a design that has been known since as "St. Andrew's Cross."

Andrew's feast day is November 30. He is the patron saint of Russia; Scotland; Greece; Catalonia, Spain; Genoa, Italy; fishermen; and gout sufferers.

Andrew introduced Peter to Jesus, who called him "Cephas," the Aramaic version of the word *rock*. Aramaic is a language closely related to Hebrew; a form of it is thought to be the language spoken by Jesus. In Greek "rock" translates as Peter.

Peter was told by Christ, "Come with me and I will make you a fisher of men." Although there were twelve apostles, the trio of Peter, James, and John was the elite—those closest to Jesus—among the chosen.

Peter was reportedly in attendance at Jesus' first miracle: at the marriage feast at Cana, when Mary told her son the guests had no wine. Jesus said to her, "My time has not yet come," but added "What would you have me do?" although he must have known what she was requesting. Soon water that had magically become wine materialized, enough to see the wedding guests happily through the day's festivities.

Peter was married, and his wife often traveled with him. He was with Jesus throughout his public life, making his boat available to him, and indeed his home as well. Jesus stayed with the apostle on a few occasions and once while at his home healed Peter's mother-in-law.

When Peter acknowledged Jesus as "the Christ . . . the son of the living God," Christ replied, "You are Peter and upon this rock I will build my church." And he added, "I will give you the keys of the kingdom of heaven: Whatever you bind on earth will be considered bound in heaven; whatever you loose [or forgive] on earth shall be considered loosed [or forgiven] in heaven." Giving Peter the "keys of the kingdom of heaven" has been interpreted in Catholic teaching as giving him jurisdiction over church affairs as the first pope. This interpretation firmly sets the concept of the papal primacy.

The Passion

At the Last Supper, Peter told Jesus, "Even though they all fall away, I will not." Yet, when Jesus was held prisoner at Pontius Pilate's palace, Peter denied him three times, an outlandish treatment by a chosen apostle. In fact, what stands out in most minds when Peter is mentioned 2,000 years later is that denial.

Peter wept after his betrayal. Later, when he heard that Jesus had risen, he went to the empty tomb to see for himself. An angel had told Mary Magdalene and the other women to take the news that Jesus had risen "to the disciples and to Peter," mentioning him by name.

It is apparent from all of Peter's too-human faults that Jesus intended his message to be more important than the messenger, more important than any pope. (This was a good thing, because Christianity has endured a few papal scoundrels over the years.)

Jesus emphasized the importance of love. He was forgiving to those who showed their love in service to others, in love of God, and in self-sacrifice. As Jesus said about Mary Magdalene, "Her sins, which are many, are forgiven, for she loved much."

The risen Christ asks Peter three times: "Do you love me?" And, of course, Peter, who had three times denied him, now says three times, "Yes, Lord, you know that I love you." Then Jesus commands him, "Feed my sheep"; that is, he wants Peter to care for those who will become the faithful in the new church.

The Early Church

Peter took the helm of the small band of Christians after the Crucifixion and was the first apostle to perform a miracle. In Jerusalem and in later travels, he combined preaching the news about Jesus with defending the faith in courts and settling squabbles among individuals and groups of believers. An especially important move for Peter was authorizing a missionary outreach to the Gentiles.

He did not stay in Jerusalem for the rest of his life, although most of the other apostles did. He went on to Lydda in Palestine, and beyond. In Antioch he met with St. Paul and worked closely with him.

Peter was arrested and imprisoned more than once during those years, and then, miraculously, was set free. Eventually he became the first bishop of Rome. During the reign of Nero (ca. 54–68), he was martyred. Death was by crucifixion, but Peter insisted that he be hanged upside down on the cross, saying he was not fit to die in the same way as his master.

The martyrs wanted to die, not to flee from labor, but to attain their purpose.

—St. Catherine of Siena

The organization of the papacy in the church's early days is hazy. It is believed that Peter and Paul founded the church in Rome and set up a system for the succession of bishops. However, it was probably not until the middle of the second century that the concept of one bishop presiding over a **diocese** came into being, rather than the Roman style of a group of bishops functioning in that role.

Peter is still considered the first bishop of Rome. To this day the pope also carries the title of bishop of Rome.

Peter's tomb is presumed to be under St. Peter's Basilica. Bones found there are still being studied.

His feast day is June 29, which he shares with St. Paul. He is the patron saint of longevity and fishermen. To read more about devotion to St. Peter, turn to Chapter 38, about basilicas, shrines and cathedrals dedicated to saints.

Suggested Additional Reading:

Saint Peter by Michael Grant (Scribner, 1994). This critically acclaimed look at the saint and his times is written by a former fellow of Trinity College, Cambridge, and professor of humanity at Edinburgh University. He has published several other works on the ancient world.

CHAPTER 20
St. Teresa of Ávila
(1515–1582)

Although Teresa lived some 300 years after Catherine of Siena, the two women had quite a bit in common besides saintliness. Both were mystics, and both lived in a time when their countries—Spain and Italy—paid little attention to the words of a woman. Yet both women managed not only to be listened to but to have their words heeded. Both left writings that have endured to the present. Teresa of Ávila was the first woman named a Doctor of the Church, and St. Catherine of Siena was the second.

But this chapter is about Teresa. Although she did have several traits in common with Catherine, she was quite her own person—and a formidable one at that.

You would have liked Teresa, hagiographers say. She was intelligent, charming, and quite witty, even tart. One time a visitor came upon her happily digging into a partridge dinner someone had sent. The visitor was appalled. A woman of God looking as if she were enjoying her food? What would people think? "Let them think what they please," Teresa responded. "There is a time for partridge and a time for penance." Another time she said, "I could be bribed with a sardine."

Life as a Carmelite

She was born Teresa Cepeda y Ahumada, the daughter of a wealthy merchant of Ávila. Teresa expressed interest in religion at an early age, although not in any traditional manner. When she was seven she and her brother ran away from home, wanting to reach land occupied by the Moors—and then be martyred for Christ there! An uncle stopped the two children and brought them home.

Teresa's mother died when she was 14, and her father arranged for her to be educated at a local convent, which was typical of the times. At 20 Teresa decided to become a nun, a vocation she later said was due more to a fear of purgatory than a love of God.

E-QUESTIONS?

What is purgatory?
Purgatory is a temporary state after death where souls go to be cleansed of past sins before becoming worthy to heaven.

Her father was not in favor of Teresa taking vows, whatever her motive, but she was willful and ran off again, this time to the Carmelite convent in Ávila. While there she became ill, and her father had to bring her home. Her health deteriorated further. She became paralyzed from the waist down from an illness that has never completely been explained. At one point she was near coma.

Eventually she rallied, and after a long and painful convalescence returned to the convent. By now her faith, rather than being strengthened by her ordeal, was tepid.

Life in the convent did not help her in finding a path to God. At that time the Carmelites and several other religious congregations led such easy, even pleasant, lives that they might have been living in a resort. Many wealthy widows and single women would enter a convent with no thought of giving up much of their prereligious life. They wore jewelry over their habits. They had special foods brought in. In fact, many women ran to convents for the freedom they provided. Young girls living in convents for schooling had quite a nice life, too. Teresa's winning personality made her quite popular in this busy, social atmosphere.

E-FACTS

If you are heading for Rome, plan to see Bernini's marble sculpture of St. Teresa of Ávila. She is leaning back with her eyes closed, lips parted, hand to head—presumably in ecstasy. An angel stands by her with an arrow, illustrating words she wrote about an angel who would drive a golden spear with a searing hot tip into her heart. "When he drew it out," she wrote, he "left me completely afire with a great love for God."

The statue, one of a group, can be found at the Church of Santa Maria della Vittoria in Rome.

But Teresa was to have her moment of truth. One day when she was in her thirties, she looked upon the image of Christ on the cross as she had done hundreds of times before. This time, however, as she thought of his suffering, she became almost disgusted with her "religious" life. She determined to spend more time in prayer and other worthy pursuits. Almost immediately after making that decision, Teresa said, she felt God's presence and love within her.

By now repelled by the ways of the Carmelites, she decided to found a new, reformed Carmelite order. After some difficult groundwork, she finally did, in 1562.

She named her new community the Discalced (shoeless) Carmelites. Actually, the nuns wore sandals, but the word referred to the vow of poverty the sisters would take, making them, figuratively speaking, shoeless. The nuns in the Discalced order lived by hard labor and by alms. They kept strict hours and slept on straw pallets. Food was simple, and there was not much of it. Prayer was stressed, for spiritual growth. (Forget about the jewelry and visits from friends.)

In most other contexts, one reforms an institution to make it more liberal or more up-to-date. With Teresa and the Carmelites, the reverse was true.

Teresa was full of common sense and had no use for pomposity. Once a young nun came to her with stories of all kinds of temptation and of how she was such a sinner. "Now, Sister," Teresa said, "remember, none of us is perfect. Just make sure those sins of yours don't turn into bad habits."

After the Ávila convent, Theresa founded another 16 religious houses throughout Spain, traveling with little or no money and enduring the hardships of the Castilian countryside. While setting up the second convent, she met a young friar named Juan de Yepes y Álvarez, who was to become St. John of the Cross. Teresa founded the first reform monastery for men and put John in charge of it and of establishing other monasteries. (Read more about St. John of the Cross in Chapter 12.)

> While I was at the monastery in Toledo, some were advising me that I shouldn't give a burying place to anyone who had not belonged to the nobility. The Lord said to me: "You will grow very foolish, daughter, if you look at the world's laws. Fix your eyes on me, poor and despised by the world. Will the great ones of the world, perhaps, be great before me? Are you to be esteemed for lineage or for virtue?
>
> —*THE AUTOBIOGRAPHY OF ST. TERESA OF ÁVILA*
> (BOOK-OF-THE-MONTH CLUB, 1995)

Mystic and Writer

Teresa of Ávila has been called one of the most profound mystics of all time. Besides experiencing ecstasies, she would on occasion levitate in full view of her nuns. It is said that at other times in church she had to hold on to the altar rail to keep from moving upward. Commenting probably on her own life, or perhaps the difficult life of the cloistered nun in general, she noted, "The sufferings God inflicts on **contemplatives** are of so unbearable a kind that, unless He sustained such souls with the manna of divine consolation, they would find their agony unbearable."

This Carmelite was a prolific writer, too, leaving much behind for historians to ponder. There is a good deal for everyone to learn, too, about God's love and how important prayer is to spiritual growth. Her autobiography includes explanations of her visions and other mystical experiences. Two of her other writings, *Way of Perfection* and *Interior Castles,* guide the reader toward grace and perfection. Teresa also wrote numerous letters that offer insight into her mind and temperament.

Tough Times

It was not all smooth sailing. Teresa ran afoul of the Spanish Inquisition, as John of the Cross, Ignatius of Loyola, and so many others did, and eventually endured a formal investigation, although charges against her were dismissed.

Her own order caused grief, too, as she surmounted a five-year bitter struggle from the so-called Calced Carmelites. Her colleague, John of the Cross, was actually imprisoned for a time in the Calced Carmelite monastery in Toledo. Finally, Pope Gregory XIII recognized the Discalced Reform Carmelites as a separate order.

Teresa died at Alba de Tormes, Spain, in 1582. As her full life drew to a close, she said "My Saviour, it is time that I set out . . . Let us go."

It is said a marvelous scent emanated from her body, and later, when one of her confessors had her grave opened, her body was still intact and there was the aroma of lilies. As was the custom of those times with saintly people, the body was cut up and pieces given to various powerful admirers of the nun as relics. The confessor kept the little finger of the left hand for himself.

E-FACTS

Teresa's left hand, minus the little finger the confessor kept, wound up with Generalissimo Francisco Franco of Spain who kept it on his night table until he died in 1975.

Teresa of Ávila was canonized 40 years after her death. In 1970 she became the first woman to be named a Doctor of the Church. Her feast day is October 15. She is a patron saint of Spain and of headache sufferers, and is invoked against heart disease.

E-FACTS

A few years back, St. Teresa of Ávila was named patron saint of AIDS patients.

Suggested Additional Reading:

The Autobiography of St. Teresa of Ávila, translated by Kieran Kavanaugh, O.C.D., and Otilio Rodríguez, O.C.D. (Book-of-the-Month Club, 1995). These are the saint's autobiographical writings.

Interior Castles: Teresa of Ávila, translated and edited by E. Allison Peers (Doubleday Image Books, 1989). This is probably Teresa's most mystical work.

Teresa of Ávila: The Progress of a Soul by Cathleen Medwick (Alfred A. Knopf, 1999). A well received work to add to the Teresa reference shelf. The author draws on the life and writings of a saint she calls "a vain and vivacious girl with a divine agenda," adding she was "a magnet for attention."

CHAPTER 21

St. Thérèse of Lisieux
(1873–1897)

If you say "the Little Flower" or "the Little Way," many will know that you are referring to St. Thérèse, a young woman who lived just 24 years, yet left behind a book still being read around the world, a work showing the way to live closer to God by performing the smallest tasks well.

The Little Flower was born Marie Françoise Martin in Alençon, in the northern part of France, on January 2. She was the youngest of nine children. Her father was a watchmaker; her mother, Zélie, had a lace business (Alençon lace is highly regarded). Her parents had each hoped to enter the religious life, but for some reason that was not to happen and they married. Both are currently candidates for beatification.

Marie's mother died when she was five. Soon afterward the Martin family moved to Lisieux, where Marie was raised by her older sisters.

She was apparently a happy child, keeping a number of pets, including doves and goldfish. She is said to have done savage imitations of neighbors and other people she and her family knew. She was quite precocious. Indeed a photograph of her when she was older shows an attractive, dark-haired young woman with an almost impish look in her eyes.

E-FACTS

When Diana, Princess of Wales died in 1997, among the reams of material printed about her was the little known fact that she had regularly lit candles at the statue of St. Thérèse of Lisieux in the Carmelite church in the Kensington section of London. Mother Teresa, whom Diana had met, is thought to have introduced her to the life and works of Thérèse.

Asked to Write

Two of Marie's sisters became Carmelite nuns, and Marie soon followed them to the convent, taking the name Thérèse of the Child Jesus and spending her time cloistered in prayer and meditation. She was ill with tuberculosis a good deal of the time, and at a certain point the **abbess** of the convent (who was also her sister, Pauline) suggested to the frail young nun that she write about her life and her faith. Thérèse began that work in 1894 and completed it in 1897, almost on her deathbed, racked with pain.

Her writings were published as *The Diary of a Soul,* which has become one of the most widely read spiritual autobiographies, translated into 60 languages. It is not a deep book—Thérèse is no Augustine; she is not a serious mystic like John of the Cross or Teresa of Ávila. In fact, her style is deceptively simple as she writes about her family, her convent, and her God. She refers to herself as a "little flower" and her faith as the "little way of spiritual childhood," based on her certainty of God's love for us. In return, we can do even small things for Him and do them well. Her childlike faith, and her acceptance of suffering—and she endured a great deal of pain, both physical and spiritual in her lifetime—have made readers respond positively and in great numbers to her message. After all, very few of us are called to do great things in life, but we can understand and take to heart her Little Way.

Thérèse had no visions, no ecstasies like other saints. She did not hear Jesus speak to her. She was, you might say, like one of us. Actually, if it were not for her autobiography, it is unlikely anyone outside her region would have known about this young woman. Here is an example of her kindness:

In Eternity

You sent me off to fetch one of Father's big glasses and had me put my little thimble alongside it; then you filled them both up with water and asked me which I thought was fuller. I had to admit that one was just as full as the other because neither of them would hold any more. That was the way you helped me to grasp how it was that in heaven the least have no cause to envy the greatest.

—THÉRÈSE OF LISIEUX

Thérèse (born Marie) had four sisters: Pauline, Thérèse, Celine, and Leonie. All of the girls were bright, attractive, and well behaved—except for Leonie. Leonie was always out of sorts. It turns out she had been subjected to much psychological abuse by the Martin housekeeper. The woman was booted off the premises once that became known, but the damage to Leonie seemed to be complete and permanent.

On her deathbed, Zélie Martin worried about Leonie, but Marie (Thérèse) told her mother not to be concerned, that she would care for her sister. Indeed, on her own deathbed, Thérèse told Leonie she would look out for her from heaven.

Thérèse of Lisieux died of tuberculosis on September 30, 1897. She once said, "After my death I will let fall a shower of roses. I will spend my heaven in doing good on earth."

Thérèse was canonized in 1925 by Pope Pius XI and was named a Doctor of the Church by Pope John Paul II in 1997, making her the third woman to be so named. Her feast day is October 1. She is a patron saint of France, foreign missions, and florists. In 1998, St. Patrick's Cathedral in New York City drew 6,000 people to a special mass celebrating St. Thérèse's elevation to Doctor of the Church.

And Leonie? Well, she tried again for admission to a convent (she had been turned down or asked to leave three convents before), and this time she was successful. When she was dying at 78 in 1941, a Parisian cardinal called her a "hidden saint." Leonie laughed it off, saying it was talking to Thérèse while she was alive that helped turn her around. In any event, Leonie lived for 44 years after her sister's death, certainly time to make her own mark. She is now, along with her parents, a candidate for **beatification**, along the road toward sainthood. She is a remarkable example of the old saying that it's *never* too late.

I am only a very little soul, who can only offer very little things to our Lord.

—THÉRÈSE OF LISIEUX

Suggested Additional Reading:

The Autobiography of Saint Thérèse of Lisieux: The Story of a Soul, translated by John Beevers (Doubleday Image Books, 1989), the saint's renowned autobiography written during her years as a Carmelite nun.

Maurice and Thérèse: The Inspiring Letters Between Thérèse of Lisieux and a Struggling Young Priest by Patrick Ahern (Doubleday, 1998). Maurice Bellière was a young seminarian when he wrote to the mother superior at Thérèse's community asking for a nun to pray for him. The nun chose Thérèse. Here is an exchange of 21 letters between the two, woven with narrative by the author, who is an auxiliary bishop of New York and considered an authority on Thérèse of Lisieux.

Thérèse by Dorothy Day, the activist and cofounder of the Catholic Worker movement in the 1930s (Templegate Publishers, 1960).

CHAPTER 22

St. Thomas Aquinas
(1225–1274)

So bright . . . a genius . . . brilliant . . .

It is rare to read about Thomas Aquinas without seeing these and other glowing testaments to his extraordinary mind. Thomas was the greatest of the Catholic theologians, and indeed one of the most brilliant minds in the Western world. Church doctrine that he wrote is still heeded today, as are his prayers and hymns.

E-FACTS

Thomas Aquinas wrote several hymns still used in church services: *"Tantum Ergo," "Adoro Te Devote,"* and *"O Salutaris Hostia,"* among others.

Family Kidnapping

Thomas was born at the family home near Aquino, in southern Italy, the youngest of four sons. The home was actually a castle, and Thomas's father was the son of the count of Aquino and also a relative of the king of France.

Befitting his station, Thomas was well educated: he was sent to a nearby monastery when he was just five years old. Later he attended the University of Naples. After a few years of study, the young man announced that he wanted to become a Dominican friar, news his family received with as much enthusiasm as Catherine of Siena's family did when she announced she wanted to become a nun. They were, in a word, appalled. He entered the order, but his family kidnapped the young man and held him in their castle for a year.

The lockup did not work (keeping Catherine tied to home as a servant was not successful, either). When his parents realized that Thomas would follow no path but the Dominican, they released him.

The Student

Thomas rejoined the Dominican order (formally the Order of Preachers, or O.P.) and was sent to Germany for further studies. He was a quiet student, never contributing much to the class, although his razor-sharp mind absorbed all that was passed on to him. His classmates called him "the dumb ox," thinking he was simpleminded—and as a reference to his plumpness.

Thomas earned a doctorate at the University of Paris and taught there as well. This was quite a learning center at the time—Ignatius of Loyola and Francis Xavier studied there, among other renowned figures in the arts, politics, and religion.

Thomas began writing then, works on philosophy and comments on Scripture. Little by little, admiration for him grew until he was recognized as a genius.

The Magnum Opus

In 1266 Thomas began his masterpiece *Summa Theologica,* which serves as the basis for Catholic theology. It was the most ambitious written work of Catholic faith ever undertaken. In the past, theologians addressed themselves to specific dogma problems within a narrow frame. Thomas took a broader view, reconciling Christian doctrine with reason, bringing in Greek philosophers, who before Thomas were not even considered in matters of faith. The saint wrote that fundamental Christian doctrines, though matters of faith and impossible to explain by reason, are not contrary to reason, and in fact can be discovered by natural reason.

Thomas allowed for differing viewpoints before deciding where most of the evidence in question lay, whereas in the past theology had to be accepted on authority. His views were often thought controversial, especially when he adapted the philosophy of Aristotle, a pagan, to Christian theology.

Vatican II, which was convened by Pope John XXIII in 1962 and concluded by Pope Paul VI in 1965, brought church leaders to Rome to discuss and update theology and policy. Up until that council Thomism—which is what it had become known as—had pretty much taken over the education of priesthood candidates in seminaries. But it was a "package" approach to Thomas's work: here are the questions, and over there are the answers. That style of learning, and teaching, went against Thomas's very spirit, and his courage to be controversial. Post–Vatican II theologians would try to restore Thomas's work as that holy man had created it: open to dialogue and not at all insular.

E-PROFILE

St. Albert the Great (Albertus Magnus) (ca. 1206–1280)

One of Thomas's teachers was St. Albert the Great, or Albertus Magnus. Albert noted Thomas's abilities early, and supposedly said, "You call him Dumb Ox. I tell you that the Dumb Ox will bellow so loud that his bellowing will fill the world."

Albert is considered one of the great intellects of medieval Christendom. He was called "the Universal Doctor" by his colleagues, and he is the only philosopher to be known as "the Great." Albert was a Dominican who studied and lectured in German Dominican priories. He preferred to concentrate on thought, writing, and teaching. Albert was especially interested in the secular sciences, and lectured on Aristotle's ethics and zoology.

Albertus Magnus was canonized in 1931. His interest in science brought opposition by those who claimed he took part in black magic. But he is now a Doctor of the Church. His feast day is November 15. He is the patron saint of scientists and medical technicians. Albertus Magnus College is a four-year institution in New Haven, Connecticut.

> Every truth without exception—and whoever may utter it—is from the Holy Spirit.
>
> —THOMAS AQUINAS

Gentle Genius

Despite his massive work output—and he wrote many other commentaries throughout his life—Thomas was a humble and holy man and is said to have experienced visions and ecstasies. He is known never to have lost his temper, even when engaged in lively debate, and was never heard to make a harmful remark about anyone.

A Prayer of St. Thomas Aquinas
Lord, bestow on me understanding to know Thee, diligence to seek Thee, wisdom to find Thee, a way of life that shall please Thee, perseverance in waiting trustfully for Thee, and confidence that I shall embrace Thee at the last. Amen.

In one often-repeated story about Thomas the man, he is attending a state dinner given by King Louis IX. He is so lost in thought that he suddenly brings his quite sizable fist down on the table and blurts out, startling all present, "And that settles the Manichaeans!" A comment he made, speaking of gardens, is poignant and revealing: "No possession is joyous without a companion. Notwithstanding the beasts and the plants, one can be lonely there."

How different the saints are, even from one other, just like the rest of us. If Francis of Assisi were in a garden, he would no doubt be followed about by animals and birds, and would engage in conversation with them and probably the flowers as well. John of the Cross and Catherine of Siena might be lost in pious thought or rapture. Thérèse of Lisieux, in her "little way," might focus on one flower to show God's goodness to us all. But then again, maybe one, or all four of them, would have understood Thomas's sentiments.

"So Much Straw"

Thomas was not to complete the *Summa*. He suddenly stopped work in 1273. He was then living in a Dominican house in Naples, where he had been assigned to get away the controversies surrounding his work in Paris. One day during mass he experienced something that caused him to put down his pen. He said, "I cannot go on. . . . All that I have written seems to me like so much straw compared to what I have seen and what has been revealed to me."

What *had* he seen or heard that day? He never did explain, leaving hagiographers to puzzle over the interpretation of his words for the next several hundred years.

> Law is an ordinance of reason for the common good, made by him who has care of the community. Man should not consider his material possessions his own, but as common to all, so as to share them without hesitation when others are in need.
>
> —THOMAS AQUINAS

Just three months after this life-changing incident, the scholar fell ill on his way to the Council of Lyon. He died two days later, on March 7, 1274, at the age of 49. He is interred in Toulouse, France, in the Cathedral of Saint-Sernin.

Thomas Aquinas was canonized in 1323 and declared a Doctor of the Church in 1567. His feast day is January 28. He is the patron saint of Catholic universities, chastity, pencil makers, students, colleges, and universities.

Suggested Additional Reading:

Saint Thomas Aquinas: "The Dumb Ox" by G. K. Chesterton (Doubleday, 1956). An excellent look at Thomas by the noted writer on spirituality (and playwright and mystery writer). Chesterton's introduction begins, "This book makes no pretence to be anything but a popular sketch of a great historical character," so it is eminently readable for those not particularly theologically inclined.

CHAPTER 23

St. Thomas More
(1478–1535)

A married man a saint? Many of the canonized were early Christian martyrs whose marital status was unknown, or they were men or women known to be virgins or hermits. Later, many if not most saints were found among the ranks of priests, brothers, and nuns, especially those who founded religious orders. Few married men, aside from the apostles, have made it into this select group. However, Great Britain's Anglican church does not acknowledge Thomas as a saint. In that country—Catholics in England excepted, of course—he is known as Sir Thomas More.

Thomas More was one of the most respected and brightest men of his time, deeply religious but not obvious about piety. He had a sense of humor, too, which would certainly come in handy when he found himself disagreeing with the terrifying King Henry VIII, around whom heads seem to drop with not too much provocation.

Occupy your minds with good thoughts, or the enemy will fill them with bad ones: unoccupied they cannot be.

—THOMAS MORE

Thomas was born in London on February 6, the son of John More, who was a lawyer and a judge, and as Catholic as England itself at the time. When he was about 12, Thomas became a page in the household of the Archbishop of Canterbury. He attended Oxford, studied law, and was admitted to the bar. He became a successful barrister (that is, a lawyer who pleads cases in court) and then entered Parliament in 1504.

When he was 27 Thomas married Jane Holt. Their home became a comfortable meeting place for the literati at the time. Besides being brilliant and scholarly, Thomas was charming and witty, all excellent qualities in a host.

Between what you might call salons at home and the birth of four children, the young lawyer was quite busy. Among his many responsibilities was tutoring the young Henry VIII before he became king. He made a favorable impression on the future sovereign. The young lawyer was, in addition to his many other talents, an outstanding writer. One of his works was titled *Vindication of Henry Against Luther* (King Henry VIII and Martin Luther). Published in 1523, it was a defense of the king.

A major sadness in More's life came when his wife died. He later married an older widow named Alice, who was a good wife and companion.

In any event, Thomas continued to move up in what could be called a government career. He became undersheriff of London, and when Henry rose to the throne he sent Thomas on a number of diplomatic missions. He appointed him to the Royal Council, and then, in 1521, he knighted him. Thomas was selected speaker of the House of Commons and then High Steward of Cambridge.

When he was in his forties, More built what was pretty much a mansion in the Chelsea section of London, which was then woods and pasture land. The house, on 27 acres of land that More had purchased, must have cost more than even he could afford: during the time it was under construction, he borrowed more than 700 pounds from the king.

Utopia

On a diplomatic assignment to Belgium for the throne, Thomas stayed in Antwerp with Peter Gillis, a close friend of Thomas's friend Erasmus. The two became friends. During the six or seven weeks More was in Antwerp he began *Utopia*, a masterpiece that has endured to this day.

Known as Desiderius Erasmus of Rotterdam, or in later centuries as just plain Erasmus, he was a renowned scholar and literary figure of the sixteenth century. When he visited England in 1499 and met Thomas More, Erasmus gained an insight into what the future might hold for him. Perhaps he could take all of those intellectual gifts and use them in Christian thought and reform.

He produced many books, including his most famous, *Praise of Folly*, about Christian love, as well as using reason and humaneness toward a gentle reform in Christian life. Writing about social injustice and peace, Erasmus believed strongly in using reason and dialogue to resolve conflict. The humanist defended Martin Luther against heresy when that monk posted his now-famous *95 Theses*.

The Christian renewal and spirit of Renaissance humanism that Erasmus had hoped for did not come about in his lifetime, which was full of violence and factionalism. He spent his later years in Protestant Basel and died there in 1536 at the age of 70.

The work was originally titled *De Optimo Reipublicae Statu* (The Best Condition of a Society). *Utopia* was certainly the better choice for a title. In the book, More describes an incredible society of equal citizens, with common ownership of property and goods, run by the Utopians. It is a country where greed, pride, and disorder have been banished. Utopia has slaves, but they are criminals or prisoners of war, and rather than being treated badly, they are handled with paternal benevolence.

The word *utopian* has come to mean perfection, especially as it applies to a society and its specific laws, political situations, and social conditions. It is derived from More's coinage.

The Problem

Even as his business brought him more and more important positions and his writing continued, Thomas's pleasant life began to show signs of unraveling. In 1529, on the death of Cardinal Wolsey, Thomas was named Lord Chancellor of England. He was a bit hesitant to take that position because by now Henry had set aside his first wife, Catherine of Aragon, to marry Anne Boleyn. To divorce Catherine, Henry had defied the pope.

Thomas, so serious a Catholic he had once considered the priesthood, stayed diplomatically quiet on the subject. But when he refused to sign a petition to the pope requesting permission for Henry to divorce Catherine (which the pope was not likely to do in any event), Henry became enraged. After opposing a few other steps Henry wanted taken against the church, Thomas resigned his chancellorship and became a full-time writer.

He was not to be left in peace. In 1534 the Act of Succession was proclaimed. All citizens were to sign an oath recognizing that any child of Henry and the new Queen Anne would be true successors to the throne. That much Thomas was willing to concede: Henry could name anyone he liked as his heir as far as he was concerned. But the document also called for swearing that the king's marriage to Catherine had not been a true one. In all good conscience Thomas could not do that. Such an oath was a break with the pope and papal authority. So in 1534, at the age of 56, Thomas was arrested and taken to the Tower of London.

As part of the Millennium 2000 celebration in London, Thomas More's cell at the Tower was opened to the public for the first time.

E-FACTS

The Scaffold

Thomas would be imprisoned for 15 months. He was repeatedly urged either to sign the oath or to account for why he would not. He said nothing at all, figuring he would get into less trouble by remaining silent.

A number of clergymen visited him, telling him that they had signed the oath (except for Bishop John Fisher, later St. John Fisher, who felt as Thomas did and suffered a similar fate).

St. John Fisher (1469–1535)

John Fisher was beheaded at the same time as Thomas More, and for the same reason, but there was much more to John Fisher's life than his martyrdom.

He was chancellor of Cambridge University and bishop of Rochester, and at one point was **chaplain** to Lady Margaret Beaufort, mother of King Henry VIII. He was noted for his educational reforms and for his preaching, and made a substantive contribution to the Counter-Reformation. He was said to have one of the finest libraries in Europe.

Fisher led the ecclesiastical opposition to King Henry VIII's effort to divorce from his first wife and his church. When he refused to accept the king's Act of Succession, which recognized that any child of Henry and Queen Anne would be a true successor to the throne, he was arrested for treason and imprisoned. While he was in jail Pope Paul III elevated him to cardinal. He shares a June 22 feast day with Thomas More.

The prisoner remained adamant about his position. At one point his wife, exasperated and fearing for his life, urged him to sign. Thomas's response: "My good woman, you are no good at doing business. Do you really want me to exchange eternity for twenty years?" The "twenty years" presumably referred to what was likely to be the remainder of his life.

At the end of the 15 months, Thomas was asked by Oliver Cromwell to comment yet again on the succession, and still he said nothing. He was then accused of treason. He did not say a word in his defense; perjured evidence was offered at trial, and he was convicted. Then he did speak, giving the reason for his persistence—and adding that he hoped to see his accusers again in the next life.

Five days later, he was beheaded. During that time he prayed and fasted. As he went to the scaffold, Thomas proclaimed to the crowd that had gathered to witness his execution, "I am the King's good servant, but God's first." His noted wit did not desert him. The steps to the scaffold were rickety. More turned to one of his guards and said, "I pray you see me safe up; for my coming down let me shift for myself."

As he knelt before the block he recited the words of the psalm that begins "Have mercy upon me, O God, according to thy loving kindness."

When More's severed head fell, the executioner picked it up and showed it to the crowd, exclaiming, "Behold the head of a traitor!" The corpse was interred by More's family, but his head was boiled and then impaled on a pole and raised high above London Bridge.

Thomas More was one of the few English laymen to be considered for sainthood. He was canonized in 1935 and is the patron saint of lawyers. His feast day is June 22, which he shares with his ally John Fisher.

Suggested Additional Reading:

The King's Good Servant but God's First: The Life and Writings of St. Thomas More by James Monti (Ignatius Press San Francisco, 1997). A scholarly approach to the saint, and a careful look at his writings.

The Life of Thomas More by Peter Ackroyd (Nan A. Talese/Doubleday, 1998). The British author of other acclaimed biographies takes the reader through the life of this saint while offering a fascinating look at the times and language of sixteenth-century England. "It must be a candidate for book of the year," said the *Observer.* Also available on audiocassette (read by Patrick Tull, Recorded Books, 14 cassettes, 19 hours, unabridged).

Chapter 24
St. Valentine
(Died ca. 269)

Here is another saint, like St. Nicholas, whose true life and works, not that well known to begin with, have been spun into a legend that today would probably amaze the man himself.

Valentine was a physician and a priest, perhaps a bishop, in Rome. It is said he secretly married people who were forbidden to wed under Roman law. At the time Emperor Claudius the Goth was attempting to raise a large army and thought that single men would make better soldiers than those who would be worrying about their families back home.

Valentine was arrested for those "misdeeds," imprisoned, and beheaded on February 14. He was buried on Rome's Flaminian Way, and a basilica was erected there in 350.

Hail, Bishop Valentine, whose day this is,
All the air is thy Diocese.
— JOHN DONNE (1571?–1631) WRITTEN FOR LADY ELIZABETH
AND COUNT PALATINE, MARRIED ON ST. VALENTINE'S DAY

The Two Valentines

Things now get tricky. It seems there was another Roman by the name of Valentine who died on the same day. This man was also a priest and was martyred in Terni, some 60 miles from Rome. This Valentine confessed his faith before the emperor, declaring that the gods Jupiter and Mercury were "shameless and contemptible characters."

While he was in prison, Valentine befriended the blind daughter of his jailer. He cured her and converted his captor to Christianity. When the emperor heard, he had Valentine beaten and beheaded.

It is now thought that the two Valentines were the same man, who was taken from one city where he was imprisoned, to the other where he was executed.

E-FACTS

In 1999 Dublin nominated itself the international capital of love. The city has the relics of St. Valentine. Pope Gregory XVI donated them to Dublin's Carmelite church in the nineteenth century.

Celebration

So how was the leap made from clergyman Valentine to our present-day romance with February 14?

Up until 200 years after Valentine's death the Roman feast of Lupercalia was celebrated on February 15. That day commemorated Faunus, one of many Roman deities. To the Romans, Faunus was the god of flocks and fertility and the protector of fields and shepherds. During the day's celebration, single women would place their names in a large bowl with each single man drawing one name. The man would then be that woman's partner during the festival. Of course, sometimes love matches resulted, with no need for either party to participate in that side of the feasting the next year, perhaps to the relief of both.

The feast of Lupercalia, with its romantic aspect, was probably combined with the feast a day earlier for Juno, the Roman goddess of women and marriage. Add to that combination the martyrdom on the same date of St. Valentine, who had married Roman couples underground, as it were, and you might—indeed scholars have—come up with the reason February 14 has become such a special day for celebrating.

Love Notes

As for the custom of sending valentines, it is thought to have originated in the Middle Ages with the belief that birds began to pair around the middle of February, so it was suggested that lovers might exchange notes and gifts then as well. Next came the melding of those romantic messages and the saint's name into one word: valentine. The word represented the card, as well as the person sending or receiving it.

> Saint Valentine is past:
> Begin these wood-birds but to couple now?
> —WILLIAM SHAKESPEARE (1564–1616), *A MIDSUMMER NIGHT'S DREAM*

After the advent of postal systems, the Valentine messages grew to the phenomenal number of today, along with the lovers' and loved ones' celebrations that accompany the holiday.

As you might expect, St. Valentine is commonly regarded as the patron saint of lovers. His feast day is February 14, although sometimes you will see a religious calendar that makes no note of it.

CHAPTER 25

St. Vincent de Paul
(1580–1660)

St. Vincent de Paul—doesn't he have something to do with . . . charities?

Charities, it is. You may have seen deposit bins around your town or notices that clothing and other items will be collected for the poor, all under the auspices of the local St. Vincent de Paul Society.

This man's interest in, and work for, the poor and other needy, including virtually any person from homeless infants to prisoners, made him an important activist saint. Vincent was no mystic, no cloistered monk. He was a doer, and indeed in many instances, he set the standard for charity work—what needs to be done and how it should be organized.

Upwardly Mobile

Vincent was born to a poor family in Gascony in southwestern France. His parents felt the priesthood was an educational and economic escape for their son. Vincent became a Franciscan, ordained at a youthful 19.

You might say he truly enjoyed the life of a priest. It opened doors to him, offering him entrée to some of the "better" addresses and homes. It was a good life. Not the same kind of life enjoyed by Francis of Assisi and Augustine before their conversions—Vincent was, after all, a practicing Catholic and religious. But it was an excellent way to live in the lavish style the "haves" enjoyed in prerevolutionary France.

He was probably in his forties or fifties when he was called to hear the confession of a dying peasant. The man worked on the grounds of the estate of a wealthy family for whom Vincent was serving as family tutor and chaplain. Before slipping away, the greatly relieved laborer told Vincent that he would have died in the state of mortal sin had he not confessed to the priest and received absolution. That gave Vincent pause. He realized the power of his vocation and the good he could do. He decided to devote himself to the poor.

The poor are your masters, terribly sensitive and exacting as you will see, but the uglier and dirtier they are, the more unfair and bitter, the more you must give them your love. It is only because of your love that the poor will forgive you the bread you give to them.

—St. Vincent de Paul

Setting the Standard

In a complete turnabout from a relatively coddled life, Vincent began to focus on doing good works, to the point that there did not seem to be anyone left out of his ministry: orphans, the physically ill, the poor, prisoners, and the mentally ill. Vincent even entered the area of war relief and, new for that time, care for the elderly. From donations he received he was able to he ransom Christian slaves in North Africa.

He also organized charities in a way no one had before, making sure that those who needed help received it. He learned how to use newspapers and magazines in asking for charitable contributions. And, in time-honored tradition, he asked for donations from his wealthy friends to do good for those who needed so much. The rich were happy to give and to feel good about themselves in helping.

With all that activity, Vincent still found time to write prolifically on spiritual topics.

E-FACTS

The St. Vincent de Paul Society was founded in 1833. In this country the National Council of the U.S. Society of St. Vincent de Paul oversees eight regional groups and 50 state offices. Volunteers are engaged in personal services, primarily on the parish level. Their work includes drop-in centers, summer camps, work with the homeless and the aged, personal visitations, and other outreach programs. The society is based in St. Louis, Missouri, and can be reached at ☎(314) 576-3993 or ✍*www.svdpuscouncil.org* or *svdpus@aol.com*.

Founding Orders

Monsieur Vincent, as he became known, also founded a religious society of secular priests known as the Vincentians, who are devoted to mission work. His fame continued among the noted and grew among the needy. While he still kept a foot in both camps, so to speak, he was revered as a simple country priest. He was a very human saint, though. He once described himself as "by nature of a bilious temperament and very subject to anger."

E-FACTS

In the years when his cause for canonization was being investigated, it was learned that Vincent used snuff. That seemed to give some investigators pause about the merits of his cause, but fortunately not for long.

Vincent worked closely with St. Louise de Marillac. Whirlwind of energy that he was, Vincent still would have had a difficult time accomplishing as much as he did without her assistance. She assisted him in founding the Daughters of Charity, an "unenclosed" congregation of women; that is, they did not live in a convent, which was a rather new concept at the time. About the work of the Daughters, Vincent said, "Their convent is the sickroom, their chapel the parish church, their cloister the streets of the city."

E-PROFILE

St. Louise de Marillac (1591–1660)

Louise was raised by her widowed father. On the advice of her confessor, she married a man attached to the household of the French queen and eventually had a son. She nursed her husband through his last illness, and after his death met Vincent de Paul. He became her spiritual director, and then the two began an informal partnership that was to become probably the most successful ever in charity work. They formed the Daughters of Charity to care for the sick and poor. By the time of her death 26 years later, the Daughters had more than 40 houses throughout that country.

Louise had worried about the future of the congregation after her death. She repeatedly urged her Sisters to be "diligent in serving the poor . . . honor them, my children, as you would honor Christ Himself."

Louise de Marillac was canonized in 1934 and was declared patron of social workers by Pope John XXIII in 1960. Her feast day is March 15.

Vincent lived to be 80. He was canonized by Pope Clement XII in 1737, and was named patron of all charitable societies by Pope Leo XIII in 1885. His feast day is September 27.

PART II

American Saints: Growing in Numbers

There aren't many American saints—who are officially canonized, that is. In fact, only five American saints have gone through church procedure. Can you name them all? The answers appear below.

Answers: St. Elizabeth Bayley Seton, St. John Nepomucene Neumann, St. Frances Xavier Cabrini, St. Rose Philippine Duchesne, and St. Katharine Drexel.

CHAPTER 26

St. Elizabeth Ann Seton
(1774–1821)

Mother Seton, as she is known, earns the first chapter in this section because she is the first American-born saint. You may even remember when Pope Paul VI announced the canonization of this New Yorker in 1975.

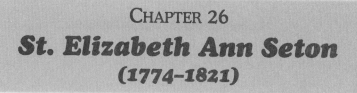

In the Calendar of Saints

In announcing the canonization of Elizabeth Bayley Seton in September 1975 to the thousands of Americans in St. Peter's Square in Rome, Pope Paul VI said:

> For the honor of the Most Holy Trinity, for the exaltation of the Catholic Faith and the increase of the Christian life, by the authority of Our Lord Jesus Christ, of the holy Apostles Peter and Paul and by Our authority, after mature deliberation and most frequent prayer for divine assistance, having obtained the counsel of many of our brother bishops, we declare and we define that Blessed Elizabeth Ann Bayley Seton is a saint, and we inscribe her name in the calendar of saints, and mandate that she should be devoutly honored among the saints in the universal Church.

She was a woman who lived through almost all that can be experienced in a lifetime: religious conversion, travel, marriage, motherhood, financial problems, discrimination, widowhood, betrayal, losing a child, founding a religious order, and taking vows. Actually, when you look back at it, all Elizabeth Seton seems to have missed experiencing was war. The recognition of her strong faith throughout what might be called a soap-opera life came in sainthood.

The Anglican Elizabeth

She was born Elizabeth Ann Bayley in New York City. Her father was a professor of anatomy at King's College, now Columbia University, and her maternal grandfather was the rector of St. Andrew's, the Anglican Church on Staten Island.

E-FACTS

After the Revolutionary War the Anglican faith became known as Episcopalian to American and Scottish people.

Elizabeth was one of three girls. Her mother died when she was just three, her father eventually remarried and soon there were six more siblings. Leading the life of a well-to-do young lady, Elizabeth learned to play the piano and to speak French. At the appropriate age—she was 19— she was married to William Magee Seton.

The couple was happy, and in fairly short order had five children: Anna Maria, William, Richard Bayley, Catherine Josephine, and Rebecca. William Seton was a prosperous merchant, so the couple was wealthy as well.

Because of the standard of comfort in her life, Elizabeth was able to involve herself in charity work in the city. Among other projects she was one of the cofounders of the Society for the Relief of Poor Widows with Small Children.

She also explored her religion during those years, under the tutelage of an assistant to Trinity Church. She spread word of her new enthusiasm for her faith among family members and was overjoyed when her husband finally joined the church. "Willy's heart seemed to be nearer to me for being nearer to his God," she wrote.

Clouds on the Horizon

A mere six years after their marriage, the Setons' placid life began to fall apart, and it was sudden. Willy's business, a family-owned company, failed, and by 1780 the firm was in bankruptcy.

Tuberculosis, a disease that had plagued the Seton family, now showed up in Willy and it was serious, perhaps exacerbated by his worry over the business. To try to halt the progress of the illness, the Setons sailed for Europe, taking their oldest child, Anna Maria, with them and leaving the other four with relatives. To finance the trip, Elizabeth sold the last of her silver, china, and whatever else she owned that would bring cash.

The desperate strategy did not work. The family landed in Leghorn, Italy, and went on to Pisa. Two days after Christmas 1803, William Seton died there.

Elizabeth buried her husband as quickly as Italian law mandated, but she was unable to return to America because of the bad winter weather and the fact that Anna Maria had caught scarlet fever. Her grief was overwhelming, but her enduring faith held fast. She wrote a friend, "If I could forget my God one moment at these times I should go mad—but He hushes all—Be still and know that I am God your Father." (Elizabeth Seton kept a journal for many years and engaged in exchanges of letters with many family members, friends, and colleagues who helped paint a rounded portrait of a deeply spiritual woman.)

She stayed in Leghorn for four months after her husband's death, befriended by two couples (the men were brothers). During that time she was introduced to Catholicism and became increasingly interested in that faith, to the point of studying the religion.

In 1804 she returned to New York, accompanied by the younger of the two brothers, Antonio Filicchi. Elizabeth was to remain in touch with that family for the rest of her life. They were instrumental in her conversion and there was much letter writing between them.

Back at home and without her beloved Willy, Elizabeth was forced to set mourning aside and turn her attention to how she would earn a living. Apparently the Bayley family resources could not stretch beyond the Bayley family, because Elizabeth seemed to have received no financial help, or at least not enough, from her father. And with the Seton family business in bankruptcy, there was not likely to be much help from that quarter.

As she looked around New York to see what she could do, Elizabeth was stunned to find friends and even some family members taking a few steps back from her now that she was interested in becoming a Catholic. She thought perhaps she could teach school, but those same friends did not want her influencing their children. Elizabeth was looked on with disdain in her Protestant circle, and indeed in all of that predominantly Protestant city.

She set about taking in boarders, a business that limped along for a while. One bright spot for her in that dark time was that she was baptized a Catholic in 1805.

An Answer

Finally the young widow was offered a position by a Catholic religious order in Baltimore asking her to found a girls' school.

E-FACTS

The colony of Maryland was welcoming to Catholics, and indeed many early Catholic institutions that would later spread across America were founded there. One of them was Mother Seton's educational system.

Other women joined Elizabeth, and by 1809, under her leadership, they founded a religious community, the Sisters of Charity of St. Joseph. They also established a school for poor children in a village named Emmitsburg, near the Pennsylvania border. Initially the women lived in a farmhouse, along with Elizabeth's children. From then on, as the order grew, the girls lived in their mother's boarding schools, her two sons in a nearby Catholic school for boys. The new community, now including 18 nuns, was approved by Archbishop Carroll of Baltimore in 1812.

Elizabeth was named superior of the order. She modeled it on St. Vincent de Paul's Daughters of Charity, with a few variations in its bylaws allowing for differences between Americans and the French. She called it the Sisters of Charity of St. Joseph. The nuns would devote themselves to the education of the poor and to teaching in parochial schools. The nuns' habit was Elizabeth's black mourning dress with a shoulder cape and a black bonnet, which was later replaced by a white one.

From her groundwork grew the huge Catholic parochial school system in the United States. Mother Seton's work spread throughout North America, South America, and Italy, where she still had ties (principally the Filicchi family).

E-QUESTIONS?

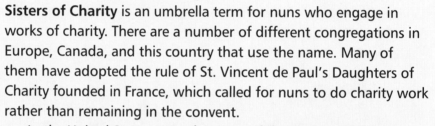

Who are the Sisters of Charity?
Sisters of Charity is an umbrella term for nuns who engage in works of charity. There are a number of different congregations in Europe, Canada, and this country that use the name. Many of them have adopted the rule of St. Vincent de Paul's Daughters of Charity founded in France, which called for nuns to do charity work rather than remaining in the convent.

In the United States several groups of the Sisters of Charity trace their origin to Elizabeth Seton's original order, but others now operate independently of her order's rules.

Another Loss

Elizabeth Seton was a strong woman, but when her daughter, Anna Maria, died at the age of 16, she experienced a totally different sorrow and test of her spiritual resources. Anna Maria was her oldest child, and the one most like her mother. An added bond between the two was the time they spent together traveling to Italy with Willy, and the months following in that country without him.

Her daughter's death was not unexpected: Elizabeth and Anina, as Anna Maria was known, spent much time together during her long illness, talking, praying, and strengthening their faith. On her deathbed Anina took vows as a Sister of Charity, and mother and daughter spoke of being reunited in eternity.

Still, Elizabeth was devastated by Anina's loss and sank into a deep depression. She wrote to a friend, "The separation from my angel has left so new and deep an impression on my mind, that if I was not obliged to live in these dear ones I should unconsciously die in her."

Serenity

The sharp anguish eventually eased. Elizabeth Seton continued in the huge task of administering and expanding her order, and continued looking after her children, who were never far from her, physically or in her thoughts. When the boys got older, she sent them to Leghorn to learn business from Antonio Filicchi.

Elizabeth died in Emmitsburg in 1821—ironically of tuberculosis.

E-FACTS

Seton Hall University in South Orange, New Jersey, was founded in 1856 by James Roosevelt Bayley, who named the college after his aunt. In 1918 the Sisters of Charity established Seton Hill College in Greensburg, Pennsylvania.

You could say Mother Seton attained sainthood for her devotion in founding and running a religious order that became so important in early American education and remains so to this day. But her canonization also reflects her deep spirituality. Here was a woman who lived more than half of her life accepted and even flourishing as a Protestant in New York. When it became apparent she was about to convert to Catholicism, she suffered discrimination in that city and was not free of it and comfortable again until she moved to Maryland. Despite prejudice, despite her financial problems, not to mention the death of her husband and two children—she lost her youngest daughter, Rebecca ("Bec"), in 1816 when the girl was 14—her faith, aside from what could be called a small blip representing the desolation she felt after Anna Maria's death, remained strong.

The move toward canonization began in 1907. In 1959 Mother Seton was given the title "Venerable." In 1963 she was beatified and she was canonized in 1975. Her feast day is January 4.

CHAPTER 27
St. John Nepomucene Neumann
(1811–1860)

Two American saints are firsts: John Neumann was the first male American saint, and Frances Xavier Cabrini was the first naturalized American citizen to be canonized. St. Rose Philippine Duchesne, like Neumann and Cabrini, was also an immigrant to this country.

John was born in Bohemia and educated in Prague. He wanted to become a priest, but, curiously, when he applied he was told there were enough clerics at the moment in that region.

In a way this was all right with him. Deep down he had an interest in becoming a missionary in the United States, and so he sailed to New York, arriving with literally his last dollar in his pocket. Ordained there, he was transferred to Buffalo, which fit his concept of "frontier priest" more than Manhattan did. He covered a sizable geographic area outside that upstate city, because he was younger and stronger than the other priest assigned there. He walked constantly to baptize, officiate at weddings, give the Eucharist, and comfort the dying.

He did not stay in the Buffalo area long but traveled to other regions as a missionary. When he was 31 he joined the Redemptorist Order. The first Redemptorist professed in this country, John Neumann served in parishes in Baltimore and Pittsburgh, until he was eventually consecrated bishop of the sprawling city of Philadelphia at age 45.

E-PROFILE

John Henry Newman (1801–1890)

It is easy to mistake John Henry Newman for John Neumann. John Newman was a British writer and theologian and was first an Anglican priest attached to Oxford University. When he was 40, he published a tract that appeared to be a Catholic interpretation of an Anglican position. The work was denounced; Newman resigned his post and retired to a religious community. After much thinking and reading, he became a Catholic, then a priest, and eventually a cardinal.

Cardinal Newman was invited to be consultant for the first Vatican Council (1869–1879). He declined. Nearly a century after Vatican I, his thoughts on ecumenism, defense of conscience, and the theology of the laity had such an influence on Vatican II that Pope Paul VI dubbed that conclave "Newman's Council."

Why is John Henry Newman not a saint? The Catholic Church in England is small and not that familiar with pushing a candidate to canonization. Also, Newman's "liberal" thinking—at least that is how it appeared to Rome—is also likely to be holding him back. As Kenneth L. Woodward says in his book *Making Saints,* "Rome does not canonize thinkers whose ideas it has not yet made its own."

In this country, Newman clubs, in which a priest serves as chaplain, are in existence in many colleges and universities.

John most emphatically did not want that post. He pleaded with his superiors in Europe to intercede for him with Pope Pius X, to keep the pope from choosing him. It didn't work. He went to Philadelphia, overseeing that city's rapid development, fueled by the growing number of immigrants. He built churches and schools—more new schools than any bishop in the country—and produced a German/English catechism for the newcomers. Describing the new bishop of Philadelphia, whom he had met for the first time while visiting America, the archbishop of Thebes reported him to Rome as "a little inferior for the importance of such a distinguished city, not in learning nor in zeal nor in piety, but because of the littleness of his person [John Neumann was five foot two] and his neglect of fashion. . . . The populous City of Philadelphia, rich, intelligent, full of life and importance, surely merits a bishop of another type."

E-FACTS

There must be something about Maryland: St. Elizabeth Ann Seton founded her Sisters of Charity there. St. John Neumann served in Baltimore. Now Francis Xavier Seelos, who was stationed in Maryland during Neumann's time, was beatified by Pope John Paul II in 2000. It is important to remember that Maryland offered Catholics freedom from religious persecution and was more or less the cradle of American Catholicism in those early years of settlement.

A few years after his death, reports of favors and cures obtained through his intercession began and have never stopped.

A man noted for his piety and humility, John Neumann is said to have lived in a tiny room and to have owned only one habit. He is buried in Philadelphia. He was canonized as recently as 1977, and his feast day is January 5.

Suggested Additional Reading:

John Henry Newman: Selected Sermons, introduction by Ian Ker (Paulist Press, 1994). Another collection of Newman writings.

Newman for Everyone: 101 Questions Answered Imaginatively by John Henry Newman; Jules M. Brody, editor (Alba House, 1996). Blends the theoretical with the abstract through editing of the saint's works.

Newman the Theologian: A Reader by John Henry Newman (University of Notre Dame Press, 1990). Another facet of the output from a brilliant mind.

CHAPTER 28

St. Frances Xavier Cabrini
(1850–1917)

The woman was a whirlwind, accomplishing so much in her lifetime, both here and abroad, that she would make the busiest person you know seem a dawdler.

She was born Maria Francesca Cabrini in Lombardy, Italy, the youngest of 13 children. Orphaned at 18, she wanted to become a nun but, in delicate health, was refused entry to two religious communities. Help was to come from another quarter, however; a local prelate asked if she'd like to take over a poorly run orphanage. Would she! After completing that assignment, she and seven followers moved into an abandoned friary and founded the Institute of the Missionary Sisters of the Sacred Heart, specializing in educating girls. (As you may have gathered reading this book, if no religious order will take you, or none suits your purposes, the thing to do is to go off and start your own.) Soon there were branches in other Italian cities.

E-FACTS

When she became a nun Maria Cabrini took the name Francis Xavier, after a missionary saint she admired. That evolved into Frances Cabrini rather than the masculine spelling Francis, although sometimes you will see the name spelled with an *i*.

In 1899, the archbishop of New York asked Frances and five of her sisters to come to New York to work. It turned out to be a peculiar offer. When the nuns arrived, the archbishop took back his invitation and suggested they return to Italy.

No thank you, said Frances. The women stayed. She went on to establish numerous schools, orphanages, hospitals, and convents, not only throughout the United States but in Central and South America, England, and France. She even returned to Italy six times to organize more convents there. In this country, Frances was especially helpful in assisting Italian immigrants.

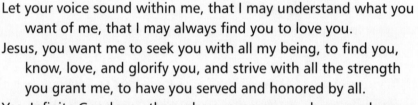

A Prayer of St. Frances Xavier Cabrini

Let your voice sound within me, that I may understand what you want of me, that I may always find you to love you.

Jesus, you want me to seek you with all my being, to find you, know, love, and glorify you, and strive with all the strength you grant me, to have you served and honored by all.

Yes, Infinite Goodness, through your mercy, you have made me a missionary of your divine Heart, and I must, I will act as a missionary, relying on your help which is never lacking.

Let your voice sound within me, and I shall go even to the farthest end of the earth, to do all that you ask, because the sound of your voice performs wonders.

In your name, Jesus, and enclosed within your Heart, I can do anything!

When faced with a seemingly insurmountable problem, she would ask, "Who is doing this? Are we—or our Lord?"

At the time of her death in Chicago, she had established more than 50 schools, orphanages, hospitals, convents, and various other charitable centers.

She was canonized in 1946. Her feast day is November 13, and she is the patron saint of hospital administrators and emigrants and immigrants.

> She is telling us that if we love Christ with all our soul, in the very conditions of our lives, we shall be holy and pleasing to Him.
> —CARDINAL SAMUEL STRITCH OF CHICAGO,
> ON THE OCCASION OF MOTHER CABRINI'S CANONIZATION

Saints for Their Times

Away from their immediate sphere of influence, neither Bishop Neumann nor Mother Cabrini is very well known in this country. Their work took place at a time when our nation was receiving a great number of immigrants from Europe. Both Bishop Neumann and Mother Cabrini were instrumental in organizing those waves of newcomers and providing services for them that are, in many cases, still in existence today. The time was right for their unique energy and talents.

CHAPTER 29

St. Rose Philippine Duchesne
(1769–1852)

Born in France, this saint entered the Visitation order at the age of 17, but persecution during the French Revolution forced the entire order into exile.

Rose then joined the Congregation of the Religious of the Sacred Heart (now the Society of the Sacred Heart) and left for America as a missionary. Heading west, in 1818 she established at St. Charles, Missouri, the first convent for her order in America.

St. Rose founded many schools and orphanages and, like Katharine Drexel, also worked among the Native Americans. Rose ministered to the Potawatomi tribe at Sugar Creek, Kansas. They called her "Woman Who Prays Always."

She was canonized as recently as 1988, and her feast day is November 18.

CHAPTER 30

St. Katharine Drexel
(1858–1955)

Katharine Drexel died in 1955, which is only yesterday compared to other dates cited in these pages. Actual film of this cannonized woman is shown on television when there is talk of her canonization. It is easy for us to recognize, and even identify with, such a contemporary person, even if she wears a nun's habit that has long since been updated by her order. She lived so recently that several of the sisters remember Katharine Drexel and speak of her with affection.

The Heiress

If the first thing to catch your attention here is the name, then, yes, you are correct in your assumption: Katharine Drexel was a member of the wealthy Philadelphia banking family. Her father was a partner of J. P. Morgan in a firm that later became the major Wall Street financial house Drexel Burnham Lambert.

Katharine's mother died just five weeks after her birth. Her Catholic father, Francis, of Austrian descent, eventually remarried and her stepmother, Emma, had a good deal of influence on the young girl.

The Drexels were a religious family, and Katharine and her two sisters, Elizabeth and Louise, were brought up learning to give to the needy. Three days a week Emma would open the doors of their town house at Rittenhouse Square to cheerfully hand out food, clothing, and cash to those who needed assistance.

Katharine led the life of a young woman of means. She had a governess and tutors. At 15 she traveled to Europe with her family for the first time and took in the typical tourist sites. (She pronounced Westminster Abbey "gloomy.")

Back at home, Katharine made her social debut. But even while her days were filled with fittings and parties, she still made time for charity.

After her stepmother died in 1883, Katharine's father took his daughters to Europe again. This time the young woman visited the home of her namesake, St. Catherine of Siena, and her growing desire to enter a religious order was reinforced.

Returning to Philadelphia, Katharine talked to her priest, a longtime family friend, who urged her to wait awhile and see if the determination was still as strong in a year or two. During that interval Katharine and her father and sisters traveled to the Northwest, exposing her to a part of the country along the way that would play a prominent role in her future.

In 1885 Francis Drexel died. He had established a trust for his three daughters of $15 million, the largest estate ever recorded in Philadelphia up to that time. Fortune hunters were tripping over themselves to get to the girls' front door. Elizabeth and Louise both eventually married, but all three girls used their money to help others.

Katharine's Choice

There were plenty who needed help. The years of Katharine's life, like the lives of John Neumann and Frances Xavier Cabrini, spanned a time of monumental growth in this country, with immigrants pouring in to both coasts, that created a movement toward settling the middle of the country.

E-FACTS

Drexel University was founded in 1891 by Anthony J. Drexel, Katharine's uncle. Members of the Drexel family are today still involved with the Philadelphia institution in one way or another. The university offers undergraduate programs in, among other specialties, business, engineering, environmental design, and computer and physical science. For more information you can call ✆(800) 2-DREXEL or visit the Web site at ✉*www.drexel.edu.*

Katharine took the road less traveled in her work for charity: She elected to concentrate on Native Americans and African-Americans. These two sectors of the population received almost no attention from government or society at the time. The Native Americans had been here for centuries, and African-Americans were not exactly the new immigrants of the moment.

The rail trip Katharine had taken with her father across America had, at least at a distance, acquainted her with the part of the country that needed her help. Katharine had also spoken with two missionaries, one from Dakota and the other from the Indian Bureau in Washington, D.C. She started small, endowing schools on Native Americans reservations around the nation with part of her inheritance.

There was another trip back to Europe, too, with her sister, Elizabeth, and this time she met with Pope Leo XIII. When she pleaded with him to send priests for the Native Americans, he responded, "Why not become a missionary yourself?"

So she did. In 1888 the young heiress entered the convent of the Sisters of Mary in Pittsburgh, Pennsylvania, to begin training for the sisterhood. She ultimately intended to found a new order, but first she had to become an "established" nun.

At the age of 37, Katharine took her final vows. By that time, with everyone now knowing about her eventual plans, she had found 12 women who wanted to work with her.

Her congregation was known as the Sisters of the Blessed Sacrament for Indians and Colored People, later to be just the Sisters of the Blessed Sacrament, or SBS. Soon even more like-minded women were joining the order.

> The accumulation of vast wealth while so many are languishing in misery is a grave transgression of God's law, with the consequence that the greedy, avaricious man is never at ease in his mind: he is in fact a most unhappy creature.
>
> —POPE JOHN XXIII

Difficult Times

The ministry had its rough moments. Walking the streets of Harlem and other big-city neighborhoods in the 1950s, the sisters often passed by whites who called them "nigger sisters." When the nuns would tell Katharine about the remarks, she would say only, "Did you pray for them?"

A particularly difficult episode occurred in 1922 in Beaumont, Texas. The Ku Klux Klan had said they would tar and feather the white pastor at one of Mother Drexel's schools—and bomb his church as well. The nuns prayed. In two days a tornado hit Beaumont and destroyed the Klan's headquarters. Two Klansmen died in the storm. The Klan never bothered the nuns again.

Making a Difference

Katharine Drexel was still allowed to administer her trust fund, which brought her somewhere in the neighborhood of $300,000 a year, a very nice neighborhood in the early days of the twentieth century. Besides funding her own projects, she readily donated money to the causes of others—a million dollars, for instance, went to the Bureau of Catholic Indian Missions. In the 1920s she contributed $750,000 toward the founding of Xavier University in New Orleans, the first Catholic college established for blacks. The archbishop there had asked her to help in providing a training college for black teachers. She had her lawyer handle the details of the purchase because she felt certain the owner wouldn't sell to her.

E-FACTS

With the help of Katharine Drexel, Xavier University was founded in 1925. The 29-acre campus is situated about two miles from downtown New Orleans. A four-year private liberal arts university affiliated with the Roman Catholic Church, it has two graduate schools as well. Today, some 90 percent of full-time undergraduates are African-American.

On her own, Katharine Drexel was responsible for building nearly 100 schools in cities and suburbs, and a dozen schools for Native Americans.

Special Acclaim

It seems remarkable even these days, but imagine how extraordinary all of what Katharine Drexel did was back then. In noting all that she gave, Augustus Tolton (1854–1897), who lived at the time of Katharine Drexel and was in those early years of her work the first African-American priest to be acclaimed by black Catholics, wrote: "In the whole history of the Church in America we cannot find one person that has sworn to give her treasure for the sole benefit of the Colored and Indians. As I stand alone as the first Negro priest of America, so you, Mother Katharine, stand alone as the first one to make such a sacrifice for the cause of a downtrodden race."

By the terms of Francis Drexel's will, when one of his daughters died her part of the Drexel trust would be divided between the other two. Katharine eventually inherited Elizabeth's share and, when Louise died in 1945, the entire income from the trust.

She lived to be nearly 100 years old. In poor health for the last 20 years of her life, she stayed close to her order's motherhouse and spent most of her time in a wheelchair. But she continued her commitment to civil rights, including funding the NAACP in some of its projects.

By the time of her death she had spent just about all of her inheritance. The capital from the trust reverted to charities specified by Francis Drexel.

Katharine Drexel is buried at the motherhouse of the Sisters of the Blessed Sacrament in Bensalem, Pennsylvania. She was beatified by Pope John Paul II in 1988, and canonized on October 1, 2000.

Her feast day is March 3. (It is possible to have a feast day when one has been beatified.)

E-FACTS

At one point when Katharine Drexel was negotiating changes in the constitution of her order, and was up against a delay in a response from Rome, she had a visit from a small woman as determined in her way as Katharine. Mother Frances Cabrini told Katharine to go to Rome herself and handle the business. Katharine did.

Her Miracles

In 1974 a 14-year-old boy in the Philadelphia area was cured of deafness in one ear. He had prayed to Katharine Drexel, and when his hearing returned it was attributed to the nun's intercession.

Then, in January 2000, Pope John Paul II issued a decree formally recognizing the second miracle. The Vatican Congregation for the Causes of Saints ruled that there was no natural cause for the curing of a 17-month-old American child's deafness. That recovery has also been attributed to the intercession of Katharine Drexel after the girl's parents began praying to the nun. The decree was the last step before canonization.

Appropriately, Mother Katharine Drexel was canonized at a jubilee mass in Rome along with Sister Josephine Bakhita, a Sudanese slave who had joined the Daughters of Charity; Sister Josepha Sancho de Buerra, a Spanish nun who founded a religious order in the late 1800s; and 120 Chinese martyrs who died in the Boxer Rebellion of 1900. More than 3,000 Americans, including members of the Sisters of the Blessed Sacrament and faculty, alumni, and students from Xavier University in Louisiana, attended the mass. The Xavier University Concert Choir sang at the liturgy. Also seated near the altar was the man whose cure for deafness in 1974 was attributed to Mother Drexel's intercession.

CHAPTER 31

Bl. Damien of Molokai
(1840–1889)

Mention the Hawaiian island of Molokai and many of us think instantly: lepers. Say the name Father Damien, and the association that flashes through the saint watcher's mind is: "Father Damien and the lepers." This priest is as identified with his life's work as Mother Teresa is with the poor of Calcutta.

European Roots

A Belgian, which may come as a surprise to you, he was born Joseph de Veuster of a farming family at Tremeloo. At the age of 20 he became a member of the Congregation of the Sacred Hearts of Jesus and Mary. Three years later he headed for Hawaii, then known as the Sandwich Islands, where he was ordained and took the name Damien.

A photograph of Joseph in those years shows a handsome man with dark hair and penetrating eyes, who looked very, very young.

The new priest's assignment was several areas on the island of Hawaii, the largest of the islands, and Molokai, considerably smaller than Hawaii and to its north. Oahu, where the capital of Honolulu is situated, is a bit larger than Molokai and lies to the west of that island.

The Outpost

In 1865, when Damien was still a boy in Europe, King Kamehameha V of Hawaii signed into law "An Act to Prevent the Spread of Leprosy." Hawaiian health authorities were anxious to control the disease for which there was no cure.

E-FACTS

Leprosy is a chronically infectious disease that principally affects the skin, although in advanced cases organs can also be affected. The disease manifests itself in skin lesions, especially on the face, arms, and legs, that grow and spread. If not treated there can be a loss of sensation and paralysis in the affected areas. The ancient Egyptians called leprosy "death before death."

Yellow flags adorned homes or the trees or fences of anyone who had, or was suspecting of having, leprosy. All of the afflicted were torn from their homes and sent by boat to Molokai. They included representatives from every segment of the population: the elderly, children, criminals, single persons, babies, married couples (who arrived together, or sometimes alone if an unafflicated spouse did not opt for a life sentence on the island).

Can there be worse sickness, than to know
That we are never well, nor can be so?
—JOHN DONNE, "AN ANATOMY OF THE WORLD,
FIRST ANNIVERSARY" (1612)

The settlement to which the lepers were banished was Kalawao. The ocean ringed three sides of that protruding land, and 1,600-foot cliffs rose on the fourth, perfectly isolating the area for government officials' intentions. It was a prison made by nature.

The "prisoners" were dropped off at the island to make a life for themselves as best they could, which was not a very good life at all. There was nothing resembling a civilized society on Molokai, just disease-ridden souls who saw death as their only release.

Damien Sets Sail

The young priest volunteered to serve at the leper colony. He arrived in 1873 and stayed 16 years until his death. Besides serving his parish's spiritual needs, Father Damien also took on the roles of physician, law enforcement officer, undertaker, and anything else that needed to be done. He eventually created a society and community the residents could take pride in.

First, he created a cemetery. Before his arrival those who died on the island were buried in shallow graves and left to be eaten by the creatures that roamed the island.

Damien built shelters and even a water supply system. He continually had to deal with the Hawaiian Board of Health, usually ending up frustrated at its bureaucracy. He also founded two orphanages for the colony.

Damien considered himself one of his flock and would *not* succumb to any fears of contact with the lepers. Thus, in 1884, he contracted leprosy himself. He continued working until just a month before his death.

> Illness is the night-side of life, a more onerous citizenship. Everyone who is born holds dual citizenship, in the kingdom of the well and in the kingdom of the sick.
> —SUSAN SONTAG, *ILLNESS AS METAPHOR* (1978)

Controversy

This seemingly saintly priest was not without controversy. Some who visited the colony considered him arrogant, crude, and even dirty. That's how he contracted leprosy, they claimed, by smoking from the same pipe as the lepers. If he hadn't been so careless—so reckless—they said, he would have lived longer and would have been able to continue serving his people.

Others refuted this with a theory that he got leprosy from his relations with women on the island (a posthumous investigation later exonerated him of that charge).

After his death, a Reverend Dr. Charles McEwen Hyde, a Congregational minister in Honolulu, wrote to a Presbyterian colleague in Australia, making these charges against Damien, and more. His letter was printed in a local Presbyterian paper in Sydney.

Hyde's allegations brought a response from an interesting quarter. In 1905 the author Robert Louis Stevenson, who had visited Molokai several weeks after Damien's death, and had met Damien four years earlier, wrote "An Open Letter to Rev. Dr. Hyde." Many pages long, it replied to what Stevenson considered slander by Hyde. If Damien de Veuster had any imperfections, wrote Stevenson, well, he was only human after all and was "a saint and a hero all the more for that."

Damien the Star

Although a long way from competing with Joan of Arc for frequent portrayal on the stage and in film, Father Damien has also been represented in films.

- Actors Kris Kristofferson, Peter O'Toole, and Derek Jacobi, with Australian David Wenham as Father Damien, starred in *Molokai: The Story of Father Damien*, a movie whose U.S. premiere was in September 1999 on the island of Molokai.
- In Vancouver, British Columbia, the award-winning Pacific Theater company has for the last 10 years included in its repertoire a one-man show titled *Damien,* about the missionary to the lepers.

Road to Sainthood

In 1936 Father Damien's remains were moved from Hawaii to Louvain, Belgium, near Brussels, for an impressive burial ceremony that probably would have stunned this simple man.

Father Damien was declared Venerable by Pope Paul VI in 1977, and was beatified by Pope John Paul II in 1995. Since the beatification was so recent, there is no reason to believe Damien's path to sainthood will not continue.

E-FACTS

Today leprosy is known as Hansen's disease. Today, some 5 to 6 million people worldwide suffer from it, notably those in tropical or subtropical climates. In the United States, fewer than 300 new cases of Hansen's disease appear each year. Although drug treatment is now effective, the stigma of leprosy remains. A famous U.S. facility for those suffering from the disease is in Carville, Louisiana.

Suggested Additional Reading:

Damien the Leper: A Life of Magnificent Courage, Devotion, and Spirit by John Farrow (Doubleday Image, 1999). A classic on the subject of Damien, which has been translated into more than 20 languages since it was first published in 1937. Farrow's book takes the priest from his birth in Belgium through his life in the islands to his return to his homeland for burial amid pomp and respect, where a king and a cardinal waited on a pier to receive his body and see it to its final resting place.

John Farrow (1904–1963) was a Hollywood film director and author of several books as well. His daughter, the actress Mia Farrow, provides an introduction to the current reissue of this work.

CHAPTER 32

Bl. Junípero Serra
(1713–1784)

Will he or won't he become a saint? His ascension at this point seems questionable. But let's learn a bit about this missionary who, like Father Damien, is now known as "Blessed."

Junípero Serra was a Spanish priest of the Franciscan order who founded eight of the 21 missions running the length of California. The first founded by Serra was in San Diego in 1769.

He was born and educated in Majorca, an island off the coast of Spain. He became a Franciscan in 1730 and was ordained a priest in 1738. For a time he taught philosophy in Majorca and then left for Mexico City to teach at San Fernando College. From there it was on to Lower California (Baja, part of Mexico), where he was named superior of the Franciscan missions. Little by little his missionary work to introduce Christianity to the indiginous people took him deeper into the California that is now part of the United States.

E-FACTS

Early in 2000, Sister Boniface Dyrda, of the Franciscan Sisters of Our Lady of Perpetual Help, died in Missouri at the age of 83. It was her miraculous cure from a blood disorder 40 years ago that helped secure the beatification of Father Serra.

The Other California Missions

The Spanish weren't the first visitors, but in 1769 the Spanish soldier and newly named governor of California, Captain Gaspar de Portolá, led an expedition that established forts first in San Diego and then in Monterey. Portolá traveled with the Junípero Serra, who was to Christianize the Native Americans. After he established the first mission in San Diego, there would be 20 more along the coast of California. The missions and the dates of their founding follow. (You will recognize that some were named for saints you read about earlier in these pages.)

San Diego de Alcalá (San Diego) 1769

San Carlos Borromeo de Carmelo (Carmel) 1770

San Antonio de Padua (near Jolon) 1771

San Gabriel Archangel (San Gabriel) 1771

San Luis Obispo de Tolosa (San Luis Obispo) 1772

San Francisco de Asís (San Francisco, more commonly known as Mission Dolores) 1776

San Juan Capistrano (San Juan Capistrano) 1776

Santa Clara de Asís (Santa Clara) 1777

San José de Guadalupe (Fremont) 1779

San Buenaventura (Ventura) 1782

Santa Bárbara (Santa Barbara) 1786

La Purísima Concepción (near Lompoc) 1787

Santa Cruz (Santa Cruz) 1791

Nuestra Señora de la Soledad (near Soledad) 1791

San Juan Bautista (San Juan Bautista) 1797

San Miguel Archangel (San Miguel) 1797

San Fernando Rey de España (San Fernando) 1797

San Luis Rey de Francia (near Oceanside) 1798

Santa Inés (Solvang) 1804

San Rafael Archangel (San Rafael) 1817

San Francisco de Solano (Sonoma) 1823

In Question

Junípero Serra was beatified in 1987. However, we are living in an age that acknowledges human rights, and one where revisionist history often comes into play when assessing icons. Father Serra's road to sainthood might be stalled, for now or forever. For the last several years Native American activists have been telling the church that the missionary did not treat the people he tried to convert well.

As you will read in Chapter 39, everything in a would-be saint's life is analyzed by the church before canonization. Whether the controversy surrounding the activists' claims will derail this Franciscan's path to sainthood might well be assumed if no news of canonization comes from Rome. Yet it takes so long for canonization, even after an individual is named "Blessed," that it would be hard to say if a delay is a deliberate stall or just the bureaucratic process at work.

E-FACTS

In all there are 29 American candidates for sainthood, most of them known and revered only in their own locality or within their religious order.

CHAPTER 33

Bl. Kateri Tekakwitha
(1656–1680)

Sometimes known as Katherine Tekakwitha, Kateri is the first Native American born in North America to become a candidate for sainthood.

Kateri was born in Ossernenon, near present-day Auriesville, New York. This is the same area where St. Isaac Jogues and a handful of other Jesuits and laypersons who worked with the Native Americans were martyred in the years 1642–1649.

Her mother was an Algonquin convert to Catholicism; her father was a Mohawk chieftain. Sadly, both of them and Kateri's brother died in a smallpox epidemic, leaving the girl an orphan at age four. While the disease spared the child her life, she suffered permanent damage to her eyesight and her face was disfigured.

Living with her uncle, she first met Christian missionaries when three Jesuits visited their home. She was finally baptized in 1676 and given the name Kateri, or Katherine.

The community of Ossernenon was not at all happy with her conversion; Kateri had to flee for her life. She walked some 200 miles to Caughnawaga, Canada, a Native American Christian enclave near Montreal. She made her First Communion there and lived a life of piety and good works. Eventually she took a vow of chastity, a rather unusual step in the Native American community at the time.

Miracles have been attributed to the woman called "the Lily of the Mohawks." In 1943 she was declared "Venerable" by Pope Pius XII and beatified by Pope John Paul II in 1980.

CHAPTER 34

Bl. Theodore Guerin
(1798–1856)

Theodore was a French-born nun who founded the Sisters of Providence of St.-Mary-of-the-Woods. She was born Anne-Thérèse Guerin in Brittany, France, on October 2, 1798, and had intentions of holy service from her early childhood. Her local priest allowed her to receive her First Communion before others in her age group, and in return, she promised to become a nun.

The Blessed Mother Theodore was home-schooled until her father was murdered by bandits. Then she began to help her mother run the household. She eagerly joined the Sisters of Providence, a group of women who offered various charitable services to the community. While working there, the Sisters asked Mother Theodore to lead a missionary group to Indiana. She accepted the job and arrived in Indiana in October of 1840.

Quickly, Mother Theodore opened a schoolhouse, fighting poverty, discrimination, hunger, and the elements for her cause. She established many other schools throughout Indiana and Illinois, gaining respect for the Sisters of Providence. She died on May 14, 1856, leaving a strong legacy of her schools and mission.

She was beatified by Pope John Paul II in 1998.

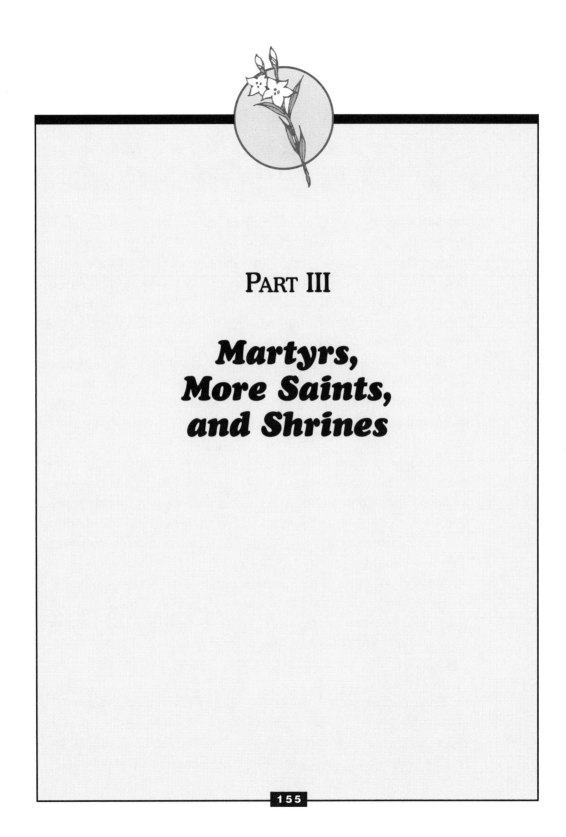

PART III

Martyrs, More Saints, and Shrines

CHAPTER 35
The Horrible Fates of Early Martyrs

Readers who attended parochial school—especially grammar school—through the 1960s, or even later, can remember listening to stories in religion class of the way early Christian martyrs died for their faith. Boiled in oil! Sliced to bits by gladiators in an amphitheater! Torn to pieces by wild beasts in an arena! Set afire! Eyes plucked out—then stabbed to death! Thrown into a body of water, tied to a boulder! As well as all the more mundane fates, such as . . . beheading!

Martyr comes from the Greek meaning "witness." In this context we are talking about a person who gives his or her life for the Christian faith. Being martyred is never what one would call a tidy death, but early Christians who perished in this fashion did suffer in a variety of horrendous ways. And keep in mind this was for a faith that was still new to them and certainly new, even unknown, to the rest of the world. There was precious little history of Christianity or years of an established church and earlier saints and martyrs for these new Christians to draw upon for strength. Yet their belief was firm enough that they refused to deny their faith when called upon to do so—and then were slain for it.

Many, if not most, of those saintly names have been forgotten or dropped from lists in prayer books to—well, to make church services go faster. Still, their names are familiar to saint watchers, who remember hearing and reading about St. Agnes, St. Perpetua, St. Felicitas, St. Polycarp, and a number of other men and women whose deaths no one would forget.

Their endings were brave and sad, but look at their ultimate reward. They were cannonized and they are still remembered in the twenty-first century. Not a bad trade-off, you might think, unless you're faced with being roasted alive or fed to a slavering beast.

The Making of a Martyr

Practitioners of the new Christian faith faced their greatest opposition from the year 33 to Constantine's edict allowing Christianity in 313, just after he was converted.

St. Stephen: The First Christian Martyr

Stephen was Jewish, spoke Greek, and was living in Jerusalem when he was chosen by the apostles to be one of seven deacons. He was to work within the Hellenic Jewish Christian community in Jerusalem. Hellenic Christians believed that Christianity had to separate itself entirely from Judaism.

Stephen was a bright, learned man who loved to talk and debate. Inevitably, in preaching in the synagogue, he angered some of the elders who charged him with blasphemy. He was arrested and brought before the Sanhedrin (the official Jewish legislative Judicial council), where he argued credibly in his own defense. Stephen was dragged outside of town, where he was stoned to death. Before dying, around the year 35, he forgave his killers.

St. Stephen

St. Stephen's feast day is December 26. He is the patron saint of Hungary, stonemasons, and bricklayers.

The persecution of the Christians came at the hands of the government. In addition, as new Christians clashed with the synagogue system of their birth, they were often turned out by the religious leaders and into the hands of civil authorities.

There were thousands of Christian martyrs during the period of persecution, since their religion refuted the legitimacy of the Roman Empire's deities (including the emperor, who considered himself divine). Civil law forbade the practice of the Christian faith or even assembling for the propagation of that belief. The treatment of the Christians, ranging from merely dismissive to outrageously cruel, depended on the mood of the emperor at the time.

Christians often met in secret. Many were caught, forced to admit their belief, and then executed. But not all admitted to being Christians, which raised an interesting question much discussed at the time: Were those who said whatever authorities wanted to hear—and therefore did not die—still true Christians? Or did they have to begin all over again in the faith with another baptism (and, presumably, hope for martyrdom the next time around)?

A martyr's date of death rather than his or her birthday is celebrated because it is the day that the martyr went on to eternal life. Some saints retain that day as their feast day.

Death Rituals

Christians brought food and other items to the graves of their loved ones or friends; pagans did, too. With Christians, the idea was to be joyous, as indeed the Christian faith was in the first few centuries. The church returned to the joy surrounding death in the years after Vatican II. Funerals were no longer conducted with the celebrant in black vestments and the service accompanied by dirge-like music—the "*Dies Irae*," for example, a hymn that starts: "Day of wrath, O day of mourning." Today, a funeral is more like those early times, celebrating the deceased's moving on into God's light. A present-day funeral and burial also stress the joy participants acknowledge at having known the deceased. White, not black, is the operative color used in services.

Interestingly, civil authorities did not interfere with early Christian graves, having a respect for death that apparently crossed religious lines. In time shrines and basilicas were built over some of those martyrs' tombs. These houses of worship remain today.

What is martyrology?
A **martyrology** is a listing of feast days. The list includes all of the saints who have been assigned that feast day. This is unlike a church calendar, which gives only one name per date. A martyrology also lists brief biographical data about each holy person.

Giving Their Lives

So who were those early souls who died for their faith? Are these true stories? Yes. Specific details of some of the early martyrs fall into the category of legend, which is understandable with stories repeated over nearly two millennia. The following sections tell about some of the better known martyrs from the early days of Christianity and distinguish legend from fact.

St. Polycarp (ca. 60–155)

St. Polycarp

This saint had more than a devout faith for which he was willing to die. He was a man of letters who made an impact on the church at that time. His is the oldest account of Christian martyrdom outside the New Testament.

Polycarp was a disciple of John the Baptist and served for many years as bishop of Smyrna. He was arrested when he was 86 years old and ordered to repeat "Caesar is Lord" and curse Christ. Polycarp refused, saying, "Eighty and six years I have served him and he never did me any wrong. How can I blaspheme my King who saved me?"

His sentence: death by burning. "Come, do what you will," the elderly bishop told his accusers, adding, "Leave me as I am, the one who gives me strength to endure the fire will also give me strength to stay quite still on the pyre, even without the precaution of your nails."

The fire blazed around this holy man but did not touch him. An executioner stabbed him to death. An account of his martyrdom claimed there was such a quantity of blood "that the fire was quenched and the whole crowd marveled."

St. Polycarp's feast day is February 23.

St. Barnabas (First Century)

A missionary, Barnabas is especially important because he went outside the Jewish faith and preached the gospel to the Gentiles. Originally a Jewish Cypriot named Joseph, he was later renamed Barnabas by the apostles after he sold his land and donated the proceeds to the new young church. The name means "son of encouragement," sometimes translated as "son of consolation."

No writings of Barnabas have survived, but what is known as the "Letter of Barnabas," by an anonymous Christian of the late first or early second century, takes a position on the superiority of Christianity over Judaism. Some scholars agreed that Barnabas wrote a New Testament letter to the Hebrews, too, but later historians believe neither work is by him. Both are too extreme in their denunciation of Jewish tradition, which did not seem likely for this saint.

Always close to the apostles, Barnabas appears to have been stoned to death in Cyprus around the year 61.

His feast day is June 11.

Sts. Perpetua and Felicitas (died 203)

Perpetua was a wealthy woman of Carthage, in North Africa, and had a son, known as Vivia or Vibia. Perpetua is usually linked with St. Felicitas (or Felicity), her pregnant young servant. The two suffered the same fate.

What makes Perpetua's martyrdom so touching is she actually recorded her thoughts as a young woman facing death, and these accounts survive. At age 22, Perpetua was arrested with Felicitas and several friends for some transgression or other having to do with the banned practice of Christianity. They were all held in a private home, where they were baptized, and were then moved to a prison.

At her trial, Perpetua was in conflict about her responsibilities. She had an aged father who pleaded for her life, and of course she had her baby boy. (Her husband is not mentioned in the narrative of her life.) When confronted with all that lies outside her religion, she said simply, "I am a Christian."

In her account, the baby is brought to Perpetua in prison and she nurses him. She notes "straightaway I became well, and was lightened of my labor and care for the child; suddenly the prison was made a palace for me, so that I would sooner be there than anywhere else." All could not be made right with her father, however. A non-Christian, he could not understand her dedication to this religion or grasp her joy in foreseeing eternity. She says to him, "What happens at this tribunal will be what God wants, for our power comes not from us but from God."

When she places her son with a person who will care for him after she is gone, she is greatly relieved. There was not much relief in hearing her sentence: to fight with wild beasts in the amphitheater. She and Felicitas would enter that arena together.

You may recall how calm Thomas More was before his execution, as he waited in the Tower of London, and how he remained calm even as he climbed the scaffold. Perpetua was equally serene and accepting. Her last words: "Thus far have I written this, till the day before the games; but the deed of the games themselves let him write who will."

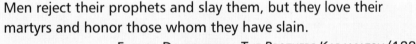

Men reject their prophets and slay them, but they love their martyrs and honor those whom they have slain.
—FYODOR DOSTOYEVSKY, *THE BROTHERS KARAMAZOV* (1880)

An eyewitness completed Perpetua's story: Felicitas was eight months pregnant when she was arrested. She prayed to go into labor so she would not be separated from her friends, and she gave birth to a daughter, whom she handed over to Christians who remained free.

On the day before their execution, Perpetua and Felicitas and their fellow prisoners and friends celebrated a "love feast" in the prison, which sounds reminiscent of the love-ins of the 1960s. It probably meant there was music and laughter, and prayer and good-byes at this feast. And joy— they were going to their death, but they found peace and happiness in those last hours despite the horror of what awaited them.

The next day the prisoners entered the arena. Again Perpetua was asked to deny her faith. Again she refused, saying, "For this cause came we willingly unto this, that our liberty might not be obscured. For this cause have we devoted our lives." They were tossed about by the animal let into the arena, said to be a wild cow, but the two women survived.

An executioner was called to put them to death by the sword, but apparently he was new at the job and was not able to strike the right, final blow. Perpetua guided his hand.

The eyewitness added, in closing the account of this saint, that just before the swordsman took aim, Perpetua and Felicitas, formerly mistress and slave, exchanged a kiss.

They share the same feast day, March 7.

St. Cyprian (ca. 200–258)

A learned man, Cyprian was a lawyer and teacher before he converted to Christianity. He became a great scholar of the Bible and is considered a major figure in early Christian literature.

Cyprian was named bishop of Carthage, and at one point he had to flee persecution. He continued to rule his see by letter.

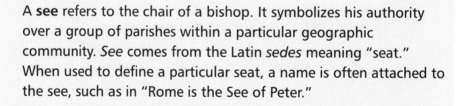

A **see** refers to the chair of a bishop. It symbolizes his authority over a group of parishes within a particular geographic community. *See* comes from the Latin *sedes* meaning "seat." When used to define a particular seat, a name is often attached to the see, such as in "Rome is the See of Peter."

That didn't set too well with his flock, who were quite critical of his taking off. When he did return, many of "the faithful" were no longer so true to the church. A priest who stayed when Cyprian left was now in schism, which is a formal breach of unity among people of the same faith. Between coping with that priest and deciding how the lapsed could be welcomed back into the church and standing firm on the primacy of the pope, Cyprian had his hands full.

More was to come. When he was 52 years old, Carthage was stricken with a plague that was to last two years. Cyprian and his Christians were blamed. At that time he wrote "On the Mortality" to comfort those in his diocese.

> We should not mourn for our brethren who have been freed from the world by the divine summons, since we know that they are not lost, but only sent on ahead.
>
> —ST. CYPRIAN

Cyprian ran into still more trouble when he ran afoul of Pope Stephen I. The saint refused to recognize the baptism of heretics, which Stephen had declared valid.

Finally compounding those difficult times, an official decree went out forbidding clerics from the practice of Christianity and requiring them to participate in the official state religion. When he refused, Cyprian was arrested and exiled to a village some distance from Carthage. In a year, a new edict came down, this one calling for death for bishops, priests, and deacons. When Cyprian continued in his refusal to recognize pagan gods, he was beheaded on September 14.

His feast day is September 16, two days after his martyrdom.

St. Sebastian (died ca. 288)

St. Sebastian

You know this holy man, even if you are not a saint watcher. Come across a painting of him and you probably think to yourself, "I've seen him before." He is the young man standing at a pillar whose hands are tied behind him, looking upward toward heaven. He has been shot with nearly a dozen arrows. His martyrdom is often depicted in writings and art dealing with Christianity and martyrdom. He is Saint Sebastian.

Sebastian is thought to have been born in Gaul (France), and was a soldier in the Roman army. Not revealing he was a Christian, he made numerous converts, including some government officials. Sebastian is said to have cured his wife, Zoe, of her deafness.

Sebastian's Christianity was finally brought to the attention of Emperor Diocletian, who was persecuting the followers of the new faith. He ordered archers to execute Sebastian. The arrows hit him and he was left for dead, but he didn't die. A Christian woman found him and nursed him back to health, only to have Sebastian once again denounce the emperor for his cruelty to Christians. He was again sentenced to die, and this time his executioner took no chances, beating him to death.

Sebastian was indeed a real person, and is buried on the Appian Way. However, some of the details of his story could be pious fiction. His feast day is January 20, and he is invoked for protection against plague.

E-FACTS

It is believed that all of the Twelve Apostles were martyred, with the exception of John.

St. Dorothy (died 303)

Yet another victim of Diocletian's scourge was Dorothy, who refused to make sacrifices to the gods. She was tortured and ordered executed. There is thought to be a legendary aspect to St. Dorothy's story. On the way to her place of execution, she met a young man, what we might call a lawyer today, named Theophilus. Teasing her, he asked her to send him fruits from "the garden" that she had claimed she would soon enter. She knelt for her execution, prayed, and an angel appeared with a basket of three roses and three apples. Dorothy had them sent to Theophilus, saying she would see him later in the garden. The lawyer converted to Christianity, and soon he, too, was martyred.

Her feast day, formerly February 6, is no longer observed.

Perhaps there is no happiness in life so perfect as the martyr's.
—O. Henry, "The Country of Elusion" (1907)

St. Agnes (died ca. 304)

A beautiful young Roman Christian, Agnes elected to consecrate her virginity to God. She suffered during the Emperor Diocletian's persecution, after unsuccessful would-be suitors brought her Christianity to the attention of authorities.

Diocletian was enraged at the girl's firmness of purpose, and though she was only 13 he sent her to a house of prostitution. No one touched her, in part because of her bearing, and on one occasion a miracle intervened.

She was eventually ordered beheaded, although some say she was stabbed in the throat. She is buried on Rome's Via Nomentana, where there is a cemetery named after her.

Her feast day is January 21, and she is the patron saint of Girl Scouts and maidens/virgins.

St. Lucy (died ca. 304)

A Sicilian, Lucy was born of noble parents. Like Agnes, she refused a marriage proposal under the reign of the anti-Christian Diocletion and was sentenced to a brothel.

But here Lucy's path diverges from Agnes's. When the guards tried to take Lucy, she could not be budged; it was as if she had become stone. She was ordered burned to death, but the flames did not touch her. Finally, she was stabbed through the throat.

Lucy is patron of those with eye diseases, perhaps because of her name, which means "light." Some stories have her eyes torn out by her judge, others say she tore them out to offer them to a suitor she did not like. In both incidents they were mysteriously and miraculously restored. In Sweden, the Christmas season begins on St. Lucy's Feast Day, with the celebration of the Festival of Light. Her feast day is December 13.

Suggested Additional Reading:

Perpetua's Passion: The Death and Memory of a Young Roman Woman by Joyce E. Salisbury (Routledge, 1997). The diary of this early Christian martyr, completed by a witness after her death.

CHAPTER 36

How the Veneration of Saints Grew

How did martyrs get to be saints, anyway? Did someone write down a Christian's name when he or she was slain, adding a note about that individual's bravery as a martyr, and then pass it along to other Christians?

Actually, that's pretty much the way it happened. However, some early Christians who were not martyred also became saints. Let's take a look now at the other sorts of holy people in those early days who would be declared saints.

The Confessors

Not everybody who admitted to being a Christian was killed for their faith. Men and women who had the good fortune to live through their ordeals or court trials were called **confessors**. They might have suffered a good deal in prison and may even have endured exile, but they survived. After their death they were accorded the same honor that went to martyrs.

Virgins and Ascetics

Around the fourth century there arose two divergent "lifestyles." Certain Christian women elected to stay unmarried and chaste, considering themselves brides of Christ (e.g., St. Agnes and St. Lucy). Choosing to remain a virgin caused problems for many women, especially if they were in a family that was not Christian. Even Christian parents often gave their daughters a difficult time about the decision, especially if a proper marriage was needed to improve the family fortunes.

These women usually entered a religious order. For many of them, remaining a virgin and becoming religious was a declaration of independence—the only way out of leading a life traditionally imposed on them. While their motives were almost certainly piety and a desire to commit their lives to God, no doubt there were women who just did not want to marry or who did not want to marry the man chosen for them.

In religious life, too, a woman could *learn*, sometimes rising to the position of superior in her convent. The convent was not always a cloistered life of prayer: some women taught, some wrote, and some did works of charity outside the convent walls.

Christian men, especially monks, chose the path of the *ascetic*. A monk, or even a man affiliated with no religious order, would walk off into the desert or woods, existing on food he could find or kill. He spent his time in prayer and contemplation—and sometimes self-flagellation and other extreme **mortifications**. All of this was done to become closer to God. The hermitlike, celibate existence was difficult and, when taken to an extreme, was likened to martyrdom.

E-QUESTIONS?

What are ascetics, and what is a hermitage?
Ascetics are those who strive to become more virtuous by practicing extreme self-denial and discipline. A **hermitage** is the dwelling place of a hermit.

Ascetics were not men who saw this way of life as a temporary measure, perhaps to atone for a sin or crime or to plead a favor with God. For example, Joachim, father of Mary, went into the desert and fasted and prayed for 40 days (see Chapter 3). More likely, this was a choice for a longer period, sometimes even the remainder of a man's life.

E-FACTS

In late 1999 the 19 Cistercian monks of Caldey Island, off the coast of Wales, welcomed a man who intended to spend an alcohol-free Christmas at the monastery. He didn't make it. Reported the abbot: "It wasn't a very silent night—even if it was Christmas. All we could do was lie in our beds and cover our ears." The monks could not reprimand the merrymaker: they take a vow of silence for 12 hours every night.

Saint Who?

Until about the fifth century, saints were honored only in the place they came from, which was usually a village. They were chosen saints by acclamation in that community; in those days the infant church had no requirements as to who should or should not be canonized. "Polycarp—the man was a saint!" someone would say with gusto. Others would agree: "No doubt about it!" The town would note his name and from then on pay him the veneration due one so worthy. This would include praying for his intercession in one matter or another, celebrating the day he died, and, of course, passing on his story orally and in writing.

See everything. Overlook a great deal. Improve a little.
—POPE JOHN XXIII

Records were kept of those who died as a martyr or as a prominent religious or, as everyone would agree, as just a particularly holy man or woman. Their names were read during church services.

This system worked fine in small towns. Naturally no one outside those hamlets knew about those particular saints. For martyrs and other Christians of note who died in large cities—Rome, say—people were specially appointed to keep track of listings of names. In times of intensive persecution, however, so many were killed that only the more famous names were recorded.

All martyrs, known and unknown, were honored in an umbrella celebration called Feast of All Martyrs, which was instituted in the fifth century. It later evolved into the present All Saints Day.

News traveled in the early centuries, certainly slower than it does now, but people were just as curious then about what went on around them as we are today. Towns and cities began exchanging lists of martyrs and other holy people, especially those famous for, say, how they died or their acclaim as preachers. They would sometimes trade relics of the person as well, which is how a relic of an Italian saint sometimes ended up in a church in another country. If a town had the name of a special martyr and a relic of him or her, the residents considered themselves twice blessed and twice as protected by that saint.

E-FACTS

The All Saints Day celebration takes place each year on November 1. It began in the early days of the church to pay respect to martyrs as well as to "confessors" who suffered but were not put to death. At that time *martyr* was equated with *saint.* Christians would go to martyrs' tombs, paying respect and sometimes conducting services at the burial site. They prayed, too, that they would have the strength to endure martyrdom if they were next. Gradually, these services were moved to a local church, where martyrs who did not have tombs could be included in veneration.

All Saints Day now pays tribute to all saints known and unknown, especially those who have not been assigned a feast day in the church calendar.

Getting Organized

The towns and cities that kept a record of native holy people, whom they could venerate and around whom they could hold festivals, were fortunate. But as Christianity spread, new nations that adopted the religion found themselves in a quandary when it came to saints. Obviously they had no Christian history, so they requested lists, usually from Rome, the largest city, with the names of many saints. From that base they added their own saints as they acquired them. Lending out lists and getting new lists from other countries is how some saints became universally known.

During the Middle Ages, the system became more organized. Lists of saints who had broad appeal were sent from the Holy See in Rome to every nation or community. For example, there was a consensus in Rome that the gospel writers should be known and venerated by Christians everywhere, so they were placed on what would become a universal list. As new Christian nations developed their own holy people, they would send those names to Rome for inclusion in the growing master list.

E-QUESTIONS?

What was the Middle Ages and what is a relic?
The **Middle Ages** is the period between the collapse of the Roman Empire in 476 and the end of the fifteenth century. Some put the latter date at the beginning of the twelfth century. Strictly speaking, religious **relics** are parts of a saint's body or of those who have been beatified. They can also be items that touched those individuals' remains or items the saints or about-to-be saints touched.

Going Overboard

Veneration of the saints was admirable, but sometimes it went to excess. **Cults** developed around certain saints; the faithful became obsessed with relics, sometimes dividing them up into smaller and smaller parts and selling them.

These were not cults as we know the term today, rather they were supporters of a particular holy person, interested in advancing his or her cause toward sainthood or venerating the saint. That was fine. But some Christians became obsessive about miracles and superstitions surrounding their favorite saint, which made the church feel there might be too much emphasis on saints at the expense of worshiping God.

Thus a practice was established of having the regional bishop decide, after reading the would-be saint's biography and account of miracles attributed to him or her, whether that person should be approved as a saint, with a feast day assigned in that region.

This was a start, but papal approval of favorite saints carried more prestige than the acknowledgment of a mere bishop. Involving Rome also allowed decisions to be made on unbiased knowledge of the life of a candidate for sainthood. Thus in 993 Ulric of Augsburg, a bishop, was declared a saint in the first papal canonization.

There are many canonized on earth, that shall never be Saints in Heaven.

—SIR THOMAS BROWN (1663–1704)

Back to Reason, and Sensible Veneration

The canonization process (see Chapter 39) was refined over the centuries until, in 1284, papal approval was the only legitimate path to official recognition of sainthood. By then lists of saints' names were pretty much in place, and the days when huge numbers of martyrs were being regularly added to the lists were over.

Relics, too, gave way to more practical symbols. After all, there were only so many bits of bone and hanks of hair to go around, and the church frowned on selling them! Also, the burial sites of saints belonging to the earliest age of the church were uncertain, and saints who were, for example, burned to death left no relics at all.

The new symbols that cropped up could be more easily seen by the faithful, or even bought by them. They could be mass-produced as well— or at least as mass-produced as those early centuries would allow. They could be sizable and expensive works of art, or they could be small reminders of a holy person—a drawing, or perhaps a medal or a ring.

Paintings depicted saints in a form unique to that person's life, or perhaps death. St. Cecilia, for example, a patron of musicians (see page 258), was painted playing an organ.

St. Peter, the first pope, holds keys, symbols of "the keys of the kingdom." St. Nicholas is portrayed with three golden balls or bags of gold, symbolizing his gift to the three young sisters without a dowry. And of course there was St. Sebastian with those punishing arrows.

The saint does everything that any other decent person does, only somewhat better and with a totally different motive.
—COVENTRY PATMORE, ENGLISH POET (1823–1896)

The Rise of Patron Saints

The practice arose of giving a child a saint's name at baptism in Germany and France in the Middle Ages and spread rapidly throughout the rest of the church. The child would grow up looking to and praying to that patron saint.

The custom was popular well into the twentieth century but is virtually ignored today. The church certainly suggests that parents name a child after a saint, but the enrollment rosters of little Jennifers and Codys in parochial schools show that often there is not all that much attention paid to that practice. Of course, a middle name could be a saint's name—Jennifer Anne, for example, or Cody Andrew. (The practice is reminiscent—although without the religious connotation—of the Jewish custom of naming a baby after an ancestor.)

As missionaries traveled the globe to spread the word of Christianity, they named sites where they landed, and eventually preached, after saints. In America, a whole state was named after one: Maryland, for Mary the mother of Jesus. A huge number of towns and cities in this country are named after saints.

The practice of appointing saints as patrons of specific occupations, or to intercede for those suffering from particular illnesses, or for other special causes came about as local people believed that a particular saint had performed miracles for them or interceded for them for a special favor, which was usually related to an incident in that holy person's life. The naming of patron saints is an ongoing, continuing practice; patrons are named for practically every aspect of life. This is an informal process, not at all like canonization.

CHAPTER 37
Later Saints, Martyred and Otherwise

Most of the martyrdom for the new Christian faith occurred in the second and third centuries under the Roman emperors Decius and Diocletian. Dying for one's faith has certainly abated since then, but it has not disappeared, as you will see in this chapter and others.

In this chapter we will look at saints who died as martyrs after the heaviest concentration of persecutions. We will also meet those fortunate saints who led an exemplary though often embattled life, but at least didn't have to endure a lighted torch setting fire to a pile of wood under them at the end of it.

St. Jerome (332–420)

St. Jerome

Born in Aquilea, Dalmatia, Jerome was educated in Rome to become one of the great scholars of the church. A thoughtful student, he was interested in learning all things, with an emphasis on classical poetry. One night the young man had a dream in which he was told the way for him was through the gospels and not the world. On awakening, Jerome decided to devote himself to studying the words of God.

As many men at this time elected to become hermits, so did Jerome. He retreated to the desert to live an austere life, although he did take his books with him. Instead of Latin he studied Hebrew, which few Christians did at this time, and spent time writing.

He lived among other hermits, who were apparently not much to his liking. After four years, disillusioned by the experience, he came out of the wild, saying, "Better to live among wild beasts than among such Christians!"

Jerome was ordained in **Antioch**, which was, until the rise of Constantinople, the third most important city of the Roman Empire after Rome and Alexandria. After more traveling and studying, Jerome eventually took a post as secretary to Pope Damasus. The pontiff gave Jerome a special assignment: translating the Scriptures from the Greek, which had been translated from the Hebrew, into Latin, which had become the more common language of the church. Jerome elected not merely to translate the Greek into Latin, but to translate the original Hebrew into Latin. The job took him the rest of his life.

During those years he also wrote *Adversum Helvidium*, which denounced a book by Helvidius declaring that Mary had had several children besides Jesus. He conducted Bible studies with noble ladies as well, encouraging them to study the Scriptures. One of them was St. Paula, who was to figure prominently in his future.

St. Paula (347–404)

Paula was a wealthy Roman aristocrat, happily married and with several children, including her daughter, St. Eustochium. When her husband died, Paula was devastated and decided to devote the remainder of her life to Christ. She met St. Jerome, who became her lifelong spiritual adviser and friend. Paula used her wealth to establish two monasteries for Jerome in Bethlehem, one for men and one for women. She oversaw the women's community.

Paula died in debt, having given all her money away. Jerome, despite his cranky reputation, wrote to Eustochium: "If all the members of my body were to be converted into tongues, and if each of my limbs were to be gifted with a human voice, I could still do no justice to the virtues of the holy and venerable Paula. Noble in family, she was nobler still in holiness; rich formerly in this world's goods, she is now more distinguished by the poverty that she has embraced for Christ."

St. Paula

Paula is the patron saint of widows. Her feast day is January 26.

Jerome was a fiery priest, ready to fight for the right reasons. He made some enemies with his sermons, especially those on the virtues of celibacy, which fell on many deaf ears, and his attacks on pagan life, which cited some influential Romans by name. Overall, Jerome was difficult to get along with; in fact he was downright cantankerous, traits more likely unheard of in saintly dispositions.

When Pope Damasus died in 384, the saint lost his protector. Now it was open season on Jerome; and a rumor surfaced, as well, about his having an improper relationship with Paula.

It was time to leave Rome. Jerome traveled to Antioch, where others of the Roman group of friends, including Paula, joined him. They all went on to Egypt and Palestine and eventually settled in Bethlehem.

Always the Scholar

Jerome remained principally a thinker and writer, keeping to his books, continuing the Latin translations and writing essays. He got into a scholarly argument with St. Augustine, who questioned Jerome's critical interpretation of the second chapter of St. Paul's epistle to the Romans.

Jerome is best known for a singularly long legacy. His translation of the Old Testament from Hebrew and his revision of the Latin version of the New Testament are still considered works unequaled in the church. His version, which is called the Vulgate, was declared the official Latin text of the Bible for Catholics by the Council of Trent in the sixteenth century, and from it almost all English Catholic translations were made until the last part of the twentieth century. Pope John Paul II replaced it with the New Vulgate in 1979.

What was the Council of Trent?
The **Council of Trent** (1545–1563) was a Roman Catholic attempt to reform the church. It became known as the **Counter-Reformation,** because the council issued decrees in opposition to what had become Protestantism.

Jerome's prolific writings included over 100 letters, which are still read and interpreted by hagiographers. He was not martyred, but died in

Bethlehem on September 30, which is also his feast day. He is a Doctor of the Church and is the patron saint of librarians and students.

E-FACTS

Sometimes a holy man and woman join together in God's work. These symbiotic relationships usually followed gender-specific roles for that time: the woman would found or run (or both) a convent, or would do charity work—or both—while the man founded a religious order for men, and possibly did good works and wrote as well. Together, the two were able to achieve more than each would have done individually, and perhaps more successfully, too. Examples of saints who worked together are St. Francis of Assisi and St. Clare; St. Teresa of Ávila and St. John of the Cross; St. Vincent de Paul and St. Louise Marillac; St. Francis de Sales and St. Jeanne de Chantal; and St. Jerome and St. Paula.

St. Simeon Stylites (ca. 390–459)

Simeon was born on the Syrian border of Cillicia. As a 13-year-old herding sheep, he had a vision that he took to mean his later life would be spent on pillars. Yes, pillars (*stylites* comes from the Greek *stylos,* "pillar"). In any event, Simon entered a monastery, but he was asked to leave because he tended to overdo mortification, which can include lengthy periods of fasting and self-flagellation.

Simeon became a hermit near Antioch; then he moved to the top of a mountain when his piety began attracting crowds. Going even farther to get away from them, he built a 10-foot-high pillar and lived on top of it. For the rest of his life he lived on successively higher pillars. The last was about 60 feet high and was his home for 20 years. None of the pillars measured more than six feet in diameter at the top.

Clad in animal skins and host to quite a number of vermin, he preached from those positions, made converts, and was considered a respected and holy man. Even emperors consulted him. Women, however, were not allowed near the pillar sitter's enclosure.

As if sitting on a post were not enough, Simeon Stylites practiced other great austerities. He ate and slept very little. He was too tall to stretch out on the platform atop the pillar, but he would not accept any kind of seat. Once in a while he would stoop for rest; other times he would just let his body go slack.

He died this way, falling forward from a praying position. The date of his death has been passed on as either July 24 or September 2, and he was the first of what would become known as the "pillar ascetics." His feast day is January 5.

St. Gregory I (the Great) (540–604)

St. Gregory

Gordianus, as he was called, was born in Rome of wealthy parents. Well educated and well connected, he became what today we call a civil servant. When his father died, he turned toward religion and transformed the family home into a monastery. He became a **monk** and went on to establish six other monasteries. But then, when he was 39, he was called on to serve as papal ambassador to the imperial court in Constantinople.

When Pope Pelagius II died unexpectedly, Gregory, to his dismay, was unanimously elected his successor. As the Roman Empire fell into ruin, Gregory took the helm and wisely steered both the region and the church through famine, plague, and war.

As pope, he promoted plainsong choral music—named Gregorian chant, after him—and was responsible for the successful mission to convert England. That particular group of 40 missionaries was led by St. Augustine of Canterbury.

Gregory's greatest legacy was seeing the church through such difficult times. He was a holy man who successfully, steadily guided the souls in his care.

His feast day is September 3. He is the patron saint of England, musicians, and teachers.

The person who acquires any virtues without humility is like someone carrying powdered spices in the open air.

—ST. GREGORY THE GREAT

St. Hildegard of Bingen (1098–1179)

We would call Hildegard a Renaissance woman—except that she lived before there was a **Renaissance**.

She was born of noble German parents in the province of Rheinhessen. A sickly child, at the age of five she was given to Bl. Jutta (an abbess, who is on the road to sainthood) to live with her in her cottage next to a Benedictine monastery. Jutta raised Hildegard, and when the girl reached 18, she became a Benedictine nun. By this time Jutta had attracted a like-minded group of women around her. When Jutta died, Hildegard, at the age of 38, became prioress of that community.

Around 1147 she and a dozen or so nuns moved their community to Rupertsberg, near Bingen, and founded a convent. She went on to found another convent some time later.

> Glance at the sun, see the moon and stars. Gaze at the beauty of earth's greenings. Now, think.
>
> —HILDEGARD OF BINGEN

Hildegard was extraordinary in many ways. For one, she had had visions since she was a child, finally telling her confessor about them when she was in her early forties. It was then that she began to accept her gifts and the fact that God was speaking to her. The visions were approved by her superiors, one of them an ambassador from the Vatican, as having come from God.

Approval meant publicity for the nun, who now had people coming to see her and consult with her.

More Talents

Hildegard was also a musician. Moreover, she possessed enormous medical knowledge, offering hundreds of cures or remedies and describing illnesses, such as heart disease, that still affect us today.

It took her 10 years, but between 1141 and 1151 she wrote her masterwork, *Scivias (Know the Way)*, in which the mystical nun presented a look at human beings and the cosmos as radiating from God's love, which she said were "rays of his splendor, just as the rays of the sun proceed from the sun itself." In the 1999 flurry by the media to come up with a "Person of the Millennium," the Pulitzer Prize–winning columnist Ellen Goodman, in noting how no women were considered for that award, suggested that Hildegard of Bingen could have been a strong contender.

Her feast day is September 17.

St. Thomas à Becket (1118–1170)

St. Thomas
à Becket

The martyr Thomas à Becket turned out to be the most popular saint in medieval England.

He was born in London, the son of the sheriff of that city, and educated locally, continuing his studies at the University of Paris. (You may recall that Ignatius of Loyola and his small band of Jesuits attended that institution as well, some 400 years later).

When Thomas returned to England, he was appointed clerk to the archbishop of Canterbury, in the Kent countryside of southeastern England. At 37 Thomas became King Henry II's chancellor, and then was asked to step up to the position of archbishop of Canterbury. Thomas was not enthusiastic about taking on that title, but to please his king he accepted. He was ordained and then consecrated to the post of primate, or religious leader, of all England.

E-FACTS

Geoffrey Chaucer's popular fifteenth-century work, *The Canterbury Tales*, follows pilgrims en route to the Canterbury cathedral, which is today a tourist, if not a pilgrimage, destination.

Thomas had some sort of religious conversion at this time, or at least a deepening of faith. He resigned his post as chancellor (he held both that and the archbishop title concurrently) to opt for an austere life.

However, soon he was in conflict with the king over government versus religious authority and, charged with treason, left England for France.

Henry eventually had his son crowned king by the archbishop of York. Over time the dispute between the king and Thomas seemed to be easing, and six years after he left, Thomas returned to Canterbury. But he refused to lift the excommunication he had imposed on supporters of the king during their dispute. Four of Henry's knights, believing they were doing their king's will (the king had said aloud at one point: "What a set of idle cowards I keep in my kingdom who allow me to be mocked so shamefully by a low-born clerk!"), killed Thomas at Canterbury Cathedral on December 29, 1170.

Thomas's problems with the king are reminiscent of Thomas More's with King Henry VIII. In both there was a struggle to define the jurisdiction of the crown and that of the church.

St. Thomas à Becket's feast day is the day of his death, December 29.

E-PROFILE

St. Augustine of Canterbury (d. ca. 605)

Pope Gregory the Great asked Augustine (sometimes known as Austin) to re-establish Christianity in the southern part of England after it had been overrun by the pagan Anglo-Saxons of Denmark and Germany.

He and 40 of his monks were received by King Ethelbert and Queen Bertha of Kent. Augustine built a church and Benedictine monastery at Canterbury, on land given to him by the king, but ran into opposition trying to get people in Britain to switch to Christianity. He did make converts, though, who were spurred on by their king becoming a Christian. He was the first archbishop of Canterbury, and the church he built was the first cathedral in England.

Canterbury remains the religious capital of England. None of today's cathedral is from Augustine's time, however. The last of several Saxon buildings on the site was destroyed by fire in 1067. Most of the current structure was then designed and completely finished in 1498.

St. Augustine of Canterbury's feast day is May 27.

I have committed my cause to the great judge of all mankind, so I am not moved by threats, nor are your swords more ready to strike than is my soul for martyrdom.

—St. Thomas à Becket

St. Elizabeth of Hungary (1207–1231)

St. Elizabeth of Hungary

There are many stories of grief and loss, among both martyrs and just plain saints, and this is a particularly sad one.

She was Queen Elizabeth, happily married to King Ludwig IV of Thuringia, in southern Germany. It was a match made in their childhood, with Elizabeth moving into the castle of her future husband when he was just nine and she even younger.

Older, married Elizabeth was a pious woman who worked hard to relieve poverty among her subjects, establishing hospitals and nursing the sick—even lepers—with her own hands. She brought bread to the hungry, too. Her husband supported her in all her good works, and the couple had two children.

Unfortunately, Elizabeth put herself in the hands of one Conrad of Marburg as her spiritual adviser. This priest had been an Inquisitor of heretics and he took the same harsh tone with Elizabeth, at times beating her with a stick for minor infractions of his rules. She bore the hurt stoically, continuing to work with the sick and the poor, while the people's affection grew for her.

Sadly, Ludwig died while in command of a force of Crusaders headed for the Holy Land. Elizabeth's scheming mother-in-law and brother-in-law saw this as the perfect opportunity to toss out the young queen, who was pregnant again. They claimed she was stealing from royal coffers to provide for the poor. More likely the reason was that she was a little too pious for them. In truth, she was perhaps guilty of both charges.

Elizabeth was beside herself with grief at the loss of Ludwig. "I have lost everything," she cried. "O my beloved brother, O friend of my heart, O my good and devout husband, you are dead, and have left me in misery! How shall I live without you? Ah, poor lonely widow and miserable woman that I am, may he who does not forsake widows and orphans console me. O my God, console me! O my Jesus, strengthen me in my weakness!"

Cast Off

Elizabeth left the castle penniless and lived in extreme poverty until her relatives, embarrassed at her situation, gave her a simple house in Marburg. She was a beautiful woman, and Emperor Frederick II, whose wife had recently died, elected to overlook the scandal surrounding the young widow and made inquiries through the aristocratic grapevine as to whether she would be interested in marriage. Elizabeth sent back a word of thanks, but informed him she would remain a widow and devote her life to good works.

Because she was quite taken with the story of St. Francis of Assisi and St. Clare, she became a Franciscan tertiary. Eventually Elizabeth was allowed to return to the castle, and her son was accorded the right of succession due him.

You might think this turbulent life encompassed many years, with Elizabeth dying at a good age. But Elizabeth of Hungary lived just 24 years.

Her feast day is November 17. She is the patron saint of bakers and is invoked against plague.

E-FACTS

Elizabeth of Hungary was buried in the church in Marburg, where pilgrims attended in great numbers. During the Protestant **Reformation**, her body was removed to an unknown location.

St. Francis de Sales (1567–1622)

Born in Thorens, France, he was educated at the Jesuit College of Clermont in Paris, later earning a law degree in Padua. Yet he felt his true calling lay in the priesthood, which caused family dissension (as it did for several other saints whose lives you have read about in these pages). Still, like the determined souls who preceded him, Francis pursued his choice and was ordained at the age of 26.

St. Francis de Sales

Into Calvinist Country

During the years of Francis's life, the Protestant **Reformation** was sweeping the region. One of Francis's first assignments as a priest was to move into an area around Lake Geneva that had become strongly Calvinist: Catholic churches had been burned and the priests exiled.

There was never an angry man who thought his anger unjust.
—St. Francis de Sales

However, in 1594 the Catholic duke of Savoy reconquered the area and asked the bishop to allow priests to return. Francis volunteered for that mission.

It was a particularly difficult assignment. Francis was alone during hard winters, trekking on foot from one end of the region to the other, often barely escaping being killed, since resentment against Catholics was high. Yet, with his positive and loving message of the gospel, he was able to bring a sizable number of people back to their original faith. More than 2,300 families were reported to have returned to Catholicism.

Fittingly, he was named bishop of Geneva in 1602. He was not allowed to live in Geneva, however, because the city remained a Calvinist stronghold and this was hardly an ecumenical period in history. Francis was based in Annecy, France, about 50 miles south of Geneva, and conducted the work of his diocese from there.

What is Calvinism?
Calvinism is a religious orientation within Protestantism that began with the French-born Swiss reformer and theologian John Calvin in the sixteenth century and flourished in parts of western Europe. Among other principles, Calvinists believed in predestination, which means God has predestined some souls to heaven and others to hell.

During this time he met a wealthy young widow, St. Jeanne de Chantal. After her husband's death left her with four children, Jeanne felt she had a vocation. Francis asked for her help in forming a new religious congregation. The women would work among the poor rather than being enclosed, much like the Daughters of Charity founded by St. Vincent de Paul with St. Louise de Marillac.

In 1610 Francis and Jeanne founded the Order of the Visitation. Jeanne was its first superior.

We do not receive a good graciously when it is presented to us by an enemy's hand. On the contrary, a present is always acceptable when a friend makes it. The sweetest commandments become bitter if a cruel, tyrannical heart imposes them, and they become most pleasing when ordained by love.

—ST. FRANCIS DE SALES

Legacy

Francis is especially remembered as a writer, notably for his *Introduction to the Devout Life*. What made this book different is that it was addressed to the average layperson, whereas other manuals of that type were for the religious.

Francis spoke of moderation and the importance of charity. His wisdom and direction were simple. He said, for example, "A single 'Our Father,' said with feeling, has greater value than many said quickly and hurriedly." He offered an especially kind admonition to sinners, asking them to say, "Alas, my poor heart, here we are, fallen into the pit we were so firmly resolved to avoid! Well, we must get up again and leave it forever."

St. Francis de Sales's feast day is January 24, and he is the patron saint of writers and journalists and the deaf.

St. Isaac Jogues (1607–1646)

St. Isaac Jogues

Born in Orleans, France, of well-to-do parents, Jogues became a Jesuit missionary and arrived in New France (Canada) in 1636, working among the Huron Indians along Lake Superior.

It was, to put it mildly, difficult being a missionary in an area in constant conflict. The various tribes were continuously at war with each other. The missionaries had the nearly superhuman task of staying neutral and removed from the battles while going about their preaching.

You may recall that when St. Francis Xavier preached in Japan, he was impressed by the people and their culture (see Chapter 8). He decided that in future missionary endeavors, he would take into consideration the country's traditions and culture rather than imposing his own background on the people. Isaac Jogues and his Jesuit missionaries adopted a similar stance. They found the spirituality of the Native Americans impressive and sought to weave the customs of that life into the Christianity they were preaching.

A Close Call

Nonetheless, Jogues found it hard to understand the brutality in the villages and the constant battles. In 1642, rather than escape the attacking Mohawks, he and his lay associate, René Goupil, a surgeon, chose to become captives with their Huron companions. Goupil was killed, and Jogues was tortured, having one of his thumbs and several fingers severed. (Many a parochial school graduate can remember listening to the story of that particular torture, digit by digit.)

Eventually, instead of being slain, Jogues was taken in as a slave by a Mohawk woman. Finally able to escape to New Amsterdam (New York) with the aid of the Dutch at Albany, he sailed back to France. But in 1646 he volunteered to return. French forces were trying to negotiate a truce among the tribes at war there and, with his knowledge of the Mohawks, Jogues agreed to return as a French ambassador. The Jesuits even secured a papal dispensation for him to celebrate mass in spite of his mutilated fingers. (A priest must be able to lift the host in consecration during mass.)

What I suffered is known only to One for whose love and in whose cause it is pleasing and glorious to suffer.

—St. Isaac Jogues

Soon after his arrival in Ossernenon, a village near present-day Auriesville, New York, Jogues was taken in by an Iroquois warrior who believed Jogues was a sorcerer making the Indians' corn crops fail. Isaac Jogues was tomahawked and beheaded. It is said he offered up his death for the salvation of his assailants. His lay assistant, Jean de la Lande, was martyred the next day. The legend is that after Jogues's martyrdom, the Iroquois brave who killed him came to the Jesuits seeking refuge from Christian Hurons. He remembered Jogues's teachings, and asked to be baptized. He took Isaac Jogues as his Christian name.

Isaac Jogues and his companions share an October 19 feast day and all are patron saints of North America.

E-FACTS

Six Jesuit missionaries and two lay assistants were killed by the Iroquois between 1642 and 1649. They were the first martyrs in the New World.

Those who died in Auriesville, New York, were St. René Goupil, a surgeon; Isaac Jogues, priest; and John de la Lande, lay assistant. In Midland, Ontario, Canada, death came to the Jesuit priests Anthony Daniel, John de Brébeuf, Gabriel Lalemant, Charles Garnier, and Noël Chabanel.

Shrines have been built to the martyrs in Auriesville and in Midland.

St. Alphonsus Liguori (1696–1787)

A saint noted for his scholarly mind, Alphonsus was born into a wealthy family near Naples. He practiced law for nearly a decade until a fixed court case turned him against that career. He left law to become a priest and was ordained at the age of 30. He did missionary work for a while and also taught for a bit.

While working with the poor around Naples, Alphonsus recognized the need for their religious education. He founded the Redemptorist order to minister to the poor. A devoted priest, he demanded of his preachers that they remain simple—in their teaching and in their lives.

Alphonsus reluctantly accepted the office of bishop of a diocese outside of Naples, where he concentrated on educating the residents and reforming the **seminary**. He was a generous man—during the famine of the winter of 1763, he opened the bishop's residence to anyone who came and gave them whatever he had.

Picking Up a Pen

What Alphonsus is most remembered for, aside from founding the Redemptorists, are his great scholarly works. He authored devotional manuals, instructions for priests, and essays replying to enemies of the church. In *Theologia Moralis* (1753), he took on the **Jansenists**, who believed God was a severe taskmaster and claimed believers were unworthy of frequently receiving the sacraments. They had a generally dark outlook on life and were pessimistic about salvation. He revised and reprinted that work nine times during his lifetime.

Alphonsus's compassionate nature was not challenged by the rigor of the Jansenists, but neither was he so lax as to allow extreme permissiveness, either in church rulings or with church members. He took the middle ground, which the church considered sound.

His writings became the basis of Catholic theology for the next 200 years.

If you embrace all things in life as coming from the hands of God, and even embrace death to fulfill his holy will, assuredly you will die a saint.

—St. Alphonsus Liguori

Tumult

Toward the end of his life, things became more difficult for this holy man. He still needed approval for his order from the Vatican and from the ruling monarch of Naples, which was now under Spanish control.

Matters worsened further. Unthinkable though it seems, Alphonsus was expelled from his own order when it was found he had failed to read an important paper before signing it. His poor health and near blindness apparently was not an acceptable excuse.

Besides physical illness, Alphonsus also suffered at times from deep spiritual depressions. When things looked bright, however, he experienced ecstasies, made predictions that came true, and performed several miracles.

Before he died problems within his community healed, the Redemptorists were recognized by the Vatican, and their numbers grew as they expanded to many parts of the world. He died quietly at the age of 90.

His feast day is August 1. Noting his contribution to the moral instruction of his parishioners and others, Pope Pius IX made him a Doctor of the Church in 1871. He is the patron saint of vocations.

Suggested Additional Reading:

Francis de Sales and Jeanne de Chantal: Letters of Spiritual Direction, edited by Wendy M. Wright and Joseph F. Power, O.S.F.S. (Paulist Press, 1988). This book is a look at these "working partners" through their letters.

Hildegard of Bingen: Scivas, translated by Mother Columba Hart and Jane Bishop (Paulist Press, 1990). Part of the Classics of Western Spirituality Series, this exhaustive (nearly 500-page) collection of Hildegard's major religious writing consists of 26 visions, which she explains fully. Introduction and translators' notes acquaint the reader with this saint's life and work.

Hildegard of Bingen's Medicine by Wighard Strehlow and Gottfried Hertzka, M.D. (Bear & Co., 1988). Feeling poorly? Maybe Hildegard can help. Here are her treatments for colds, the flu, nerves, rheumatism, and more. For example, wash your mouth out in the morning with clear, cold water. Hold the water in your mouth until the film on your teeth dissolves. The authors stress Hildegard's use of cold water: using warm water softens teeth.

Hildegard: Prophet of the Cosmic Christ by Renate Craine (Crossroad Publishing, 1997). This selection from the Crossroad Spiritual Legacy Series introduces this mystic and her words in an approachable, readable text.

Indian and Jesuit: A Seventeenth-Century Encounter by James T. Moore (Loyola University Press, 1982). This book is no longer in print, but you might be able to obtain a copy at a used-book store or your public library.

CHAPTER 38
Shrines and Other Saintly Stops

Shrines, Cathedrals, and Basilicas

Which is which?

A **shrine** is a building or complex that is a pilgrimage destination; the main focus is a cult figure, such as a saint. An example is Lourdes, with its dedication to the Virgin Mary. A shrine can also be located in a church, marked by a special artifact or statue that the faithful visit for purposes of veneration.

A **cathedral** is a church where a bishop, archbishop, or cardinal presides and is the seat of that particular diocese or **archdiocese**. It is usually, but not always, the most prominent religious edifice of that faith in a particular geographic area. Cathedrals are usually centrally located; you are not likely to find one in the countryside.

A **basilica** is a church with historical significance and one that continues to play a role in the religious life of a region. Basilicas are, one could say, more serious than churches. They celebrate more historical feast days and generally with more solemnity. They are expected to be models of liturgical celebration and are also places of **pilgrimage**.

"Major" basilicas are principal papal churches found only in Rome. They are of special historic note and are also pilgrimage destinations. Among them are St. Peter's, St. Mary Major, St. John Lateran, and St. Paul's Outside the Walls.

"Minor" basilicas carry that special recognition from the Holy See. In this country they include the Sacred Heart Basilica on the campus of the University of Notre Dame in Indiana, the Cathedral of St. Augustine in St. Augustine, Florida, and the Mission Dolores in San Francisco (one of the chain of missions originally established by Bl. Junipero Serra). Confusing though it may seem, a church does not have to have basilica in its name to be considered a minor basilica.

You don't have to actually visit the shrines cited here to enjoy knowing about them and to understand how they fit into what you have been reading about individual saints.

There are more shrines around the world than you can shake a censer (incense holder) at, and here are some of the most popular. Admission is usually free, although a donation is always appreciated.

Shrines in the United States
Washington, D.C.

National Shrine of the Immaculate Conception

The patron saint of America is Mary, under the title of the Immaculate Conception. The National Shrine of the Immaculate Conception in Washington is a fascinating complex. The basilica, the largest Roman Catholic church in the Western Hemisphere, is Romanesque and Byzantine in style and is highlighted by a blue-domed roof.

The bell tower is somewhat reminiscent of St. Mark's in Venice, and holds a 50-bell carillon. Regularly scheduled carillon concerts increase in number during the summer tourism months.

The shrine also houses the largest collection of contemporary Christian art in the United States, most of which honors Mary. Some 50-plus chapels are part of the complex, each of them also featuring an aspect of Mary or her life. Guided tours are available, and the shrine also has a gift shop and cafeteria.

For more information: The shrine is at ✉4th Street and Michigan Avenue in the northeast section of the city: ✆(202) 526-8300. The Web address is ✍*www.nationalshrine.com/NAT_SHRINE/index2.shtml.*

E-FACTS

Another shrine to the Blessed Mother is the National Shrine of Our Lady of the Snows, in Belleville, Illinois. This is a sizable outdoor complex with nine devotional areas, restaurant, gift shop, and even a motel. The shrine claims one million visitors each year. It's at ✉422 South DeMazenod Drive; ✆(618) 397-6700; ✍*www.snows.org.*

Baltimore, Maryland

A well worn path leads to this St. Jude Shrine, which honors the patron saint of lost causes and desperate situations. In the heart of Baltimore, the shrine has been welcoming visitors since 1917. Besides areas for prayer, especially prayers of thanks, it features a Millennium Room in the visitors' center that offers a unique mix of history of the shrine and futuristic interactivity, including a virtual Wall of Honor, which memorializes friends and family, and celebrates birthdays, anniversaries, and other milestones. There is also a gift shop.

The shrine is run by the Pallottine priests and brothers.

For more information: The St. Jude Shrine is at ✉ 512 W. Saratoga St., Baltimore, 21201; ✆toll-free (877)-2ST-JUDE; ✍*www.stjudeshrine.org.*

Emmitsburg, Maryland

In the northwestern part of this state, just below the Pennsylvania border, is the National Shrine of St. Elizabeth Ann Seton. It was built in 1965, a full decade before Mother Seton's canonization in anticipation of that event.

A rotunda-topped basilica greets visitors, where Mother Seton's remains have been reinterred. On the grounds are the Stone House where the saint lived with her companions in 1809 and the White House where they resided after 1810. It was here that she founded the first parochial school in the country.

You'll find a museum, too, dedicated to her life and work, and an information center. The nearby cemetery marks the place where Mother Seton was originally buried after her death in 1821.

A handful of miles from the Seton shrine is the Grotto of Lourdes, at the foot of the Catoctin Mountains. It is a shrine to Mary, a simple mountain sanctuary that was a favorite spot of Mother Seton's, a refuge she called "wild and picturesque." It offers a perfect opportunity for meditation on this woman's exceptional life. Stone and bronze Stations of the Cross lead the way along original pathways to the Grotto and the Corpus Christi Chapel.

For more information: National Shrine of St. Elizabeth Ann Seton, ✉333 S. Seton Avenue, Emmitsburg, 21727; ✆(301) 447-6606; ✎*www.setonshrine.org.*

Grotto of Lourdes

St. Augustine, Florida

When you're next in the Sunshine State, you might want to stop in this town of 20,000 along Florida's northeast coast, just off Interstate 95. It is the oldest permanent European settlement in the United States, dating from 1565. St. Augustine is commonly called America's oldest city.

In town, the waterfront Mission of Nombre de Dios is reputedly the site of the first Catholic mass in this country, celebrated in 1565. You can see its huge cross, rising 200 feet, from several miles around. As for the saint in this complex, there is a shrine to Our Lady of la Leche, dating from 1615. There is also a charming, very small ivy-shrouded chapel, built in 1918, and a gift shop.

For more information: Mission of Nombre de Diós, ✉30 Ocean Ave., St. Augustine, 32804; ✆(904) 824-3045.

Churches are best for prayer
that have least light:
To see God only, I go out of sight.

—JOHN DONNE (1573–1631)

Darien, Illinois

The National Shrine of St. Thérèse is situated in this town west of Chicago. Contemporary in design, it features a chapel and museum dedicated to the "Little Flower," as well as special programs honoring Thérèse of Lisieux.

For more information: National Shrine of St. Thérèse, ✉ 8501 Bailey Rd., Darien, 60561; ✆ (630) 969-3311; ✍ *www.saint-therese.org.*

Lake Zurich, Illinois

Prefer the good old days when the mass was said in Latin? You can attend the Latin Tridentine mass celebrated regularly at St. Pius V Traditional Roman Catholic Shrine. To really bring back memories, there is a Latin mass held on First Fridays as well, along with a regular schedule of masses and special devotions throughout the week.

The shrine, located in Chicago's northwest suburbs, is named after a sixteenth-century pope who enforced the decrees of the Council of Trent; strengthened the Index of Forbidden Books, as well as the Roman Inquisition; and published a catechism, breviary, and missal. His feast day is April 30.

For more information: St. Pius V Traditional Roman Catholic Shrine, ✉ 30 Miller Rd., Lake Zurich, 60047; ✆ (847) 438-4909.

Libertyville, Illinois

The St. Maximilian Kolbe Shrine is situated in the community of Marytown, home of the Conventual Franciscan Friars of St. Bonaventure Province. The shrine honors the Polish saint who died in a Nazi prison camp in World War II.

Marytown is also the center of the Militia of the Immaculata Marian consecration movement, which was founded by that saint in 1917.

For more information: Marytown/St. Maximilian Kolbe Shrine, ✉ 1600 West Park Ave., Libertyville, 60048; ✆ (847) 367-7800; ✍ *www.marytown.com.*

St. Maximilian Kolbe (1894–1941)

He was born in Zdunska Wola, Poland, and, although a sickly youth suffering from tuberculosis, entered the Franciscan order at 16.

After his ordination he instituted a movement called the Knights of Mary Immaculate, a Marian devotion, and launched a series of journals. Maximilian Kolbe also organized a community called City of the Immaculate, which grew to be the largest religious community of men in the world.

When the Nazis invaded Poland, Kolbe was arrested and in 1941 was sent to Auschwitz, the notorious Nazi prison camp. A few months after he arrived, a prisoner escaped. The commandant selected 10 men for punishment. One man, Francis Gajowniczek, wept aloud that he would never see his wife and children again.

At that point Maximillian Kolbe offered to take the man's place. The nightmare began. Through it all, Kolbe counseled his fellow inmates, kept them from despair, and prepared them to die. Kolbe and three other prisoners were eventually killed by injections of carbolic acid.

In 1982, when Pope John Paul II canonized Maximilian Kolbe, he stated the words from the Gospel of St. John: "Greater love hath no man than this: that he lay down his life for his friends." The man whose life Kolbe had saved was at the ceremony.

St. Maximilian Kolbe's feast day is August 14.

Golden, Colorado

Sacred Heart

The Mother Cabrini Shrine can be found just beyond the foothills of Golden, a western suburb of Denver. It was founded by St. Frances Xavier Cabrini as a sort of summer camp for orphan children.

Mother Cabrini arranged large white stones in the shape of a heart, surrounded by a smaller stone cross and a crown of thorns. Nearly 800 steps lead to a 22-foot-high statue of the Sacred Heart. The steps are adorned by the stations of the cross, the mysteries of the rosary, and the Ten Commandments. Mother Cabrini found a spring of water on a barren hilltop at the site, and the water still flows.

The shrine is administered by the Missionary Sisters of the Sacred Heart of Jesus, founded by Mother Cabrini, the first naturalized American citizen to be canonized.

For more information: Mother Cabrini Shrine, ✉ 20189 Cabrini Blvd., Golden, 80401; ✆ (303) 526-0758; ✑ *www.den-cabrini-shrine.org*.

A prayer in its simplest definition is merely a wish turned Godward.
—PHILLIPS BROOKS (1835–1893), EPISCOPAL BISHOP OF MASSACHUSETTS WHO WROTE "O LITTLE TOWN OF BETHLEHEM"

Shrines in Canada
Montreal, Quebec

St. Joseph's Oratory is a magnificent basilica and shrine dedicated to the patron saint of Canada. It is situated on the north slope of Mount Royal and, at 860 feet above sea level, is the highest point in Montreal. It is said to have the second-largest dome in the world, after St. Peter's Basilica in Rome.

Founded as a tiny chapel in 1904 by Brother André, a member of the Holy Cross Order of Roman Catholic brothers (see sidebar), by 1922 it had grown into a 5,000-seat basilica. Its carillon of bells was designed for Paris's Eiffel Tower but was found unsuitable for that landmark. The carillon came to the oratory on loan in 1955 and is now a permanent fixture. Carillon concerts are held during the week and on weekends. There is a museum as well.

For more information: St. Joseph's Oratory, ✉ 3800 Queen Mary Rd., Montreal (Quebec) H3V 1H6; ✆ (514) 733-8211; ✑ *www.saint-joseph.org*.

Bl. Brother André (1845–1937)

Born southeast of Montreal, Alfred Bessette's father died when he was nine. His mother died three years later. Forced to leave school at age 12, Alfred found work as a baker, a tinsmith, and eventually in the textile mills in New England. At 22 he returned to Canada and joined the Congregation of the Holy Cross, where he took the name Brother André.

André had always been in poor health, so he was assigned the position of porter at Notre Dame College. Devoted to St. Joseph, Brother André began to welcome the sick and the disheartened, and invited them to pray to that saint with him. He also visited homes and hospitals. A number of cures were attributed to him, but he always said St. Joseph was responsible.

His fame spread. In 1904 André and his friends built a chapel across from the college. Visitors grew in number, and by the 1930s the chapel had become a basilica. When he died more than one million people filed past his coffin. He is buried in the basilica.

In 1982 Brother André was beatified by Pope John Paul II. His feast day is January 6, the day on which he died.

Quebec City

Basilica of St. Anne de Beaupré

The famed Basilica of St. Anne de Beaupré is in the village of Beaupré, about 25 miles northeast of Quebec City, although it is usually included in "What to See in Quebec City" listings. Now quite large, the shrine began as a small monument of thanksgiving. In the 1650s, shipwrecked sailors rescued from the waters of the Gulf of St. Lawrence showed their gratitude to St. Anne, mother of the Virgin Mary, by founding a chapel in her name. It attracted the faithful in such large numbers that within a few years the little wooden structure was replaced by a fieldstone church. By 1876 the shrine had become the size of a basilica. Destroyed by fire in 1922, it was rebuilt the next year in a neo-Roman style.

Today the basilica can accommodate more than 3,000 and has over a million visitors a year. Some leave behind crutches, canes, and folding wheelchairs as a testament to their faith and the intercession of St. Anne. The fountain in front of the basilica is believed to have healing powers.

There are an information bureau, tour guides, and a gift shop. The shrine is particularly crowded the week before St. Anne's feast day (July 26), as pilgrims make a nine-day novena ending in a candlelight procession on the eve of the feast.

For more information: Basilique Ste-Anne-de-Beaupré, ✉ 10018 Av. Royale, Ste-Anne-de-Beaupre, Quebec G0A3C0; ✆ (418) 827-3781).

E-FACTS

While you are in the Montreal area you might want to visit the Kateri Tekakwitha shrines. Yes, that's plural—there are three of them: in Auriesville, New York, where the Indian girl was born; nearby Fonda, a few miles up the Mohawk River where she was baptized; and her tomb at Kahnawake, the Mohawk reservation in Canada. Her remains are enshrined at the St. Francis Xavier Mission, on the banks of the St. Lawrence River. Kahnawake is just a handful of miles from Montreal; the others are farther away.

Shrines in Mexico
Guadalupe

Our Lady of Guadalupe

Our Lady of Guadalupe is one of the major shrines in the world and is an important attraction in Mexico City. This is where the Blessed Mother appeared to Juan Diego, a young Indian boy, in December 1531 and requested that a shrine be built on that spot in her honor.

It was 10 years after the Spanish devastated the Aztecs, and the lady's message was one of compassion. The people took her appearance to signal the beginning of a new time and new church that would merge, peacefully, the culture of the Spaniards and the indigenous Mexicans.

Do not be afraid, you have nothing to fear. Am I not here, your compassionate Mother?

—Virgin Mary to Juan Diego

Juan Diego told his bishop about the apparition, but the older man was skeptical. A few days later, the youth returned to the site of the apparition and the lady once again appeared. He relayed the bishop's request for proof of her visitation, whereupon Mary instructed Juan to gather roses from the frozen, stony ground and take them to him. To his surprise Juan saw a great many roses strewn about and gathered them up in his sackcloth. When he stood in front of the bishop and opened his cloak, the roses tumbled out. But that was not all that surprised his excellency. Imprinted on the sackcloth was an image of the Virgin. The same image hangs above the main altar of the shrine today.

Juan Diego is buried at the site. The shrine, in the north of Mexico City, is always crowded, but particularly so on December 12, the feast of Our Lady of Guadalupe.

Shrines in Europe
Knock, Ireland

Our Lady of Knock has become a major shrine in the west of Ireland, near Connemara, in County Mayo. In 1859, in the small village of Knock, the Blessed Virgin appeared to 15 villagers near the local parish church. It was a "silent" apparition: Mary did not speak. The spot has since become a major point of Irish Catholicism, and in fact Knock now has an airport to welcome visitors.

While in Ireland you might want to slip on your walking shoes—sturdy ones—and visit another monument to a saint, this one not manmade. Croagh Patrick is a mountain 2,500 feet high a few miles inland from Clew Bay on the west coast in County Mayo. The statue of St. Patrick guards the ascent to the mountain, the most sacred in Ireland.

It has been a pilgrimage site since the fifth century, when Patrick spent the 40 days of Lent on its peak, praying and fasting. Today, every year on the last Sunday in July, as many as 60,000 people climb the mountain, some in bare feet, many ailing.

The first part of the climb is not that difficult, but the second can be tiring, as movement slows and becomes labored. Be prepared: It takes five hours to climb Croagh Patrick, going up and then back down. At the summit, however, is a magnificent view of the west and a small chapel, which, besides offering an opportunity for prayer, is a welcome refuge on a drizzly or chilly day.

Lourdes, France

This town of 18,000 in southwestern France on the fringe of the Pyrenees is the site of the most famous shrine in Christendom. Between February and July 1858, the Virgin Mary appeared 18 times to a young shepherdess, Bernadette Soubirous, who at the time of the first apparition was collecting firewood along the river Gave. One month after that vision, some 20,000 people were there with Bernadette, but she was the only one who could see Mary.

In one of the early apparitions, Bernadette was instructed to drink and bathe from a spring that wasn't there. It started flowing the next day. This spring evolved into the miracle baths at Lourdes. Reportedly, there have been 5,000 cures from the waters at the grotto at Lourdes, but the church officially recognizes only 66 of them.

In March, just a month after the apparitions began, Bernadette was asked to have a chapel built to honor the Virgin Mary, who also told the girl, "I am the Immaculate Conception."

Today the complex at Lourdes attracts several million pilgrims and tourists annually.

E-PROFILE

St. Bernadette of Lourdes (1844–1879)

Born Bernadette Soubirous, she was one of six children, living in a town so remote it was 80 miles from the nearest railroad. Her chronic asthma was not helped by the family's cold, damp home.

On the day of the first apparition, Bernadette said she saw bushes shaking around the grotto, and "a girl in white, no taller than I, who greeted me with a slight bow of the head." Bernadette began to pray.

Initially, people didn't believe her. But her life changed drastically. Hundreds of the faithful and the press wanted to meet her, even after the apparitions stopped. Bernadette was polite to everyone and spoke to as many visitors as she could. She refused to take any money.

She likened herself to a broom, saying, "Our Lady used me. They have put me back in my corner. I am happy there, and stop there." She did long to see Lourdes, but she knew she could not with the dreaded publicity that would accompany her appearance.

Bernadette died at the age of 35. She was canonized as recently as 1933 and her feast day is April 16. She is the patron saint of shepherds.

Fatima, Portugal

Located in a small town about 100 miles north of Lisbon, this is probably the second most popular shrine in Europe after Lourdes. Fatima is the site where the Virgin appeared on May 13, 1917, to three shepherd children: Lucia dos Santos and her two cousins, Francesco and Jacinta Marto. The three claimed to have seen a woman standing on a cloud in an evergreen tree. Her message directed the faithful to pray for peace (at that time the Great War was being waged in Europe). She asked the children to return on the thirteenth of each month until October.

As you can imagine, word of the vision spread. And on October 13 there were an estimated 70,000 people in the field awaiting the apparition. Mary was visible only to the children, but many claimed to have seen the "miracle of the sun," where that golden ball of light twirled in the heavens and then, alarmingly, plunged, stopping very close to earth before rising back to the sky. Since the sight was seen by persons miles away who had nothing to do with the apparition, it cannot easily be termed mass hysteria.

An intriguing part of the Fatima apparition has been the "three secrets" Our Lady passed on to Jacinta. The first was revealed to be a terrifying vision of hell and a prediction that while the Great War would end, a worse one would follow. That was interpreted to be World War II. The second secret was a call for piety and the consecration of Russia.

The third secret was supposed to be revealed in 1960, but when Pope John XXIII opened the message, he read it and quickly resealed it. Every pope since then has read the message, but none revealed its contents. This has led the faithful to believe the message foretells an apocalyptic event and, especially at the turn of the millennium, many called for the disclosure of the secret. That finally took place in Fatima in May 2000 when Pope John Paul II presided at the beatification ceremony of Francesco and Jacinta Marto. The third secret, he revealed, predicted the shooting of a bishop dressed in white, which the pope took to be the assassination attempt on his life in 1981 in Rome (the pope is the bishop of Rome).

Like Lourdes, Fatima is viewed as an "official" miracle by the church, but the faithful do not have to believe in the apparitions or the healings associated with the site.

Of the three children Lucia is the only one still alive. Now in her nineties, she is a nun living in a Carmelite convent near Fatima.

E-FACTS

Both Jacinta and Francesco Marto died just a few years after the apparitions.

Rome, Italy

St. Peter's Basilica

With all the magnificent churches dedicated to saints, it's hard to know where to look first. As the papal seat, St. Peter's Basilica naturally leads the list. Originally constructed as a church to house the tomb of St. Peter, the first pope, it was built by Emperor Constantine in the fourth century. The original building was repeatedly damaged by fire and then rebuilt. Then in the sixteenth century Pope Julius II asked the noted architect Bramante to draw up plans for a new basilica.

The structure is, of course, breathtaking. The dome was designed by Michelangelo, who also painted the ceiling. The magnificent canopy over the altar is from the later architect and master, Gian Lorenzo Bernini who, in the seventeenth century, also designed the ellipse outside that is St. Peter's Square. The basilica contains the tombs of many popes besides Peter. All of the buildings in the religious complex are part of Vatican City, an independent state within the city of Rome.

Outside the Vatican there are other "must-see" churches in Rome: the basilicas of St. Mary Major and St. John Lateran, and St. Paul's Outside the Walls, where St. Paul of Tarsus is buried. All are major basilicas, and if it has been awhile since you've been to Rome, you are likely to be pleasantly surprised. They were all spruced up in anticipation of the jubilee year 2000.

Czestochowa, Poland

The shrine is called Our Lady of Czestochowa (pronounced chesh-ta-HO-va), or the Jasna Gora shrine, named for the abbey of the Pauline Brothers where it is situated. It is also known as the Shrine of the Black Madonna. The "Black Madonna" is not, as some think, of African origin. The icon, probably brought from Byzantium, has never been cleaned or polished.

Czestochowa is an industrial city of about 250,000 in south-central Poland. The Madonna's role in nearby Jasna Gora (Hill of Light), came about in the fourteenth century when Prince Ladislaus Opolszyk was transporting the icon, which historians say is a ninth-century Greek or Greek-Italian work, from the Ukraine to Opala. At Czestochowa he stayed overnight at the Jasna Gora abbey, storing the portrait. In the morning the wagon holding it would not move. Ladislaus took that as a sign it was meant to stay in Czestochowa, and he built a chapel there to display it and a monastery for Pauline monks to look after it.

There are three cuts on the cheek of the image of Mary that have resisted attempts at restoration. One legend says the cuts were made by fifteenth-century Hussite bandits.

After Swedes unsuccessfully attacked the abbey in 1655—another legend says one of their swords caused the damage to the Virgin's face— Our Lady of Czestochowa was declared the Queen of Poland in 1656. It is the nation's principal shrine.

Its fame continues to grow. On major Catholic feast days as many as 500,000 people make the pilgrimage to Jasna Gora.

E-FACTS

Pennsylvania also has a shrine to Our Lady of Czestochowa. It is near the center of Doylestown, in Bucks County, and is under the auspices of the Pauline Brothers. The shrine in Poland is also situated at the abbey for the Pauline Brothers.

Medjugorje, Herzegovina

Yes, there is a shrine in this war-ravaged country. On June 24, 1981, in the Croatian mountain village of Medjugorje (med-JOO-gaw-ree), the Blessed Mother appeared to six children—and continues to do so.

The apparitions are either at the original site or in the village church, St. James. Identifying herself as the Blessed Virgin Mary, Queen of Peace, her message has been to ask for peace with God and man. And, she adds, "I have come to tell the world that God exists."

Since that time lives of many pilgrims to the shrine have been changed. Ever cautious, the church has no formal position on these apparitions, although Pope John Paul II has visited the site, and some bishops have spoken favorably about it.

The children, known in the world of apparitions as "seers" or "visionaries," are grown now, but they still reside in the area.

Medjugorje has become so popular it is now competing with Lourdes and Fatima as a tourism/pilgrimage destination.

E-FACTS

Several large travel agencies in this country conduct pilgrimages to particular shrines, such as Medjugorje, sometimes to several in one country, such as Italy or France. Other tours cover a few countries in one trip. Check your local travel agent. Here are two leads: All Star Travel Pilgrimages at *www.allstartours.com* and Unitours at *www.unitours.com*.

Suggested Additional Reading:

The Final Harvest: Medjugorje at the Turn of the Century by Wayne Weible (Paraclete, 1999). The journalist author of this book converted to Christianity after covering the story in Medjugorje for several years, so he is a believer in the apparitions there. He has also written several other books about Medjugorje.

Lourdes: Body and Spirit in the Secular Age by Ruth Harris (Viking, 1999). An Oxford historian who considers herself a secular Jew takes a different approach to writing about Lourdes. She accompanied a blind, paralyzed man whose mother brought him to Lourdes hoping for a cure. The experience affected her deeply, and the result is an interesting, moving book for believers and skeptics. Illustrated.

Magnificent Corpses: Searching through Europe for St. Peter's Head, St. Chiara's Heart, St. Stephen's Hand, and Other Saintly Relics by Anneli Rufus (Marlowe & Co., 1999). An intriguing look at the remains of saints throughout Europe. While certainly offbeat travel, the concept fits in nicely for those interested in further exploration of the saints.

Shrines of Our Lady: A Guide to 50 of the World's Most Famous Marian Shrines by Peter Mullin (St. Martin's Press, 1998). This guide covers the most popular to the least known shrines and is richly illustrated.

Here are two books for budget travelers as they visit saintly spots.

Bed and Blessings, Italy by Anne and June Walsh (Paulist Press, 1999). Lists more than 130 convents and monasteries in Rome that take overnight guests for around $30, and even cheaper, similar accommodations in the rest of Italy. The mother and daughter authors caution this is adventurous travel: English is not always spoken, some houses impose a curfew, and, worst of all, some places do not take credit cards!

A Guide to Monastic Guest Houses by Robert J. Regalbuto (Morehouse Publishing, 1999). Lists 120 lodgings in the United States and Canada as you make your way from shrine to shrine (with a bit of other sightseeing tossed in). Rates can be as low as $35 per night for two.

Vision Video offers these videocassettes on the shrines mentioned in this chapter:

- *Apparitions at Fatima.* 90 minutes, $19.99.
- *Medjugorje: The Miracles and the Message.* 60 minutes, $29.99.
- *The Miracle of Our Lady of Fatima* (a Warner Brothers movie of the 1950s). 102 minutes, $19.99.
- *Miracles . . . of Lourdes, Fatima, Guadalupe, and Knock.* 60 minutes, $19.99.
- *Our Lady of Guadalupe.* 70 minutes, $19.99.

For more information, including current prices, contact Vision Video at (800) 523-0226 or *www.catholicvideo.com.*

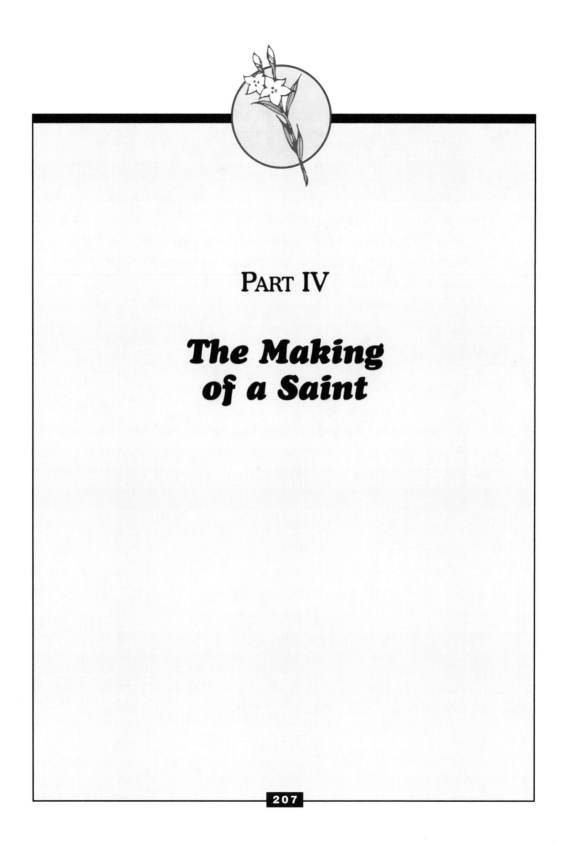

Part IV

The Making of a Saint

CHAPTER 39

How the Canonization Process Works

These pages have told of the qualities that belong to every saint: a determined faith in God and His plan for them, and charity toward others. But how is an individual officially named a saint? Why is this person tapped and not that one? How does the system work?

Formalization

By the fourth century the veneration of saints was widespread. Holy men and women were declared saints by acclamation until the thirteenth century, when the saint-naming process was formalized, and Pope Gregory IX decreed that papal canonization would be the only legitimate process. A few centuries later, in 1588, Pope Sixtus V charged the Sacred Congregation of Rites with the duty of processing candidates for canonization.

Fast-forward to 1983, when Pope John Paul II simplified many procedures called for in the canonization process, now handled by the Congregation for the Causes of Saints. The congregation is composed of a group of some 25 cardinals and bishops.

A Global Process

You have read about Americans who have been canonized. But it's a big world, and there are candidates all over the globe whom we in the United States hear nothing about as they inch toward sainthood.

Mary MacKillop

Pope John Paul II has canonized over 300 men and women since he took office in 1978. The present pope's record total is more than half of the 592 added to the church's roster of saints in the last 500 years.

John Paul is responsible for giving Nigeria and Papua New Guinea their first saints. One of those he beatified in 1995 was Mary MacKillop (1842–1909), cofounder of the Sisters of St. Joseph of the Sacred Heart. When she is canonized, she will become Australia's first saint. Mary MacKillop dedicated her order to providing free education to all those who needed it, particularly in rural areas of that country. The order spread to include New Zealand. John Paul is especially interested in conferring sainthood on men and women outside Europe, which has provided such fertile ground for canonization since the early days of Christianity.

E-QUESTIONS?

What does venerate mean?
Venerate is the word for how the faithful are to pay homage to the saints. *Worship* and *adore* are reserved for God.

Advancing the Cause

It usually takes years—generations—for a canonization to take place after initial interest is shown in a particular holy man or woman. The first requirement, which may seem obvious, is that the person to be considered must be dead. Living saints just have to wait.

Also, the path to sainthood cannot start until five years after an individual's death. That allows time for the possible flood of initial enthusiasm to die down and to see if serious interest is maintained in the cause. It also allows for those pushing a particular canonization at the local level to plan the path of their cause.

E-FACTS

In 1999 Pope John Paul II announced the five-year waiting period would be waived for Mother Teresa of Calcutta. Now her cause for canonization is under way. This is a sign of the pope's interest in providing saintly role models who are universally popular, and also of his interest in naming saints in countries that do not have many, or any.

The process might be compared to a court trial, in which the candidate either wins canonization or is denied it.

On the Local Level

The canonization process begins in the individual's diocese where he or she lived or worked. A "petitioner" approaches the local bishop to seek permission from Rome just to begin the canonization process. The petitioner can be anyone. Perhaps the candidate saint was a member of a religious order. The superior of that order locally or at a higher level, regionally, might start the ball rolling.

When permission is received, a "postulator of the faith" in that diocese is named. Similar to a defense attorney, he or she can be a member of the clergy or a layperson but must be familiar with the workings of the Congregation for the Causes of Saints. The postulator brings the case to a panel of judges appointed by the local bishop. A "promoter of the faith," similar to a prosecuting attorney, stands up for the church's position and can challenge all evidence with objections. The promoter of the faith replaces what used to be called "the devil's advocate."

The investigative process covers an extensive biography of the person in question, depositions from those who knew him or her, if witnesses are still alive. All kinds of paperwork are required to look into every facet of the individual's life. This is to make doubly, even triply, certain that canonization is warranted. It is also important to avoid any embarrassment cropping up in the future about the individual once he or she is named a saint. Alleged miracles are noted but must be proven in another step in the canonization process, which takes place in Rome. All of the documents, now known as "the Acts of the Cause," are sent to Rome.

In Rome

As a man or woman's case is accepted in Rome by the Congregation for the Causes of Saints, he or she is given the title "Venerable." Now, all of the evidence of that person's life is vetted even more stringently. If there is a reason to, the evidence is challenged by the promoter of the faith.

The Slightly Faster Track

Some potential saints are helped along in their cause by active boosters at the local level or in Rome.

E-FACTS

A few groups in America are pushing their candidates for sainthood. Most of those about-to-be saints were members of religious orders and are being promoted by their congregations. Two, however, are laypeople.

- Kateri Tekakwitha, a young Indian girl from the New York State-Canadian border (see Chapter 33) is now at the "Blessed" stage. There are some 4,000 members nationwide of the Blessed Kateri Tekakwitha League encouraging her canonization. They publish a quarterly periodical called *Lily of the Mohawks,* which features news of miracles claimed through her intercession. Selling products is often needed if the backers of a candidate are unable to afford heavy promotion.
- Pierre Toussaint, a layperson (featured in this chapter) has been named "Venerable." Many are rooting for his cause through the Pierre Toussaint Guild. It operates out of the chancery headquarters of the Archdiocese of New York, his adopted city.

For example, some saintly candidates move extremely slowly through the various layers of canonization or may be, in fact, stalled in the process. Their cause languishes in musty files in Rome because there is no group pushing for their canonization.

Money can also help a would-be saint's cause. No, not in the way you might be thinking. No one who is worthy will be sidelined because of a lack of funds to advance the cause. But backers have much to spend their dollars on: fundraisers to bring in more money for their cause; high-quality—and fast—research on their candidate's life; the ability to fly witnesses and supporters to Rome when needed for testimony; publicity, perhaps with a regularly published newsletter that can also bring in word of miracles to be studied; and in general, public relations, never letting the candidate's name drop from sight for too long. If all else is equal, these folks can often steer their saintly candidates to canonization more quickly than those with no public relations effort behind them.

The Miracle Requirement

Evidence of miracles received after having prayed to the saint in waiting is an important step in making saints. This part is extremely demanding. Potential saints must have at least two posthumous miracles attributed to them.

E-QUESTIONS?

What is a miracle?
A **miracle** is an extraordinary happening showing divine intervention in human affairs.

The miracles must be instantaneous cures; there must be no medical explanation, or medical interference, and they must be complete. No partial cures are considered, even if, say, 90 percent of a claimant's health is restored. No remission is accepted, either, so in some instances it can take as long as 10 years to be certain that a sufferer claiming a miracle is indeed permanently cured. Medical specialists are consulted for their testimony. However, no evidence of miracles is needed if the one considered for canonization is a martyr.

When a Cause Holds Up

When it seems—finally—that everything checks out for the holy person being considered for canonization, and one miracle has been confirmed, the pope publicly beatifies that individual, with veneration permitted in a particular religious community or geographic area. The candidate is given the title "Blessed."

After the second miracle has been documented, which could be many years after the acceptance of the first one, the pope issues a bull of canonization, declaring the person in question to be a saint and recommended for universal veneration.

E-QUESTIONS?

What is a papal bull?
A **papal bull** is a document of importance from the pope stamped with a lead seal. The seal is embossed with the facial imprints of Sts. Peter and Paul on one side and the signature of the pope opposite. It is all held together with cords of silk, and looks and is quite official.

This is followed by an elaborate, solemn liturgy in Rome, attended by the newly canonized's family and friends and, if he or she was a religious, members of that community and others. It is a day of great joy and celebration, the culmination of many years of study by Rome and by the local diocese—and years of waiting for the cause of the honored holy person to move on to the next level.

Wanted: People Like Us

Besides issuing more canonizations from new parts of the world, the pope has expressed interest in seeing more laypeople become saints. As you may have noticed reading these pages, most of the saintly were members of religious orders, perhaps even the founders of their order.

So the call is out not for those who have lived in religious communities but for holy people who, when living, went by Mr. or Ms. and who, as saints, can set an example that many will relate to more easily.

Look for more of these "just folks" (though with a little extra) to appear in future beatification announcements.

E-PROFILE

The Venerable Pierre Toussaint (1766–1853)

Pierre Toussaint was born a slave in Haiti, a French colony at the time, and was brought to New York City by his owner, John Berard du Pithon. Du Pithon apprenticed the black man to a hairdresser to earn a living. Pierre became quite popular and the story is he even styled Martha Washington's hair.

The young stylist, still not a free man, did well financially. He used his money to buy Haitians out of slavery, to feed and clothe the poor, and to support orphans. He risked his life nursing those afflicted with yellow fever and other contagious diseases.

Du Pithon eventually returned to Haiti and died of pleurisy. Still a slave, Pierre Toussaint took over the support of du Pithon's widow for 20 years. On her deathbed, his mistress gave him his freedom, and Pierre later married. He and his wife, Juliette, were known in New York for their good works.

At his death Toussaint was interred at old St. Patrick's Cathedral on the Lower East Side, where he had lived. In 1990 Cardinal John O'Connor, ordered him reburied at the uptown St. Patrick's Cathedral. He is the only layperson, and the only black, to be buried— along with bishops, archbishops, and cardinals —under the main altar of the cathedral.

Do you think this man was a saint? The pope does. Pierre Toussaint is no longer "Mister." He has been elevated to "Venerable," on the path to canonization.

Pierre Toussaint

Suggested Additional Reading:

Making Saints: How the Catholic Church Determines Who Becomes a Saint, Who Doesn't, and Why by Kenneth L. Woodward (Simon & Schuster, 1996). Written by *Newsweek* magazine's religion editor, this book is a classic on this subject—a fascinating look at just what goes on behind closed doors in the saint-making process.

CHAPTER 40

Waiting to Be Tapped for Sainthood

Around the world there are numerous men and women at some stage of the canonization process, even if it is only talk at the local level. Here are saintly souls who are either prominent or of special interest to us in this country. They range from the beatified to those about whom we wonder, "Do you think it might be possible . . . ?"

Bl. Padre Pio (1887–1968)

Bl. Padre Pio

He was a remarkable man who lived at a time many of us can remember. Padre Pio da Pietrelcina was a Capuchin friar who for some 50 years bore the stigmata of Jesus. For that reason he became quite famous, tracked down by the curious and the devoted, and forced to bear up under the burden of being called "a living saint."

A humble priest, Padre Pio served most of his life in a monastery in southern Italy. He was almost constantly in physical pain from his wounds, yet perhaps most hurtful was having to withstand the skepticism of his own church. Some in the Vatican were quite embarrassed by the stigmata, saying it was caused perhaps by concentrating too hard on the passion of Christ. The priest's reply: "Go out into the fields and look very closely at a bull. Concentrate on him with all your might. Do this and see if horns grow on your head!"

The power of prayer is indeed wonderful. It is like a queen, who having free access always to the king, can obtain whatever she asks. To secure a hearing there is no need to recite set prayers composed for the occasion—were this the case, I should indeed deserve to be pitied!

—SAINT THÉRÈSE OF LISIEUX

Miracles too numerous to count have been attributed to this priest. In confession it has been said he was able to read a penitent's heart. He was a mystic and had frequent conversations with Jesus, Mary, and the saints. He could also tell the future: in 1947 he told a young Polish priest, Karol Wojtyla, that he would become pope.

In 1999 that priest, now Pope John Paul II, beatified Padre Pio at the Vatican in front of a crowd of 200,000 people, with another 100,000 watching on huge television screens in an open area across the city.

The pope looked very small atop the Vatican balcony, below which he hung a banner of Padre Pio's photograph that was at least a few stories high. He told those gathered: "By his life wholly given to prayer and to listening to his brothers and sisters, this humble Capuchin friar astonished the world."

One Shaken Churchgoer

Christopher Buckley, in an essay in *Once a Catholic: Prominent Catholics and Ex-Catholics Reveal the Influence of the Church on Their Lives and Work* (ed. Peter Occhiogrosso, Houghton Mifflin, 1987), relates a story told to him by a friend of the noted English novelist and Catholic convert Graham Greene:

Padre Pio had become almost an embarrassment to the Church. You know, the Church is very wary of miracles. . . . But here they have this guy with the stigmata, and the crowds were starting to come. His hands would bleed at the moment of the elevation of the host; otherwise, he wore gloves. So they sent him to a very remote parish in Italy that was hard to get to—precisely because they didn't want headlines saying, you know, "THE AMAZING BLEEDING PRIEST." Anyway, Graham Greene heard about Padre Pio and he went to visit. He located the village on a Sunday. Everyone was packed into Mass, and he got into the back of the church. At the moment of the elevation, sure enough, Padre Pio began bleeding. Greene was horrified by it and he fled, he had to get out of there. He went to the edge of town and had a drink. He was sitting there with a bottle, getting ready to leave when he saw a young priest running in the street. The priest ran right up to him and said, "I have a message from Padre Pio. The message is this: 'Be at peace. God does not ask anything from us that we cannot give Him.'" And he left.

That's a true story. I'm not sure if Greene has ever told it—he may possibly still be freaked out. But it was told me by someone very close to him, who is also a Catholic.

Padre Pio may be canonized soon. It had been thought earlier that the church would hold off for a while after his death to discourage a personality cult from forming, and to ensure that the faithful knew that it was holiness, not the stigmata and not a spate of miracles, that made a saint (although those miracles are needed as well).

Mother Teresa of Calcutta (1910–1997)

Mother Teresa

Many of us could supply a good deal of the biography that goes here, since Mother Teresa lived so recently and her good works have been so publicized. It's interesting to have someone rising to sainthood whose later years have flashed before us on television screens and have been covered so completely in the press.

She was not a native of India, but was born Agnes Gonxha Bojaxhiu in Skopje, Yugoslavia. At 17 she left for Ireland to become a nun and shortly after that, as Sister Agnes, began teaching in India. When she was in her thirties she received "a call within a call," as she later explained it. God, she felt, was asking her to be not just a nun but a nun with a special mission. "He wanted me to be poor with the poor," she said, "and to love him in the distressing disguise of the poorest of the poor."

Kind words can be short and easy to speak, but their echoes are truly endless.

—MOTHER TERESA

With permission, Sister Agnes left her convent, went to Calcutta and, with others willing to work with her, formed the religious order, the Missionaries of Charity. She became Mother Teresa; the nuns' habit was a white sari with blue trim.

Mother Teresa toiled for years with the homeless and the desperately sick, but she seemed to have a particular affinity for working with the poor who were dying. She wanted those who had lived such hard lives, to "die like angels."

Remember that all of this took place a few decades before the media discovered the diminutive (she was an inch shy of five feet tall) religious. Once the press did find her, coverage of her and her work became extensive. In 1979 Mother Teresa won the Nobel Peace Prize and, like Padre Pio, became regarded as "a living saint."

> Don't search for God in far lands—he is not there. He is close to you, he is with you. Just keep the lamp burning and you will always see him. Watch and pray. Keep kindling the lamp and you will see his love and you will see how sweet is the Lord you love.
> —MOTHER TERESA, TO VOLUNTEERS FROM OTHER COUNTRIES
> WANTING TO WORK WITH HER AND HER SISTERS

She had a few critics, although they would emphasize that she was engaged in wonderful work that certainly no one else was lining up to do. Some claimed she did not take full advantage of modern medical equipment that could have been hers for the asking from donations. Others felt she did not "campaign" enough to change existing social structures, to which she replied, "We are not social workers."

Mother Teresa did not care for the administrative end of her job and in fact disliked, and sometimes refused, checks from donors, since it involved more paper pushing. It kept her from the ones who needed her, she explained.

The Missionaries of Charity spread eventually to 82 countries, doing, as their founder said, "small things with love," which was the philosophy of the already canonized St. Thérèse of Lisieux, who fostered the "little way."

Mother Teresa died peacefully in India on September 5, 1997. As you read in the preceding chapter, Pope John Paul II has waived the five-year wait to begin the canonization process on her behalf.

Pope John XXIII (1881–1963)

He was pope from 1958 to 1962, a warm, friendly man, in photographs almost always smiling and quite a change from his predecessor, the usually serious-looking Pius XII. Pope John XXIII has since been called the most beloved pope of modern times, maybe of all time.

Born Angelo Giuseppe Roncalli, he served as a papal diplomat for 25 years in Bulgaria, France, and Turkey, then spent several years as patriarch of Venice. As Cardinal Roncalli he was elected pope just before his seventy-seventh birthday. His was to be a transitional papacy, a few years sandwiched between the brilliant Pius XII and Giovanni Battista Montini, a younger cardinal who seemed to be the best bet for the pope who would follow John.

But Cardinal Roncalli surprised everyone. True, he had a brief papacy, but it certainly wasn't a quiet one. This pope was no mere caretaker for the next holder of that office.

We cannot know whether we love God, although there may be strong reasons for thinking so, but there can be no doubt about whether or not we love our neighbor.

—St. Thérèse of Lisieux

Changing Times

John XXIII's most important step as pontiff was, just six months into the office, to call Vatican Council II (the first council was held several centuries earlier). This was a meeting at St. Peter's Basilica of the world's cardinals and other high dignitaries. It opened in October 1962 and met in four separate sessions of a few months each, ending in December 1965.

The council did not convene to condemn errors or heresy. It was instead a positive meeting, concentrating on mercy, promotion of peace, and an ecumenical outreach. In a few words: Vatican II updated the church.

It was the first council that made full use of electronics. There was no World Wide Web in 1962, but cameras, lights, television, and print media were out in full force, every day bringing the council's work into millions of the faithfuls' homes.

Change was whipping around the world in the 1960s in every area of life, those winds blew through the Vatican too. The result was to make the church more open and accessible. A few conservatives at the council held out for the status quo, but their votes were swept away by the mandate of the majority for change. Revisions were implemented in doctrine, liturgy—the mass would now be said in the vernacular, or language of that country, instead of the centuries-old celebration in Latin—and a vision for the church in the world that looked forward to the new rather than nostalgically clinging to the old.

The Roman Catholic Church has never been the same—a pleasant surprise to most, though some say the council did not go far enough; a disaster to others who believe the church—and everything else for that matter—started a downhill slide from the last day of the council.

"This Big Ship"

John XXIII himself, before and during the council, was conciliatory to religion's and Catholicism's enemies, including Communist governments. He was quite disarming; everyone was eager to have an audience with him.

Unfortunately Pope John did not live to see the second year of the council or to conclude it. Diagnosed with stomach cancer, he died in June 1963. At that time he remarked to a friend: "At least I have launched this big ship—others will have to bring it into port." The second phase of the council opened in September 1963, headed by Cardinal Montini, who had become Pope Paul VI.

Status

In February 2000, the pope beatified John XXIII, who is now known as "Blessed." At least one miracle has been attributed to him. After verification of a second, he will be formally canonized.

This is interesting because his cause did not appear to have had front-burner attention. The ever-cautious Vatican seemed to have been waiting for the final verdict of whether the Vatican II was good or bad for the church and the faithful. After 35 years the jury still appears to be out on that, but apparently opinions one way or the other are not standing in the way of John XXIII's path toward sainthood.

E-FACTS

A priest in Great Britain has finished seven years' work transcribing diaries by George Spencer, the great-great uncle of the late Diana, Princess of Wales, in preparation for Spencer's possible canonization. They are apparently ready to be sent to the Vatican. Spencer was born in 1799 and raised at Althorp, the family seat in Northamptonshire. He was ordained an Anglican priest but converted to Catholicism in 1830. Ordained in Rome two years later, he went on to live and work in the Midlands, where he helped some of the poorest workers during the Industrial Revolution. He died in 1864.

Pope Pius XII (1876–1958)

Pius XII was the first pope to be heard widely on radio and seen on television. He was John XXIII's immediate predecessor. Talked about for canonization, his cause seems to hit snags every once in a while, and always for the same reason, his policy during World War II.

The Diplomat

Pius XII was born Eugenio Pacelli. Ordained in 1899, his was not to be the path of the typical Italian parish priest. Just two years after his ordination he entered the papal service, teaching international law to papal diplomats in Rome. He became nuncio to Bavaria in 1917, and then to the new German Republic in 1920 and finally, before his accession to the papacy, held the post of papal secretary of state.

Eugenio Pacelli enjoyed his time in Germany and admired the strength of German Catholicism. When he became pope on March 2, 1939, he chose Germans for his close advisers.

As Pope Pius XII, he promoted Marian devotion and declared a Marian year, and defined the church dogma known as the Assumption. The number of dioceses during his papacy grew from 1,696 to 2,048. Pius XII also appointed many native bishops in Asia and Africa and bestowed a cardinal's hat on some bishops from those two continents. He had to deal with the growing menace of Communism, which he strongly opposed, during those years as well. He served as pope until his death on October 9, 1958.

The status of his candidacy for sainthood is dicey. Although the Vatican seems eager to move things along, don't look for canonization soon. In recent years Pius XII has been accused by various groups of appeasing Germany during World War II. The Vatican defends the sounds of silence from the papacy at that time as discretion: the pope could accomplish more by not facing down the Nazis. He was, after all, a trained diplomat.

But his opponents say the pope could have done much more to save the Jews during the Holocaust—he could at least have spoken out against Hitler. On the other hand, some Jewish leaders support the pope, saying he did manage to save Jewish lives during the war and filter financial aid to those most in need.

Whether revisionist history will eventually pin down the truth, Pius XII's canonization is not likely to be soon. Every time there is a spate of newspaper or magazine articles or a book published about the pope and/or his role in the war, there are a flurry of defenses from the Vatican. We will probably never know what was in the mind and heart of Pius XII during those tumultuous war years. Did his affection for Germany keep him from recognizing evil in the rise of Hitler? Did it blind him from doing more? Or did he accomplish more than anyone has thought, but quietly? The issue is not likely to be resolved to the satisfaction of both sides in this continuing drama.

Dorothy Day (1897–1980)

Dorothy Day, one of the foremost American women of the twentieth century, has a story that will be told at some length here, for several reasons. First, it is rare that a layperson, and an American as well, is considered for sainthood. Her life was radically different from those who live in a religious community, as so many saints have, and for that matter, her life was different from the average layperson's.

She lived in our time, not a few centuries ago, and her experiences are instructive in that her directionless early years still led to a purposeful second half of life.

Finally, in March 2000, she was mentioned by the Vatican as being on a firm road to sainthood, which surprised quite a few people.

Dorothy Day

Nonreligious Beginnings

Born in Brooklyn and baptized an Episcopalian, her mother's religion (her father claimed to be an atheist), Dorothy Day had little to do with religion in her youth.

She attended college for two years, and then landed a job in Manhattan writing for a socialist daily newspaper. When that one folded, she worked for another one. The young journalist made many friends during this time in New York, folks who would sit around Greenwich Village coffeehouses and talk about politics, socialism, and the war that America had just entered.

During those days her rising awareness of inequality brought her to join a group going to Washington, D.C., to stage a protest for women's suffrage. Dorothy and the other women were arrested. While serving a 10-day prison sentence she asked a guard for a Bible. In writing about the incident later, she said she told herself she was not interested in religion, just in reading the Good Book as literature.

> Whatever I had read as a child about the saints had thrilled me. I could see the nobility of giving one's life for the sick, the maimed, the leper. . . . But there was another question in my mind: Why was so much done in remedying the evil instead of avoiding it in the first place . . . ? Where were the saints to try to change the social order, not just to minister to the slaves, but to do away with slavery?
>
> —DOROTHY DAY

Released from prison, Dorothy spend the next several years adrift. She wrote and even published a novel, *The Eleventh Virgin.* She enrolled in a nurses' training program. She had a lover, then a pregnancy that she aborted, a deed she said haunted her for the rest of her life. There was a short-lived marriage, too, followed by divorce. Through all of it was a growing interest in Catholicism, although she had no one to talk with about religion: most of her friends were atheists who had not given much thought to any religion.

When a new love affair came along, a deepening of religious faith came along with it. When she was 29, Dorothy gave birth to a baby girl she named Tamar.

The years of her growing acceptance of Catholicism brought her to have her child baptized. She broke off with Tamar's father, who was not interested in Catholicism, and then she herself became Catholic.

By 1932 the country was in the midst of the Depression. She and Tamar were living in an apartment in Manhattan she shared with her younger brother and his wife. Dorothy was 35 and still feeling there was no serious purpose to her life.

Then one day opportunity knocked, literally. She opened the apartment door to find 55-year-old Frenchman Peter Maurin on the other side. Maurin had taught in France, but left to try his luck in Canada. In 1911 he moved to the United States, drifting from job to job and reading constantly. He talked to Dorothy about spiritual values and the materialism of the world.

He told her he was convinced he should publish a newspaper, but he needed someone to work with him. Dorothy was trained as a journalist, so a lifelong partnership began.

Peter Maurin told Dorothy Day that St. Francis of Assisi was his ideal, for choosing voluntary poverty.

E-FACTS

The Newspaper

Together, Dorothy and Peter started *Catholic Worker*, a newspaper that sold for a penny a copy. It carried articles condemning racial inequality, the crime of child labor, the plight of West Virginia coal miners, the homeless, and just about any group of people that was suffering. The funding for the paper came from contributions.

With the help of these donations, Dorothy was able to move to a home in Greenwich Village that became a "hospitality house." Anyone who knocked on that door looking for food or shelter was welcome, no matter how bedraggled, disruptive—or even downright crazy—they seemed. "They are a member of the family in Christ," she would say.

Each day during the Depression hundreds of men came to the hospitality house, for coffee and bread. By 1941 there were some 30 hospitality houses in this country and one in England.

In 1949 Peter Maurin died quietly. Dorothy deeply believed he had been a saint.

She continued with speaking engagements, still devoted to her original belief in the dignity of every individual. Her last major trip was in August 1973 when she flew to California to join a demonstration led by Cesar Chavez, for his United Farm Workers Union. Photographs at the time show her seated on a folding chair, protected from the sun by a large straw hat, and flanked by police and farmworkers. She was arrested that day for violating an injunction limiting picketing. She was 76.

On November 29, 1980, Dorothy Day died, with Tamar at her side. She was 83 years old.

> It is not love in the abstract that counts. Men have loved brotherhood, the workers, the poor—but they have not loved "personally." It is the hardest thing in the world to love. . . . It is never the brothers next to us, but the brothers in the abstract that are easy to love.
>
> —DOROTHY DAY

After Dorothy

The movement continues. By the mid-1990s there were more than 100 *Catholic Worker* houses of hospitality and farms across the United States and around the world. Each operates independently, although all conform to the vision Dorothy Day expressed in her talks and books. There is still a *Catholic Worker* newspaper. Published in New York City, it has a circulation of 90,000 and the price of a copy is whatever the purchaser cares to donate.

Although her name has been mentioned for sainthood since her death, until recently it was felt she did not have much of a chance. It was not only her early days as a socialist, her lovers, and out-of-wedlock child (in the tradition of St. Augustine, it could be said) but her abortion, which would never be forgiven by the conservative Vatican. Also, there did not seem to be any serious supporters for Day's canonization among her *Catholic Worker* or biological family. They felt she would not have wanted to become "a stained-glass window." Dorothy herself asked friends not to "trivialize" [her] by trying to make [her] a saint.

Thus it was a surprise in March 2000 when the Vatican announced it had approved starting the canonization process on Dorothy Day's behalf. The request for it came from Cardinal John O'Connor of the New York archdiocese. Cardinal O'Connor died in May 2000.

Upon the news of her acceptance for study by Rome, Cardinal O'Connor wrote at the time that he considered her a model for everyone, "but especially for women who have had or are considering abortion." He added, "She regretted it *every day of her life.*"

Dorothy has a long way and many years to go before achieving certified sainthood, but she has achieved Vatican approval for considering her cause. She represents, throughout her later years, a life devoted to promoting the equality and worth of every man and woman.

Popularity Surge

Prior to the March 2000 announcement, Dorothy Day's name was included in a 1999 list that named the most prominent Catholic people and events of the century.

E-FACTS

Catholic Top 10

Raymond L. Flynn, former Boston mayor and U.S. ambassador to the Vatican, offered his list of the 50 leading Catholics and events of the twentieth century for *American Forum,* the talk show he hosts on the Catholic Family Radio network. His top 10 includes several who have been mentioned for sainthood:

1. Pope John Paul II
2. Mother Teresa of Calcutta
3. Second Vatican Council
4. Padre Pio
5. Archbishop Fulton J. Sheen
6. St. Frances Xavier Cabrini
7. The prominence of Catholic colleges and hospitals in the United States
8. The Miracle of Fatima
9. Dorothy Day
10. Pope John XXIII

Another end-of-the century poll asked nine church historians and theologians in this country to name the most outstanding lay Catholics in the world during the twentieth century. Eight of the nine placed Dorothy Day first. The "winner" was supposed to have made the church better during his or her life, or lived the faith in an exemplary way. The poll and responses were compiled by and published in *Evangelist,* the newspaper of the Albany, New York, diocese.

Archbishop Fulton J. Sheen (1895–1979)

Some of you who are old enough may remember television in the 1950s featuring a popular weekly half-hour program called *Life Is Worth Living*. In it, Archbishop Sheen (he was then a bishop in New York City) spoke to the viewing audience about various spiritual matters of interest to anyone of any faith or none at all. He used only a blackboard and chalk as props. This was not at all like a Sunday morning talking-heads show.

Life Is Worth Living ran in prime time on ABC from 1951 to 1957. But Archbishop Sheen isn't being considered for sainthood because he scored high in the ratings.

Multiple Talents

A native of El Paso, Illinois, his first venture into the media was the radio, where he preached over the airwaves in the 1930s. He was also head of a national Catholic project known as the Propagation of the Faith, and he led a successful convert ministry.

But he was most attracted to communications and the spoken and written word. Besides television, Archbishop Sheen wrote newspaper columns and was the author of many books, most of which are still in print (some are listed on pages 230 and 231) and consistently reissued.

Fulton Sheen died in New York City in 1979.

His Cause

In February 2000, New York City's Cardinal John O'Connor gave provisional approval to begin the archbishop's move toward sainthood. His cause has been taken up by the Archbishop Sheen Foundation in his hometown in Illinois. The foundation is looking for anyone who has letters, photos, film, or reports of physical or spiritual favors from the archbishop. The group and its board of directors, which includes Father Thomas J. McSweeney (president of the Christophers, an award-winning nondenominational group based in New York City that advances personal spirituality in the Judeo-Christian tradition through the media) and the former entertainer Lola Falana, have other ambitious plans. They hope to put together a traveling exhibit of the archbishop's memorabilia, to produce a book and provide scholarships in the archbishop's name for low-income students of theology, philosophy, or media arts.

If you have any material that could help the foundation realize its goals, they ask that you send it to the Archbishop Fulton Sheen Foundation Cause, c/o The Sheen Foundation, P.O. Box 313, El Paso, IL 61738.

Suggested Additional Reading:

Padre Pio's Words of Hope, edited by Eileen Dunn Bertanzetti (Our Sunday Visitor Books, 1999). The priest's words are arranged around points for meditation.

Padre Pio: The Priest Who Bore the Wounds of Christ is a 13-part series from the cable channel EWTN. Father Andrew Apostoli explores the life of the beatified priest in a program that also includes interviews with his fellow priests and contemporaries. Thirteen 30-minute programs cost $39.99, from Vision Video, P.O. Box 540, Worcester, PA 19490. For more information and shipping charges, call (800) 523-0226 or check *www.catholicvideo.com.* The company offers about a half-dozen other videos about Padre Pio.

At Prayer with Mother Teresa by Eileen Egan (Liguori Publications, 1999). A portrait of Mother Teresa and a collection of prayers that influenced, or were written by, that holy woman. The author, a writer and editor who has worked with Catholic Relief Services and the *Catholic Worker,* was a traveling companion of Mother Teresa's.

Mother Teresa: 1919–1997: Beyond the Image by Anne Sebba (Doubleday, 1997). A British journalist and biographer presents a balanced and very readable biography of this "living saint."

Dorothy Day by Robert Coles (Addison-Wesley, 1987). The Pulitzer Prize–winning author of *Children in Crisis* knew Dorothy Day as a medical student and worked at one of her hospitality houses. He remained a friend until her death. A *Washington Post* reviewer said of this book: "For those who are not familiar with Day, Coles is the best introducer around."

Dorothy Day: Selected Writings, edited by Robert Ellsberg (Orbis Books, 1998). Day's reflections on many areas of her life, especially her love for her *Catholic Worker* family.

On Pilgrimage by Dorothy Day, foreword by Michael O. Garvey, introduction by Mark and Louise Zwick. (Wm. B. Eerdmans, 1999). These diary entries written by Dorothy Day in 1948 will help the reader understand her personal life and the background of the *Catholic Worker* movement.

The Life and Times of Archbishop Fulton J. Sheen by Myles P. Murphy (Alba House, 2000). A detailed look at Fulton Sheen's life by an author who was inspired by him.

Lift Up Your Heart: A Guide to Spiritual Peace by Fulton J. Sheen (Triumph Classic, 1997). Archbishop Sheen shows how only God can provide the kind of peace and happiness all of us seek.

Vision Video offers videocassettes of Archbishop Sheen's *Life Is Worth Living* television series. Each volume contains two half-hour shows for $19.99.

Vision Video also offers the A&E *Biography* presentation "Mother Teresa: A Life of Devotion." The 50-minute film is $14.99.

CHAPTER 41

Disappearing Saints: Whatever Happened to . . . ?

They were saints for a while, often for centuries. Then we got word they had been, well, demoted. What happened here?

Saints who are considered obscure are sometimes dropped from the church's liturgical calendar. The deed is done to protect the saints with universal appeal, the saints about whom more is known than merely their names.

In many instances details of demoted saints' lives, beyond name and perhaps date and place of death, are legend rather than fact. They have not been declared fictional characters; it is still thought there is a kernel of truth to their existence. Nor is the church tossing them out, but just relegating them to what you might call another list—sort of a B-list. The church wants to be fair to the public in presenting saints who have a fairly well documented life.

The men and women who follow still show up on some calendars of saints' feast days (the difference between those calendars and a liturgical calendar is explained in Appendix C) and are patron saints of specific causes.

St. Barbara

Her birth and death dates are unknown, but it is said she lived in the Middle Ages. According to legend, Barbara was martyred by her pagan father because of her faith. Before her death she was held prisoner in a tower where, during one of her father's absences, she had three windows built to explain the Trinity. When her father returned, he took her before a judge, who had her tortured. Still not satisfied, her father took her to a mountaintop and killed her. He was destroyed by fire as he came down the mountain. Her feast day of December 4 is still listed in some reference works, and she is the patron saint of architects and builders. However, the church says her existence is doubtful.

St. Catherine of Alexandria

St. Catherine of Alexandria

Catherine was said to have lived in the early fourth century, the daughter of an aristocratic family in the Egyptian city of Alexandria. She studied philosophy, rather unusual for a young lady at the time, and became convinced of the truth of Christianity. At 18, determined to convert the emperor, she allowed him to have her tested by 50 of the top minds of his court. They could not dispute anything she argued, and so they converted. Then they were burned to death.

The emperor was so impressed with Catherine he asked her to be his consort. She declined and was imprisoned. While incarcerated, Catherine converted the emperor's wife. Then the torture began. The legend goes that everyone who came in contact with her—her jailer, the imperial guards—was killed.

Catherine was next. She was subjected to four wheels, each studded with sharp nails. Two wheels turned in one direction and two in the other, two of them coming down on her body from the top and the other two mauling her from below. She was to be mangled to death. To this day, a wheel with spikes projecting from the rim is known as a *Catherine wheel.*

It didn't work. An angel struck the contraption before it hurt Catherine. There is no happy ending here, however, unless you consider her moving on to glory: she was finally beheaded.

St. Catherine of Alexandria is the patron saint of librarians, lawyers, maidens/virgins, and craftsmen. Her feast day, November 29, was dropped from the liturgical calendar in 1969.

E-FACTS

Joan of Arc is said to have heard Catherine of Alexandria's voice among the voices that came to her.

St. Christopher

St. Christopher

The most famous disappearing saint is Christopher. In 1969, four years after the end of Vatican Council II, Christopher was demoted. What has been handed down of his life, the church says, appears to be primarily legend.

How many drivers in days of old (pre-1969) carried St. Christopher medals or statues of him on the dashboard of their car so that the patron saint of travelers would protect them? How many still do, despite his having been downgraded? These drivers must think, "Well, it can't hurt."

The patron saint of travelers has also appeared on medals in the wallets of tourists and business travelers, and small statues tucked in their luggage. A going-away gift to a relative or friend was often a St. Christopher medal. Here was a saint who sold a lot of product in religious stores.

The Bible on travel: Many shall run to and fro, and knowledge shall be increased.

—DANIEL 12:4

Legend dates Christopher back to the early third century. It is said he was a giant of a man, so large he was able to ferry people across a river in his arms or on his shoulder. On one trip, the legend goes, he nearly drowned carrying a child—who turned out to be Jesus. Christopher became a Christian and set out to convert others. Unfortunately for him, as you have read throughout this book, those early few centuries of Christianity were particularly difficult for the newly converted, and Christopher was martyred by the Roman emperor Decius. He was burned at a stake, but the flames did not touch him. Beheading accomplished the job.

St. Christopher no longer has a feast day, but the church still recognizes that people venerate him as the patron saint of travelers, bus drivers, and porters. He is also invoked against tempests and plague.

E-FACTS

In Brussels there is a small society, now at nine members, of Jesuit priests known as the Bollandists. Since the seventeenth century they have conducted exhaustive investigations of the 10,000-plus saints found most often in most texts. Some of those studies have led the group to conclude a saint probably did not exist (the church never comes down quite that hard when they demote a saint). For example, dropping St. Christopher from the liturgical calendar was the result of Bollandist research. The same with St. Catherine of Alexandria. The society has nixed some other saints, too, but they were so obscure the faithful are not likely to be appalled at their downgrading.

St. Julian the Innkeeper (or Hospitaler)

His is a darned good story, so good it probably is fiction.

Julian was a nobleman who lived in the Middle Ages (no dates for his life are known). One day while hunting he was told by a deer he was stalking that there would come a day when Julian would kill his mother and father. Impossible, thought Julian, but he moved to a faraway land to avoid any possibility of that happening.

He eventually married a wealthy widow and moved into her castle. One day while he was away his parents came to visit. His wife gave them her bed. When Julian returned later that night rather than in the morning when he was expected, he saw a man and woman in his bed and assumed it was his wife and a lover. He killed them both. Imagine his surprise when he saw his wife walk in from church and realized his mistake. Overcome by guilt, he left the castle to do penance, accompanied by his spouse, who had apparently forgiven his mistrust.

The two used their money to build an inn for travelers near a river and a hospital for the poor.

One day Julian found a dying man on the banks of the river and brought him home, putting him in his own bed. The man turned out to be an angel who assured Julian that God had forgiven him, adding that soon both Julian and his wife would be going to their reward. Both died within a few days.

It is thought that perhaps a clergyman made up this tale to show God's mercy and forgiveness no matter what the sin. But even that cannot be documented.

Julian of Norwich (1342–1423)

Female—and a real person—the English Julian (sometimes Juliana) was a serious mystic who lived a reclusive life as an anchoress, a religious woman whose days are filled with prayer and penance. Because an anchoress is not allowed out of the cell in which she resides, the room must be attached to a church, where she can take Communion through a window. An anchoress can talk through that window, do sewing for the poor, or, as Julian did, write.

Julian's cell was attached to the Church of St. Edmund and St. Julian. She experienced some 16 visions of Christ's passion and the Trinity. Over the next 20 years she put pen to paper and wrote *Revelations of Divine Love,* based on what she saw, touching on God's love, sin, penance, and divine consolation. The work made her an important English spiritual writer.

Julian's reputation for piety spread over Europe. Although she is called "Blessed," that title is an honorific. Julian of Norwich is not formally on the road to canonization. May 13 is her feast day.

St. Julian's feast day of February 12 remains on some listings but not on the liturgical calendar. He is the patron saint of innkeepers and hotel workers and boatmen.

Were the happiness of the next world as closely apprehended as the felicities of this, it were a martyrdom to live.

—Sir Thomas Browne (1605–1682)

St. Philomena

Philomena was a virgin and martyr in the early days of Christianity. A cult developed around her when bones of a young girl were found along with a small vial of what was thought to be blood. A tablet nearby carried an inscription that when translated read "Peace be with you, Philomena." All of this turned up in the St. Priscilla catacomb in Rome.

Early in the nineteenth century, miracles began to be reported at Philomena's tomb, which had been moved from the catacomb. Devotion to this saint grew to the point where Pope Gregory XVI legitimized her cult in 1837 and gave her the feast day of August 11. Philomena was a favorite saint of St. John-Baptiste Vianney, the Curé of Ars, known for his kindness as a confessor, who lived during her most popular years.

However, her name is no longer on the liturgical calendar. The church "suppressed" her feast day because there was so little known about her.

APPENDIX A
Saintly Lives in Historical Context

It is easy enough to recall major events that occurred in the world during Mother Teresa's lifetime, a holy woman who seems to be on the path to sainthood. But what was happening when Augustine of Hippo was writing his *Confessions?* When Ignatius of Loyola was founding the Jesuits?

Here is a chronology of historic events of varying importance that also shows the life span dates for notable people who affected those times. Interspersed with these listings are the birth and death dates of the saints who have figured most prominently in this book. This will help you put the saints' lives in the context of their times. The chronology only runs through the 1800s, since major events of the twentieth century are still within recent memory.

DATE	EVENT
A.D. 33	Jesus crucified
ca. 35	St. Stephen, a follower of Jesus, is stoned to death for his faith, becoming the first Christian martyr
ca. 60	The term *Christian* comes into common use
ca. 60–155	St. Polycarp
64	Emperor Nero blames Christians for the Great Fire of Rome; persecutions follow. Sts. Peter and Paul are martyred in that city at that time
1st cent.	Mary, Mother of Jesus
1st cent.	St. Andrew
1st cent.	St. Barnabas
1st cent.	St. Joseph
1st cent.	St. Joseph of Arimathea
1st cent.	St. John the Baptist
1st cent.	St. John the Evangelist
1st cent.	St. Jude
1st cent.	St. Luke

DATE	EVENT
1st cent.	St. Mark
1st cent.	St. Mary Magdalene
1st cent.	St. Matthew
1st cent.	St. Paul
1st cent.	St. Peter
ca. 177–312	Persecution of Christians continues in Rome under three emperors; growth of the cult of martyrs
ca. 200–258	St. Cyprian
ca. 203	Sts. Perpetua and Felicita
died ca. 269	St. Valentine
died ca. 288	St. Sebastian
died ca. 303	St. Dorothy
died ca. 304	St. Agnes
died ca. 304	St. Lucy
311	Emperor Constantine converts to Christianity and signs an edict of religious tolerance throughout the Roman Empire
324	Constantine moves to the city of Byzantium and renames it Constantinople, making it the seat of the New Roman Empire
328–387	St. Monica
331–420	St. Jerome
340–397	St. Ambrose
347–404	St. Paula
died ca. 350	St. Nicholas of Myra
354–430	St. Augustine of Hippo
381	Christianity becomes the legal and official religion of Rome when Emperor Theodosious I publishes a decree establishing the orthodoxy of Christian faith
389–461	St. Patrick
ca. 390–459	St. Simeon Stylites
395	The Roman Empire divides into Eastern and Western
400	Entire world population estimated at just over 250 million
450–525	St. Brigid
476	The last western Roman emperor falls; Eastern Roman Empire will survive until 1453; during the Middle Ages the rift between the Roman church, headed by the pope, and Eastern Christianity, based in Constantinople and headed by the patriarch of Constantinople, widens

DATE	EVENT
487–577	St. Brendan of Clonfert
540–604	St. Gregory I (the Great)
560–636	St. Isidore of Seville
died ca. 604	St. Augustine of Canterbury
ca. 610	Mohammed starts a new religion, Islam, in Arabia
ca. 618	St. Kevin of Glendalough
800	Charlemagne is crowned Holy Roman Emperor
1000–1001	Norse explorer Leif Ericson, sailing from Greenland, reaches North America
1054	After centuries of drifting apart, the Eastern Orthodox churches finally break from the Roman church over the issue of papal authority
1066	William of Norman defeats the Saxons and becomes king of England
1085	William the Conqueror orders a census in England that creates what has become known as the Domesday Book
1095	Papacy, under Urban II, launches the Crusades to reclaim holy sites from the Muslims
1098–1179	Hildegard of Bingen
1118–1170	St. Thomas à Becket
1150	University of Paris is founded
1167	Oxford University is founded
1181–1226	St. Francis of Assisi
ca. 1185	Kyoto, Japan, is the world's largest city, with a population of 500,000
1194–1253	St. Clare of Assisi
1195–1231	St. Anthony of Padua
1206	Beginning of Genghis Khan's largest land empire in history, reaching from Mongolia west to eastern Europe
ca. 1206–1280	St. Albert the Great (Albertus Magnus)
1207–1231	St. Elizabeth of Hungary
1209	Cambridge University is founded
1211	Construction of Rheims Cathedral, on the site of crowning of French kings, begins
1225–1274	St. Thomas Aquinas
1295	Marco Polo returns to Venice after 25 years in Asia and begins his memoirs
1309	Pope Clement V, a Frenchman, moves the papal seat from Rome to Avignon, France

DATE	EVENT
1334–1351	Black Death (bubonic) plague kills one-third to one-half of Europe's population
1337–1453	Hundred Years' War (actually a few more) between English and French kings for the control of France
1347–1380	St. Catherine of Siena
1377	Papacy returns to Rome
1387	Geoffrey Chaucer writes *The Canterbury Tales*
1412–1431	St. Joan of Arc
1414–1476	The Medicis of Florence are bankers to the popes
ca. 1438	The Incan Empire begins in Peru
ca. 1440	Disintegration of the Mayan Empire
1446–1450	Johann Gutenberg invents moveable type for printing (it had been in use in the Far East, but Europeans didn't know that)
1453	After Turks conquer Constantinople, Byzantine Empire crumbles; new center of the Eastern Orthodox Church is Moscow
1469–1535	St. John Fisher
1475–1564	Michelangelo, architect of St. Peter's Basilica
1478–1535	St. Thomas More
1483	Spain's Inquisition under Tomás de Torquemada sees 2,000 "heretics" executed
1491–1556	St. Ignatius of Loyola
1492	Columbus sails from Spain to the New World
1499	Trade in African slaves begins in Lisbon, as Portugal explores the west coast of Africa
1500	World population is now about 400 million
1504–1572	St. Pius V
1506–1552	St. Francis Xavier
1510–1572	St. Francis Borgia
1515–1582	St. Teresa of Ávila
1517	Martin Luther nails his 95 theses to a church door in Wittenberg, Germany, initiating the Protestant Reformation, which divides Western Christianity into the Roman Catholic Church and Protestantism
1519	Aztec Empire is at its height; the Spaniards arrive
1519–1522	Ferdinand Magellan circumnavigates the globe
1521–1597	St. Peter Canisius

Date	Event
1533–1554	King Henry VIII denies the pope's authority so he can marry Anne Boleyn; the next year he has Parliament declare him the head of the Church of England, marking the beginning of Anglican Church
1541	Spanish conquistador Hernando de Soto becomes the first European to see the Mississippi River
1542–1591	St. John of the Cross
1555	The French physician and astrologer Nostradamus begins his prophecies of what the future holds
1564–1616	William Shakespeare, English playwright
1567–1622	St. Francis de Sales
1580–1660	St. Vincent de Paul
1582	Pope Gregory XIII introduces the Gregorian calendar, which no longer considers April 1 as New Year's Day; those who do not note this are known as "April fools"
1591–1660	St. Louise de Marillac
1599–1658	Oliver Cromwell, English Revolutionary soldier
ca. 1600	Adherents to the philosophy of John Calvin, French-born Swiss Protestant thinker, break away from the English Puritans to form the Reformists
1605	Cervantes's *Don Quixote*, the first modern novel, is published
1607–1646	St. Isaac Jogues
1607	First permanent English colony on mainland America established at Jamestown, Virginia, by John Smith
1608	First permanent French colony in North America established in Quebec
1611	The King James version of the Bible is published in England
1613	Galileo Galilei says the earth revolves around the sun rather than being the fixed center of the universe; in 1633, the Inquisition finds Galileo, a Catholic, guilty of disobeying the Church by publishing his thesis and calls for him to publicly recant; he does not and is sentenced to life imprisonment
1620	Pilgrims land at Plymouth, Massachusetts, to pursue religion freely
1636	Harvard College is founded in Cambridge, Massachusetts
1644–1718	William Penn, English Quaker, founds Pennsylvania as a colony of religious freedom

DATE	EVENT
1682	Edmund Halley first notes the comet that will later bear his name, predicts its future appearances
1696–1787	St. Alphonsus Liguori
1700	Population of largest American city, Boston, is around 7,000; Native American population in all of what is now United States: 1 million
1723	First commercial valentines appear
1729	John Wesley, an English clergyman, begins a reform movement within the Church of England that leads to Methodism
1758–1843	Noah Webster, author of *An American Dictionary of the English Language*
1760	Industrial Revolution begins in England
1769–1852	St. Rose Philippine Duchesne
1770	James Cook claims Australia for Great Britain
1773	Boston Tea Party
1774–1821	St. Elizabeth Ann Seton
1775	Start of American Revolution
1776	Declaration of Independence is drafted
1781	Immanuel Kant writes *Critique of Pure Reason*, in which he establishes his theory of rational experience
1789	French Revolution begins
1801–1890	John Henry Newman
1804	Meriwether Lewis and William Clark set out to explore the new Louisiana Purchase and the land to the west, all the way to the Pacific
1811–1860	St. John Nepomucene Neumann
1815	Battle of Waterloo sees Napoleon defeated
1825	First regular train service begins in Great Britain
1837	Queen Victoria begins a lengthy reign in Great Britain that will last until 1901
1844–1879	St. Bernadette of Lourdes
1846	Famine hits Ireland as a result of potato crop failure and other factors; there are one million deaths
1848	Gold discovered in California; population of San Francisco soars from 1,000 to more than 25,000 in two years
1850–1917	St. Frances Xavier Cabrini
1858–1866	Laying of transatlantic cable

DATE	EVENT
1861	U.S. Civil War begins
1864–1869	Leo Tolstoy writes *War and Peace*
1865	President Abraham Lincoln is assassinated
1867	Japan ends 675-year-old Shogun rule
1869–1948	Mohandas "Mahatma" Gandhi
1873–1897	St. Thérèse of Lisieux
1876	Alexander Graham Bell patents the telephone
1879	Thomas Alva Edison invents the electric light
1890–1902	St. Maria Goretti
1893	New Zealand becomes the first country to give women the vote
1894–1941	St. Maximilian Kolbe
1896	First modern Olympic games are held in Athens, Greece
1899–1900	World population at around 1.5 billion
1999	World population hits 6 billion with great fanfare; 2 billion people call themselves Christians, and Christianity is the world's largest religion

Doctors of the Church

These are the 33 men and women who have been recognized by the church as pre-eminent theologians, those the faithful can learn from.

Albert the Great (Albertus Magnus) (ca. 1206–1280); Dominican
Alphonsus Liguori (1696–1787); Redemptorist
Ambrose (ca. 340–397); Bishop of Milan
Anselm (1033–1109); Archbishop of Canterbury
Anthony of Padua (1195–1231); Franciscan
Athanasius (ca. 297–373); Bishop of Alexandria
Augustine (354–430); Bishop of Hippo
Basil the Great (329–379); Cappadocian
Bede the Venerable (ca. 672–735); monk
Bernard of Clairvaux (1090–1153); Cistercian
Bonaventure (1221–1274); Franciscan
Catherine of Siena (1347–1380); Dominican
Cyril of Alexandria (ca. 376–444); Patriarch of Alexandria
Cyril of Jerusalem (ca. 315–386); Bishop of Jerusalem
Ephraem (ca. 306–373); Deacon of Edessa
Francis de Sales (1567–1622); Bishop of Geneva
Gregory I (the Great) (ca. 540–604); pope
Gregory Nazianzen (329–389); Cappadocian
Hilary of Poitiers (ca. 315–368); Bishop of Poitiers
Isidore of Seville (560–636); Bishop of Seville
Jerome (ca. 342–420); monastery head
John Chrysostom (ca. 347–407); Patriarch of Constantinople
John Damsacene (ca. 675–749); monk
John of the Cross (1542–1591); Discalced Carmelite
Lawrence of Brindisi (1559–1619); Capuchin
Leo I (the Great) (ca. 400–461); pope
Peter Canisius (1521–1597); Jesuit
Peter Chrysologus (ca. 406–450); Bishop of Ravenna
Peter Damian (1001–1072); Benedictine
Robert Bellarmine (1542–1621); Jesuit
Teresa of Ávila (1515–1582); Discalced Carmelite
Thérèse of Lisieux (1873–1897); Carmelite
Thomas Aquinas (1125–1174); Dominican

Calendar of Saints' Feast Days

The Roman Catholic liturgical calendar denotes the Sundays of Advent and Lent, Easter, the Sundays from Easter to Pentecost, and other feasts that are celebrated annually (of course, exact dates change each year). Saints' feast days are listed only for dates not given over to what is known as the "temporal cycle"—the "official" annual celebrations.

What follows is not a liturgical calendar, but rather a calendar listing by month of feast days for the saints you have read about in these pages. Sometimes you'll see two or more saints sharing the same date. This is accurate, but not something you'll find in a liturgical calendar (unless the saints are paired and share a joint feast day, such as Anne and Joachim, Perpetua and Felicita).

JANUARY	
1	Mary, Mother of Jesus
2	St. Adalhard, St. Basil the Great
3	St. Genevieve
4	St. Elizabeth Ann Seton
5	St. John Nepomucene Neumann, St. Simeon Stylites
15	St. Paul the Hermit
17	St. Devota, St. Anthony of Egypt
19	St. Canute, St. Henry of Uppsala
20	St. Sebastian
21	St. Agnes
22	St. Vincent of Saragossa
24	St. Francis de Sales
26	St. Paula
27	St. John Chrysostom
28	St. Thomas Aquinas
30	St. Aldegonda
31	St. John Bosco

FEBRUARY	
1	St. Brigid
3	St. Blaise, St. Ansgar
5	St. Agatha
6	St. Amand St. Peter Baptist St. Dorothy
9	St. Apollonia
10	St. Scholastica
12	St. Julian the Innkeeper
14	St. Valentine
21	John Henry Newman
23	St. Polycarp
25	St. Walburga

MARCH

1	St. David
3	St. Cunegund, Bl. Katharine Drexel
4	St. Casimir
7	Sts. Perpetua and Felicitas
8	St. John of God
9	St. Dominic Savio, St. Frances of Rome, St. Catherine of Bologna
13	St. Ansovinus
15	St. Louise de Marillac
17	St. Agricola of Avignon, St. Gertrude of Nivelles, St. Joseph of Arimathea, St. Patrick
19	St. Joseph
20	St. Cuthbert
21	St. Benedict
25	St. Dismas

APRIL

2	St. Francis of Paula
3	St. Adjutor
4	St. Isidore of Seville
5	St. Vincent Ferrer
7	St. Jean-Baptiste de la Salle
11	St. Gemma Galani, St. Stanislaus of Cracow
14	St. Peter González, St. Lidwina
16	St. Benedict Joseph Labre
23	St. George
25	St. Mark
27	St. Zita
29	St. Catherine of Siena
30	St. Pius V

MAY

1	St. Joseph the Worker
4	St. Florian
8	St. Plechelm
10	St. John of Ávila, St. Antonius of Florence, St. Catald, St. Isidore the Farmer
13	St. Julian of Norwich
15	St. Dymphna
16	St. John of Nepomuk, St. Honoratus, St. Brendan of Clonfert, St. Peregrine of Auxerre, St. John Nepomucene
19	St. Dunstan, St. Ivo, St. Celestine V
20	St. Bernardino of Siena
22	St. Rita, St. Julia of Corsica
26	St. Philip Neri
27	St. Augustine of Canterbury
28	St. Bernard of Montjoux
29	St. Bona
30	St. Joan of Arc, St. Ferdinand

JUNE

1	St. Theobald
2	St. Elmo
3	St. Kevin of Glendalough, St. Morand
5	St. Boniface
8	St. Medard
9	St. Columba of Iona
11	St. Barnabas
13	St. Anthony of Padua
15	St. Vitus
21	St. Aloysius Gonzaga
22	St. Nicetas, St. John Fisher, St. Thomas More
23	St. Joseph Cafasso
24	St. John the Baptist
29	Sts. Peter and Paul

JULY

3	St. Thomas
4	St. Elizabeth of Portugal
6	St. Maria Goretti
7	Sts. Cyril and Methodius
8	St. Kilian
11	St. Benedict II
12	St. John Gualbert
14	St. Camillus de Lellis
15	St. Swithun, St. Vladimir I of Kiev
19	Sts. Justa and Rufina
22	St. Mary Magdalene
23	St. Bridget of Sweden
25	St. James the Greater
26	Sts. Anne and Joachim
27	St. Pantaleon
29	St. Olaf, St. Martha
31	St. Ignatius of Loyola

AUGUST

1	St. Alphonsus Liguori, St. Friard
3	St. Hippolytus
4	St. John Vianney (Curé of Ars)
5	Sts. Addai and Mari
8	St. Dominic
10	St. Lawrence
14	St. Maximilian Kolbe
15	Feast of the Assumption
16	St. Roch
19	St. Sebald
20	St. Bernard of Clairvaux
23	St. Rose of Lima
24	St. Bartholomew, St. Ouen
25	St. Genesius the Actor
27	St. Monica
28	St. Augustine of Hippo, St. Moses the Ethiopian
31	St. Raymond Nonnatus

SEPTEMBER

1	St. Fiacre, St. Giles
3	St. Gregory I (the Great)
7	St. Gratis of Aosta
8	St. Hadrian
9	St. Peter Claver
10	St. Nicholas Tolentine
11	St. Hyacinth
16	St. Ludmilla, St. Cyprian
17	St. Hildegard of Bingen
18	St. Joseph of Cupertino
19	St. Januarius
21	St. Matthew
22	St. Phocas
23	St. Adamnan
26	Sts. Cosmas and Damian
27	St. Vincent de Paul
28	St. Wenceslas
29	Archangels Gabriel, Michael, and Raphael
30	St. Jerome, St. Gregory the Illuminator

OCTOBER

1	St. Thérèse of Lisieux
4	St. Francis of Assisi
6	St. Bruno
9	St. Denis, St. Louis Bertrand
10	St. Francis Borgia, St. Gereon
15	St. Teresa of Ávila
16	St. Gall, St. Gerard Majella
18	St. Luke
19	St. Isaac Jogues and the North American Martyrs
20	Bl. Contardo Ferrini
22	St. Peter of Alcántara
23	St. John Capistrano
24	St. Anthony Claret
25	Sts. Crispin and Crispinian
27	St. Frumentius
28	St. Jude

NOVEMBER	
3	St. Hubert of Liège,
	St. Martin de Porres
4	St. Charles Borromeo
5	St. Kea
6	St. Leonard of Noblac
7	St. Willibrord
8	Four Crowned Martyrs
10	St. Aedh Mac Bricc,
	St. Gertrude the Great
11	St. Martin of Tours
13	St. Brice, St. Homobonus,
	St. Frances Xavier Cabrini,
	St. Stanislaus Kostka
15	St. Albert the Great (Albertus Magnus)
16	St. Margaret of Scotland
17	St. Elizabeth of Hungary,
	St. Gregory the Woodworker
18	St. Rose Philippine Duchesne,
	St. Odo of Cluny
22	St. Cecilia
26	St. Leonard Casanova,
	St. John Berchmans
30	St. Andrew

DECEMBER	
1	St. Eligius
2	St. Bibiana
3	St. Francis Xavier
4	St. Osmund, St. Barbara
6	St. Nicholas of Myra
8	Feast of the Immaculate Conception
11	St. Damasus
13	St. Odilia, St. Lucy
14	St. John of the Cross
21	St. Peter Canisius
23	St. Thorlac, St. John Cantius
26	St. Stephen
27	St. John the Evangelist
29	St. Thomas à Becket

On the Job: Saints by Occupations

What's your line? Are you a butcher? Baker? Candlestick maker? Whatever your life's work, you are likely to find a patron saint for your occupation listed here. Well, maybe not the candlestick maker, but St. Barnard of Clairvaux and St. John the Baptist are patron saints of candlemakers. So it seems that almost all bases are covered here.

As veneration of the saints became popular, so did the idea of asking them for intercession. Today we have patron saints for a particular job category because something in the saint's life—not necessarily the same job category, which may not have existed then—touched upon that line of work. For instance—although this is an extreme example—St. Lawrence, a third-century martyr, was roasted on a grid and became the patron saint of cooks. Really.

In the listing of patron saints that follows, the brief biography will note how the saint came to intercede in a particular career, life situation, health problem, and so on. Naturally there was a good deal more to that holy person's life to make them merit canonization.

Sometimes a saint's biography, especially saints whose lives are little known, shows no evidence why that man or woman was chosen for patronage in a particular area. Perhaps the reasons are lost in the mists of history. Or maybe patronage was just divine inspiration on someone's part.

Every once in a while you may notice two or more patron saints for the same occupation or cause. The lives of all of those holy people might have touched that specific category of intercession. Or perhaps the cause involved needs as many helping hands as it can get!

Saints whose biographies have appeared in other parts of this book are cited in bold print, with a page number noted so you can read or reread the life of that man or woman.

In the listings that follow of saints that have *not* been mentioned before in this book, the date in parentheses is that saint's feast day. If you want to know more about saints and patronages, see the books listed at the end of this appendix.

E-FACTS

If you're named Tiffany or Jared, you're out of luck. But if you are an Elizabeth or Thomas or Margaret or Francis or if you have another more common first name, you can probably find a saint who also has that name. Perhaps more than one saint is your namesake. You can read the biographies of those saints, choose the one you feel more comfortable with, and pick him or her to be your patron.

This book, the definitive work on saints, can help you in your search: *Butler's Lives of the Saints* by Alban Butler (1711–1773). In four volumes, *Butler's* offers brief biographies of thousands of canonized saints. Check your public library; most carry those volumes.

Accountants	**St. Matthew (page 44).**
Actors	St. Genesius the Actor (August 25). Actor in Rome at the time of Emperor Diocletian. Killed for his faith by beheading. St. Vitus (June 15). His story dates back to 300, when Vitus, a Sicilian, was converted to Christianity at age 12 and became known for his conversions and miracles. In Rome he freed Emperor Diocletian's son from an evil spirit. His thanks was having the gesture taken as sorcery and Vitus, his tutor, and servant were subjected to torture. In one account all three were boiled in oil. In a cheerier version, they were not harmed, and during a storm an angel led them back to their home. Some details of Vitus's story may be legend. The nervous disorder St. Vitus's Dance (chorea) was named after him, apparently after he was able to assist those suffering from it and from epilepsy.
Advertising workers	St. Bernardino of Siena (May 20). Preacher of fiery sermons, denouncing, among other things, gambling and witchcraft. This saint, who lived from 1380 to 1444, also rejuvenated and reformed the Friars of the Strict Observance, increasing their number from about 300 to more than 4,000 during his lifetime.
Agricultural workers	St. Phocas (September 22). A gardener at Paphlagonia in the Early Christian era, Phocas lived a pious life. When an army came to his house looking for him, he told them to wait and they would find Phocas in the morning. He then prepared spiritually for death, dug his grave, and told the soldiers who he was. They were hesitant to harm him—he had been a good host—but he urged them to behead him and they did.
Anesthetists	**St. René Goupil (see page 185).**
Apprentices	St. John Bosco (January 31). Italian saint (1815–1888) who established a refuge for boys, teaching them trades. Also published catechismal materials to instruct the youths in his care.

Archaeologists	St. Damasus (December 11). Fourth-century pope who restored catacombs, shrines, and tombs of martyrs.
Archers	**St. Sebastian (see page 163).**
Architects	**St. Barbara (see page 232).** St. Thomas (July 3). First-century apostle and saint who built many churches.
Artists	Fra Angelica. St. Catherine of Bologna (March 9). A member of the Poor Clares, Catherine (1413–1463) is said to have experienced visions of Mary with the infant Jesus in her arms, later reproduced often in art. **St. Luke (see page 46).**
Astronauts, pilots	St. Joseph of Cupertino (September 18). Seventeenth-century Italian Franciscan (1603–1663) known as "the flying friar." His ecstasies and levitations had him "flying" over altars, at one time whipping through a church from one end to the other over the heads of the congregation.
Astronomers	St. Dominic (August 8). Founder of the Order of Preachers (Dominicans). A Spaniard, Dominic (1170–1221) took a new tack with his order. Rather than living in a monastery, Dominicans took the gospel message on the road, preaching as they traveled and living on very little. The Dominican order produced such theological giants as St. Thomas Aquinas; however, Torquemada, in charge of the Spanish Inquisition, was also a Dominican, taking the search for truth too far.
Athletes	**St. Sebastian (see page 163).**
Bakers	**St. Elizabeth of Hungary (see page 181).** St. Honoratus (May 16). Sixth-century French bishop noted for this miracle: while he was celebrating mass, the hand of God appeared above the chalice and held out bread. **St. Nicholas (see page 75).**
Bankers	**St. Matthew (see page 44).**
Blacksmiths	St. Dunstan (May 19). English bishop and great reformer (910–988) who was also a skilled metalworker and harpist. **St. John the Baptist (see page 66).**
Boatmen	**St. Julian the Hospitaler (see page 235).**
Bookkeepers	**St. Matthew (see page 44).**
Bookbinders	St. Celestine V (May 19). Thirteenth-century Italian-born Peter de Marrone became a hermit, a priest, and founded the Celestine order. Against his better judgment, he accepted the papacy after political bickering left the seat vacant. A holy but simple man not meant for the demands of the papacy, he soon abdicated and returned to the monastery. Pope Boniface VIII, his successor, felt threatened by Celestine's popularity and put him in prison, where he died 10 months later.
Booksellers	St. John of God (March 8). Sixteenth-century Portuguese who did varied work before becoming a Christian, then built a hospital and cared for the sick.

While there may be more of them noted in little-used history books, there are some 65 saints named John who are still mentioned in modern times. They range alphabetically from St. John the Almsgiver (sixth century) to St. John Zedazneli (sixth century).

Brewers	**St. Augustine of Hippo (see page 18).**
	St. Nicholas of Myra (see page 75).
Bricklayers	**St. Stephen (see page 157).**
Broadcasters	St. Gabriel the Archangel (September 29). In the Bible he brings news and is a heavenly intercessor. He was sent to Zachary's wife, Elizabeth, to tell her she would have a child—St. John the Baptist—who would prepare the way for the savior. Gabriel also appeared to Mary to tell her she would be the mother of Jesus.
Builders	**St. Barbara (see page 232).**
	St. Vincent Ferrer (April 5). A Spanish Dominican priest, Vincent (1350–1419) is best known for preaching in Europe and for bringing unity to the church from the Great Schism, when first two and then three rival popes claimed authority.
Bus drivers	**St. Christopher (see page 234).**
Businesspeople	St. Homobonus (November 13). Twelfth-century Italian businessman; scrupulously honest, he also gave away a good deal of his profits. His name in Latin means "good man."
Butchers	St. Anthony of Egypt (January 17). An ascetic, Anthony (251–356) spent a good deal of his life living in the desert, practicing severe austerity, even living in a cemetery for a time. After 20 years he emerged to found a community of monks, then several branches of the monastery, fueled by the interest of men impressed by his holiness. He lived to be 105 and was remarked upon (favorably) by St. Augustine in his *Confessions*.
	St. Hadrian, a.k.a. Adrian (September 8). A third- or fourth-century martyr. Once a pagan military officer who converted to Christianity, he died being torn limb from limb.
	St. Luke (see page 46).
Cab drivers	St. Fiacre (September 1). Seventh-century Irish saint who built a refuge for the sick and poor. Patron saint of cab drivers of Paris, whose taxis are called *fiacres*. The first taxi rank there was located near the Hotel Saint-Fiacre.
Cabinetmakers	**St. Anne (see page 12).**
Candlemakers	St. Bernard of Clairvaux (August 20). An eleventh-century Burgundian nobleman, Bernard had poetic leanings but eventually became a Cistercian monk, a strict order. Beset by physical problems, no doubt exacerbated by his austere lifestyle, he founded his own monastery and wrote "sweetly" in his poetry and preaching, earning the title Doctor Mellifluous. Thus the connection from sweet to honey to bees, to wax and candles.
	St. John the Baptist (see page 66).
Carpenters	**St. Joseph (see page 8).**
Craftsmen	**St. Catherine of Alexandria (see page 233).**

Communications workers	St. Bernardino of Siena (see Advertising workers). St. Gabriel (see Broadcasters).
Cooks	St. Lawrence (August 10). One of the seven deacons of Rome, this third-century saint was born in Spain and served as deacon to Pope Sixtus II, who was eventually condemned to death. When Sixtus told Lawrence that he would follow the pope to the grave in three days, Lawrence gave away money and many of the church's possessions to the needy. When the emperor asked for the return of the church's treasures, Lawrence collected the poor, sick, and other needy, presented them to the emperor, and told him they were the church's treasures. This was enough for the emperor. Lawrence was bound to a hot griddle. Apparently, in the middle of this agony, he managed to tell his tormentors that they should turn him over, he was quite done on that side. Later, historians agreed he was actually beheaded, but the link to cooks understandably persists. It is said his death led to the conversion of Rome. St. Martha (July 29). First-century friend of Jesus, she was fussing in the kitchen while her sister, Mary, listened to Christ preach in the next room. Martha was mildly rebuked by Jesus for her choice.
Customs agents	**St. Matthew (see page 44).**
Dairy workers	**St. Brigid of Ireland (see page 84).**
Dancers	St. Vitus (see Actors).
Dentists	St. Apollonia (February 9). Third-century Alexandrian martyr. This elderly deaconess was beaten so severely that her teeth were either smashed or pulled out with pincers. Still refusing to denounce her faith, she flung herself into her captors' bonfire.
Dietitians	St. Martha (see Cooks).
Diplomats	St. Gabriel the Archangel (see Broadcasters).
Dockworkers	**St. Nicholas (see page 75).**
Domestic workers	St. Martha (see Cooks). St. Zita (April 27). Thirteenth-century Italian servant who took food from her wealthy household to give to the poor. When stopped once by her mistress, she opened the apron she had filled with food and rose petals spilled onto the floor.
Druggists	Sts. Cosmas and Damian (September 26). Fourth-century Arabian martyrs. These twin physicians took no money from their patients. They died by beheading. Their story could be legend, although miracles were attributed to them centuries after their death.
Ecologists	**St. Francis of Assisi (see page 32).**
Editors, publishers	St. John Bosco (see Apprentices).
Engineers	St. Ferdinand (May 30). Castilian king (Ferdinand III 1199–1252) who founded a university and a cathedral.
Farmers	St. George (April 23). A perhaps legendary knight who killed a dragon that had been terrifying the town of Sylene in Libya. Thought to be martyred under Emperor Diocletian, he became particularly popular in the Middle Ages, especially among the Crusaders. St. Isidore the Farmer (May 10). Twelfth-century Spanish hired hand who helped the needy.

Firefighters	St. Florian (May 4). Fourth-century officer of the Roman army. Some accounts say when he declared his Christianity he was set on fire; others that he was scourged and cast into a river with a rock tied around him.
Fishermen	**St. Andrew (see page 93).** **St. Peter (see page 92).**
Flight attendants	St. Bona (May 29). Thirteenth-century religious zealot from Pisa who from age 14 guided many on the journey from Pisa to Palestine, where she had first gone to visit her father.
Florists	St. Rose of Lima (August 23). First canonized saint of the Americas. Born in 1586 in Lima, Peru. Patronage comes from her name, and the fact that she loved tending her parents' garden. She died at 31. **St. Thérèse of Lisieux (see page 103).**
Foresters	St. John Gualbert (July 12). Eleventh-century Florentine abbot who built a monastery from the wood of a nearby forest.
Funeral directors and undertakers	St. Dismas (March 25). Known as "the good thief," he was crucified next to Jesus. **St. Joseph of Arimathea (see page 73).**
Gardeners	St. Adalhard (January 2). A monk, Adalhard (753–827) was brought to court by his cousin, Charlemagne, and became one of his advisers. Presumably for supporting a revolt against Emperor Louis the Debonair, he was exiled to Aquitaine. Brought back by Louis, he was exiled again for some other transgression. A pious man who seemed to roll with the punches, Adalhard established two monasteries that became learning centers. **St. Dorothy (see page 164).** St. Fiacre (see Cab Drivers). St. Phocas the Gardener (See Agricultural Workers).
Glassworkers	**St. Luke (see page 46).**
Governors	St. Ferdinand (King Ferdinand III; see Engineers).
Gravediggers	St. Anthony of Egypt (see Cemetery Workers).
Grocers, and Supermarket workers	St. Michael the Archangel (September 29). Leader of the heavenly army of angels who defeated Satan and his followers and hurled them from heaven. He metes out punishment but tempers it with divine justice. Usually he is represented with a sword, standing over a conquered dragon (that is, Satan). Since the sixth century September 29 has also been known as Michaelmas Day, celebrated to honor the dedication of a basilica in Michael's honor in Rome. It is no longer commemorated, and today all three named archangels—Michael, Gabriel, and Raphael—have been given the feast day. It is still occasionally called Michaelmas Day.
Hairstylists	St. Martin de Porres (November 3). Born in 1579, this saint was a Peruvian whose father was a Spanish nobleman and mother a free black woman. He was a barber before becoming a Dominican lay brother. He did many good works, was extremely pious (given to self-flagellation), and, like Francis of Assisi, had an affinity for animals. **St. Mary Magdalene (see page 72).**
Homemakers	**St. Anne (see page 12).**

Hospital administrators	St. Basil the Great (January 2). Born in Asia Minor (329–379) and educated befitting his station, Basil taught awhile and then became a hermit. He attracted disciples and founded the first monastery in Asia Minor. He was active in helping the poor and the sick, building what would today be called a hospital. A holy man, he was enormously effective in fighting heresy and issuing doctrinal writings. He is a Doctor of the Church. **St. Frances Xavier Cabrini (see page 135).**
Hotel workers/ innkeepers	St. Amand (February 6). A French missionary, Amand (ca. 584–679) lived as a hermit for 15 years after his ordination then became active in missionary work in Flanders, Ghent, and most likely Germany. He founded numerous monasteries in Belgium. **St. Julian the Hospitaler (see page 235).** St. Martha (see Cooks).
Janitors/porters	St. Theobald (June 1). A twelfth-century Italian layman who worked as a janitor in a cathedral and gave most of his money to the poor.
Jewelers	St. Dunstan (see Blacksmiths). St. Eligius (December 1). French saint (588–660), also known as Eloi, was a metalworker who created two thrones for King Clotaire in Paris with gold and jewels enough for just one. He used his wealth to found a monastery and a convent.
Journalists	**St. Francis de Sales (see page 182).**
Laborers	St. John Bosco (see Apprentices).
Lawyers	**St. Catherine of Alexandria (see page 233).** St. Ivo, also known as Yves Kermartin (May 19). A thirteenth-century Breton who studied law in Paris and practiced in Brittany, he defended the rich as well as destitute prostitutes. He became a fair, incorruptible judge and eventually a priest, helping parishioners with legal problems. **St. Thomas More (see page 112).**
Leatherworkers	**St. John the Baptist (see page 66).**
Librarians	**St. Catherine of Alexandria (see page 233).** **St. Jerome (see page 173).**
Locksmiths	St. Dunstan (see Blacksmiths).
Maids	St. Zita (see Domestic workers).
Manual laborers	**St. Joseph (see page 8).**
Medical technicians	**St. Albert the Great (see page 109).**
Merchants	**St. Francis of Assisi (see page 32).** **St. Nicholas (see page 75).**
Messengers	St. Gabriel the Archangel (see Broadcasters).
Metalworkers	St. Eligius (see Jewelers).
Midwives	St. Raymond Nonnatus (August 31). Thirteenth-century Spanish cardinal who was born by cesarean section after his mother died in labor. His surname means "not born"— an odd but interesting choice, since he obviously was.

Military	**St. Joan of Arc (see page 56).**
Military chaplains	St. John Capistrano (October 23). Fifteenth-century Italian nobleman ordained in 1420 and sent on frequent papal diplomatic missions; preached in Bavaria and Poland. When Turks captured Constantinople, he preached against them but was not successful. Led the Christian army in the Battle of Belgrade in 1456, which kept the Turks from taking that city, and stemmed their overall progress.
Monks	**St. John the Baptist (see page 66).**
Musicians	St. Cecilia (November 22). Early Roman martyr. Legend is that she was unable to hear music played at her wedding because she was singing to God. She later converted her bridegroom to her faith. Both were martyred. St. Dunstan (see Blacksmiths). **St. Gregory I (the Great) (see page 177).** St. Odo of Cluny (November 18). French abbot (879–942); a musician who, among other talents, composed hymns.
Naval officers	St. Francis of Paola (April 2). Italian (1416–1507) who founded the Minims order. At one time he tossed his cloak on the water and sailed across the Straits of Messina on it.
Notaries	**St. Luke (see page 46).** **St. Mark (see page 45).**
Nurses	St. Agatha (February 5). Dates of her birth and date are unknown, but she is said to have been a wealthy Sicilian who dedicated her life to God and to chastity. When she refused the advances of a government official during the latest spate of Christian persecutions, he condemned her to a brothel, beat her, and then rolled her on a bed of hot coals until she died. St. Agatha is said to scold women who work on her feast day by appearing as an angry cat. She is known as Santo Gato (Saint Cat) in northern Spain. St. Camillus de Lellis (July 14). Hospital bursar in Italy who lived from 1550 to 1614. He was ordained and founded the Ministers of the Sick, a lay order that cared for patients in hospitals and at home. He pioneered such now-common nursing practices as isolating infected patients and a sensible diet. St. John of God (see Booksellers).
Nursing and nursing services	**St. Catherine of Siena (see page 27).** **St. Elizabeth of Hungary (see page 181).**
Obstetricians	St. Raymond Nonnatus (see Midwives).
Painters	**St. Luke (see page 46).**
Paratroopers	St. Michael the Archangel (see Grocers, Supermarket Workers).
Parish priests	St. John Vianney (August 4). French clergyman (1786–1859) best known as Curé of Ars. Named parish priest in 1818 in the village of Ars-en-Dombes, he spent his life with those 250 residents, doing good works. His fame as a confessor—he sometimes heard confessions 18 hours a day and had a special talent for drawing out penitents—brought trainloads of pilgrims to Ars. He is considered the paradigm of a parish priest.
Pawnbrokers	**St. Nicholas of Myra (see page 75).**
Pencil makers	**St. Thomas Aquinas (see page 107).**

Pharmacists	Sts. Cosmas and Damian (see Druggists).
	St. Gemma Galani (April 11). Early-twentieth-century Italian mystic whose father was a pharmacist. She experienced stigmata and died at 25.
	St. Raphael the Archangel (September 29). The third of only three of the seven archangels mentioned by name. The name Raphael means "God hath healed," and he is patron saint of all those in the healing professions.
Physicians	Sts. Cosmas and Damian (see Druggists).
	St. Luke (see page 46).
	St. Pantaleon (July 27). Raised a Christian in the fourth century, became a doctor and then personal physician to the Roman emperor. H enjoyed court life perhaps a bit too much and lost his faith. Finding his way back, he offered his medical services to the poor at no charge. He suffered martyrdom during the reign of Diocletian. He was beheaded after six other methods were used to kill him, but he was miraculously saved each time.
	St. Raphael (see Pharmacists).
Plasterers	St. Bartholomew (August 24). One of the Twelve Apostles. The little that is known about him may be apocryphal. He was to have founded a Christian community in India, where he is known to have preached. He also traveled to Armenia, where he was beheaded.
Poets	St. Cecilia (see Musicians).
	St. Columba (see page 84).
	St. David (March 1). Also known as St. Dewi. Sixth-century Welsh abbot and bishop of a monastery now called St. David's in Pembrokeshire. Many Welsh churches bear his name.
Police officers	St. Michael (see Grocers, Supermarket Workers).
Porters	**St. Christopher (see page 234).**
Postal workers	St. Gabriel (see Broadcasters).
Preachers	St. John Chrysostom (January 27). Patriarch of Constantinople who lived ca. 349–407. He went from early life as a Christian ascetic to the **bishopric** (the office of bishop). He is remembered as one who wrote sermons that moved his congregation to tears. A prolific writer in explaining the faith, his brilliance led to being named a Doctor of the Church.

E-QUESTIONS?

What is a chrysostom?
The surname **Chrysostom** was given to this particular St. John in the sixth century. It is Greek for "golden mouth."

Printers	**St. Augustine (see page 18).**
	St. Genesius (see Actors).
Prostitutes, repentant	**St. Mary Magdalene (see page 72).**
Public relations	St. Bernardino of Siena (see Advertising workers).
Radio workers	St. Gabriel the Archangel (see Broadcasters).

Radiologists	St. Michael the Archangel (see Grocers, Supermarket workers).
Road workers	St. Francis of Paola (see Naval Officers).
	St. John the Baptist (see page 66).
Sailors	**St. Brendan (see page 84).**
	St. Cuthbert (March 20). Seventh-century Irish (or possibly Scottish) monk who became a hermit, then was brought out to take on the see at Hexham, and later Lindisfarne. At the end of his life, he cared for the sick and worked many miracles of healing.
	St. Elmo (June 2). Fourth-century bishop in Compagna, Italy, also known as Erasmus, who—another victim of Diocletian's persecution—was martyred. Some accounts say he was rolled in pitch and set on fire, which may account for his association with the phenomenon known as St. Elmo's fire, in which a blue light appears around a ship's mast during an electric storm.
	St. Nicholas (see page 75).
	St. Peter Gonzáles (April 14). Spanish-born Benedictine (1190–1246), he served as chaplain to King Ferdinand III (who was also later canonized). He preached a crusade against the Moors, then urged mercy for them. He was particularly concerned about sailors, hence this patronage.
Scholars	**St. Brigid (see page 84).**
Scientists	**St. Albert the Great (see page 109).**
Sculptors	Four Crowned Martyrs (November 8). These are either four Persian stonemasons, known by name, slain by Emperor Diocletian for not sacrificing to the gods, or they are four Roman soldiers martyred by the same emperor for the same reason. The Venerable Bede records that a seventh-century church in Canterbury was dedicated to them and contained their remains.
Seminarians	St. Charles Borromeo (November 4). Sixteenth-century son of a count and the sister of a pope (who was a Medici), Charles, as you might expect with a pope uncle, moved along quickly in his career. Within a week of his elevation to pope, his uncle named him a cardinal and archbishop of Milan. At this point Charles was still a layman but he went on to become ordained and used his power and considerable intelligence to build schools and churches and hospitals, sometimes using his own money for projects. He also established seminaries for the clergy, and made many reforms. It was he who was finally able to bring the Council of Trent to a close in 1562. During the famine of 1570 in Milan, he managed to find food and feed 3,000 people a day.
Shepherds	**St. Bernadette of Lourdes (see page 201).**
Shoemakers	Sts. Crispin and Crispinian (October 25). Possibly legend, these two third-century Roman brothers went to Gaul to preach. At night they worked as shoemakers. Martyrs, they were beheaded by the order of Emperor Maximian.
Singers	St. Cecilia (see Musicians).
	St. Gregory I (the Great) (see Musicians).

Skaters	St. Lidwina (April 14). A Dutch holy woman (1380–1433) who was injured at 16 while ice skating and became an invalid for the remainder of her life. She suffered a great deal, offering her pain for the reparation for sinners. Eventually she experienced visions, ate little or nothing, and became almost totally blind.
Skiers	St. Bernard of Montjoux (May 28). An Italian who lived ca. 996–1081, he was a priest who spent most of his time doing missionary work in the Alps. He built schools and churches, but is best remembered for erecting hospices (in this context, these were inns, not services for the fatally ill) to aid lost travelers in mountain passes now named Great and Little Bernard after him. The St. Bernard dog is said to be named after him.
Social workers	**St. Louise de Marillac (see page 124).**
Soldiers	St. George (see Farmers). **St. Ignatius of Loyola (see page 49).** **St. Joan of Arc (see page 56).** **St. Sebastian (see page 163).**
Speleologists	St. Benedict (July 11). Sixth-century nobleman born in Norcia, Italy. After his first miracle as a youth he took to an underground cave where he lived for three years, constantly tempted by the devil. On returning aboveground, he founded the Benedictine order, which made manual labor part of the day's schedule. He built a great monastery, Monte Cassino, affected monastic life for centuries, and went down in church history books as a founder of Western Monasticism. As recently as the 1970s Pope Paul VI named him patron of all Europe.
Stonemasons	**St. Stephen (see page 157).**
Surgeons	Sts. Cosmas and Damian (see Druggists). **St. Luke (see page 46).**
Tailors	St. Homobonus (see Businesspeople).
Tapestry makers	**St. Francis of Assisi (see page 32).**
Tax collectors	**St. Matthew (see page 44).**
Teachers	**St. Gregory I (the Great) (see page 177).** St. John-Baptiste de la Salle (April 7), A French priest born in 1651, Jean-Baptiste founded the Brothers of the Christian Schools—or Christian Brothers as they came to be known. The order trained young men to be brothers and also ran a reform school for boys, then stepped into educating adult prisoners. He had avant garde ideas about education, one of them grouping children in classes rather than receiving individual instruction. He also started teaching classes in the local language—Italian, French—rather than Latin, which had been standard. He died in 1719.
Telecommunication workers	St. Gabriel (see Broadcasters).
Television workers	St. Gabriel (see Broadcasters).

Television writers	**St. Clare of Assisi (see page 35).**
Theologians	**St. Alphonsus Liguori (see page 186).**
	St. Augustine of Hippo (see page 18).
Watchmen,	**St. Matthew (see page 44).**
Security guards	St. Peter of Alcántara (October 22). A native of Spain, Peter (1499–1562) joined a religious order at 16, then founded a friary six years later. He preached, then lived as a hermit for a time. He founded an offshoot of the Order of the Conventuals that was more interested in penance and austerity, and eventually became the Alcatrines. He was also an adviser to St. Teresa of Ávila, helping her with her reform of the Carmelites.
Weavers	St. Paul the Hermit (January 15). Born in Egypt, Paul (ca. 229–342), who is sometimes known as Paul the First Hermit to distinguish him from later Pauls, fled persecution from Emperor Decius, and fled again when he learned his own brother-in-law planned to report him as a Christian. He became a hermit and liked the life—certainly safer than staying out in the world—and became a holy and admired man. St. Jerome visited him and wrote about his life, which ended, it is said, when he was 113.
Winegrowers	St. Martin of Tours (November 11). Martin (ca. 316–397) is considered also a founder of Western monasticism, along with St. Benedict. Born to pagan parents, he was 12 when he began studying Christianity and 18 when baptized. He became a monk in Milan, and then moved to Gaul, and established the first French monastic community south of Poitiers. He became bishop of Tours for a while, living at the cathedral, then returned to the monastic life he preferred. Many miracles were attributed to him.
	St. Morand (June 3). Twelfth-century nobleman born in Germany who became a Benedictine monk and later confidant to a count in Lower Alsace. He was known for his holiness, kindness to the people, and his miracles. It is said he fasted through Lent eating nothing but a bunch of grapes.
Wine merchants	St. Amand (see Hotel Workers/Innkeepers).
Workers	**St. Joseph (see page 8).**
Wool workers	**St. John the Baptist (see page 66).**
Writers, authors	**St. Francis de Sales (see page 182).**
	St. Lucy (see page 165).

Suggested Additional Reading:

Dictionary of Saints by John J. Delaney (Doubleday, 1980). Offers brief biographies of some 5,000 holy men and women.

All Saints: Daily Reflections on Saints, Prophets, and Witnesses for Our Time by Robert Ellsberg (Crossroad Publishing, 1999). The author offers a short biography of a saint for each day of the year. Besides honest-to-goodness saints, he includes other holy or spiritual people: Gandhi, Dietrich Bonhoeffer, Pierre Teilhard de Chardin, and Anne Frank, among others.

Saints: Who They Are and How They Help You by Tessa Clark, Elizabeth Hallam, and Cecilia Walters (Simon & Schuster, 1994). A lavishly illustrated book.

The Directory of Saints: A Concise Guide to Patron Saints by Annette Sandoval (Dutton, 1996). Easy reference guide to saints for everybody and every occasion.

Saints Preserve Us! by Sean Kelly and Rosemary Rogers (Random House, 1993). An irreverent look at the canonized and their patronages.

Patriotic Saints: For Nations, Cities, and Regions

Many spots around the globe have a patron saint. He or she may intercede for an entire country, but occasionally for a city, town, or province.

Africa	Moses the Ethiopian (August 28). Born a slave, Moses (ca. 330–405) was a servant in the home of a government official but was dismissed for stealing and being just plain unpleasant. After he left he did worse, becoming leader of a band of thieves. It is not known exactly who or what was instrumental in his conversion, but he did become a monk and became known for extreme austerities. Totally reformed at the end, he and six other monks were murdered by a roving gang when Moses refused to defend himself with force.
	Our Lady Queen of Africa.
Albania	Our Lady of Good Counsel.
Americas, Central and South	**Our Lady of Guadalupe (see page 198).**
Angola	**Immaculate Heart of Mary (see page 2).**
Argentina	Our Lady of Lujan.
Armenia	St. Bartholomew (see page 273).
	St. Gregory the Illuminator (or the Enlightener) (September 30). He was the son of a man who killed King Khosrov I of Armenia when Gregory was a baby in the third century. Gregory was taken out of town after the dying Khosrov ordered the whole family slain. He was baptized, later married, and when King Khosrov's son took over his father's throne, allowed back into Armenia. Gregory converted the son and declared Christianity the religion of the land. He and his spouse eventually entered religious orders. Gregory worked unstintingly in establishing Christianity in the country, performing, it is said, many miracles. He eventually retired to a hermitage.
Asia Minor (Near East)	**St. John the Evangelist (see page 47).**
Australia	Our Lady Help of Christians.
Austria	St. Kilian (July 8). A seventh-century Irish missionary (his name in Gaelic means "church", who became bishop of Wurzburg, Germany, and was martyred there after a dispute with the local ruler.
Bavaria	St. Kilian (see Austria).
Belgium	**St. Joseph (see page 8).**

Bohemia	St. Ludmilla (September 16). The daughter of Slav royalty, Ludmilla (ca. 860–921) married the duke of Bohemia and the two converted to Christianity. When the duke died, their son, Ratislav, succeeded him and, for some reason, put his son, Wenceslas, in Ludmilla's care. She raised the boy, but when Ratislav died, his wife, Drahomira, was named regent. Threatened by Ludmilla and not wanting to restore Christianity, which was being attacked at the time, Drahomira ordered her strangled to death. St. Wenceslas (September 28). Also known as Vaclav, he was Ludmilla's grandson. When his father, Ratislav, was killed, the draconian Drahomira took over the government and put into place anti-Christian policies. She was deposed, and in 922 Wenceslas became ruler. He was fair and just, encouraging Christianity, but got into trouble with both his faith and with politics and was slain by his brother and his brother's political allies. He is considered a martyr.
Bolivia	Our Lady of Copacabana.
Borneo	**St. Francis Xavier (see page 39).**
Brazil	**Immaculate Conception (see page 2).** **St. Anthony of Padua (see page 14).** St. Peter of Alcántara.
Canada	**St. Anne (see page 12).** **St. Joseph (see page 8).**
Central America	**St. Rose of Lima (see page 256).**
Chile	Our Lady of Mount Carmel. St. James the Greater.
China	**St. Joseph (see page 8).**
Colombia	St. Louis Bertrand (October 9). Spanish Dominican known for his missionary work in South America in the sixteenth century and for his gift of prophecy. He was canonized in the seventeenth century, but his feast day is no longer observed. St. Peter Claver.
Corsica	**Immaculate Conception (see page 2).** St. Julia of Corsica (May 22). Fifth-century Carthaginian Christian sold into slavery to a Syrian master who took her with him on a trip to Corsica. The pagan ruler the Syrian had traveled to see told Julia if she would sacrifice to his idols, he would free her. She refused, was tortured, and then crucified. Her relics rest in a church in Brescia, Italy, although she is the patron of Corsica.
Crete	St. Titus (January 26). First-century missionary who worked with St. Paul, apparently smoothing things over between Paul and the Corinthian Christians. Was also thought to be the first bishop of Crete.
Cuba	Our Lady of Charity.
Cyprus	**St. Barnabas (see page 160).**
Czech Republic	St. John Nepomucene, (May 16). Fourteenth-century martyr who, as vicar general of Prague, disagreed with King Wenceslas IV (not St. Wenceslas) over the running of an abbey. He was hauled off by royal troops, tortured, and drowned.

	St. Wenceslas (see Bohemia).
Denmark	St. Ansgar (February 3). A ninth-century missionary and then bishop, he worked in both Denmark and Sweden to convert the Scandinavians. Considered the "Apostle of Scandinavia."
	St. Canute (January 19). Eleventh-century Danish king killed by rebels (among them his brother) who were against Canute's policy of taxation. Almost king of England: his uncle, King Canute, had reigned there, but St. Canute was unsuccessful in his bid to succeed him.
Dominican Republic	Our Lady of High Grace.
	St. Dominic (see page 253).
East Indies	**St. Francis Xavier (see page 39).**
	St. Thomas the Apostle.
Ecuador	Sacred Heart of Mary.
Egypt	**St. Mark (see page 45).**
El Salvador	Our Lady of Peace.
England	**St. Augustine (see page 18).**
	St. George (see page 255).
	St. Gregory I (the Great) (see page 177).
Ethiopia	St. Frumentius (October 27). Fourth-century native of Tyre, he survived a shipwreck, washing up on the shores of Ethiopia. He became secretary to the king and, upon that ruler's death, stayed to work in that country, bringing Christianity to the people. He was called "Abbuna" in Ethiopia, which means "Our Father" and is still the title of the primate of the Ethiopian church.
Europe	St. Benedict II (July 11). Seventh-century Roman who became pope in 684. Known for his knowledge of the Scriptures, piety, and good works for the poor. He was pope for just 11 months, but during that time Emperor Constantine IV set aside his mandate that papal elections had to be approved by the emperor.
	Sts. Cyril and Methodius (July 7). Ninth-century "Apostles to the Slavs," these were two brothers—Constantine, later known as Cyril, and Methodius—born to an aristocratic family and well educated. Constantine was ordained a priest and became a professor of philosophy; Methodius held a government position before becoming a monk. Constantine joined him and the two translated documents into a Slavonic alphabet invented by Cyril. In 1862, Ratislav, duke of Greater Moravia, commissioned them as missionaries. When Cyril died, Methodius became a bishop and continued the translations.
Finland	St. Henry of Uppsala (January 19). An Englishman living in twelfth-century Rome, he accompanied the cardinal who would later become Pope Adrian IV to Scandinavia and was made bishop of Uppsala, Sweden, the next year. He was slain by an unrepentant penitent: the man did not like the penance Henry gave him for committing murder, so he killed him. Henry does not seem to have been formally canonized, but he is the patron saint of Finland.
France	Our Lady of the Assumption.

St. Denis.

St. Joan of Arc (see page 56).

St. Martin of Tours (see page 262).

St. Thérèse of Lisieux (see page 103).

Paris   St. Genevieve (January 3). A Paris nun, a doer rather than a contemplative, Genevieve (ca. 422–500) had visions and prophecies that fostered belief among government and military leaders. She cared for the people during wartime occupations and worked for the release of prisoners. She predicted that Attila II and his Huns would leave Paris alone, and, leading the people in prayer, she saw that happen. She is credited with saving Paris a number of times from catastrophes.

Alsace   St. Odilia.

Avignon   St. Agricola of Avignon (March 17). French bishop Agricola (ca. 497–580) lived a placid, if austere, life enlarging and enhancing the churches in his **diocese**.

Brittany **St. Ivo (see page 270).**

Germany	St. Boniface (June 5). An Englishman (ca. 680–754), he was ordained to teach and preach, but wanted to do missionary work. Sent by Pope Gregory II to convert the pagans in Germany, he changed his name from Winfrid to Boniface, and established several monasteries in Germany, reformed the Frankish church, and in general was quite important in that country. The Vatican named him to various posts. In old age he was murdered in Friesland (northern Netherlands) when attacked by a group of pagans. He is called the "Apostle of Germany."

St. Michael (see page 259).

St. Peter Canisius (see page 52).

Nuremberg   St. Sebald.

Greece	**St. Andrew (see page 93).**
	St. Nicholas (see page 75).
Guatemala	St. James the Greater (see Chile).
Hungary	**Blessed Virgin Mary (see page 2).**
	St. Stephen (see page 157).
Iceland	St. Thorlac (December 23). Twelfth-century founder of a monastery, later named bishop of Skalholt, one of two dioceses in Iceland.
India	Our Lady of the Assumption.
Iran	Sts. Addai and Mari (August 5). Addai was sent by St. Thomas the Apostle in the second century to cure King Abgar the Black of Mesopotamia of a presumably incurable illness. Addai did so, then went on to convert Abgar and his people to Christianity. Addai sent his own disciple, Mari, to do missionary work along the Tigris. Mari did well, building churches and monasteries and razing pagan temples. Both seem to have died of natural causes, and both did exist, although some details of their lives are presumably legend.
Ireland	**St. Brigid (see page 84).**

St. Columba (see page 84).

St. Patrick (see page 80).

Italy

St. Bernardino of Siena (see page 252).

St. Catherine of Siena (see page 27).

St. Francis of Assisi (see page 32).

Genoa   St. Andrew (see page 93).

Naples   St. Januarius.

Rome   St. Frances of Rome.

St. Philip Neri (May 26). Sixteenth-century Italian priest best known for founding the Confraternity of the Most Holy Trinity, which aided the sick, and his concept for the Congregation of the Oratory, an association of priests whose aim it was to become better religious. A holy man and a generous one, he also experienced ecstasies.

Sicily   St. Lucy (see page 165).

Siena   St. Catherine (see page 27).

Venice   St. Andrew (see page 93).

Japan

St. Francis Xavier (see page 39).

St. Peter Baptist (February 6). Sixteenth-century Franciscan born in Spain, who became a missionary in Mexico and Japan, where he was crucified with 25 other Christians. In 1862 they were all canonized as the Martyrs of Japan.

Korea

Sts. Joseph and Mary (see pages 8 and 2).

Lesotho

Immaculate Heart of Mary.

Lithuania

St. Casimir (March 4). Fifteenth-century Polish nobleman, Casimir resisted marriage, as well as holy orders, to live a life of prayer and good works. He died in Lithuania on a visit and is buried in its capital city, Vilna.

St. Cunegund (March 3). After the death of her husband, Henry II, who was emperor of Germany, Cunegund (978–1033) became a Benedictine nun, caring for the sick.

St. John Cantius (December 23). Born in Kanti, Poland, John (1390–1473) was known for being a scholar of Scripture; he held a chair in theology at Cracow. He devoted time to the poor as well.

Luxembourg

St. Willibrord.

Madagascar

St. Vincent de Paul (see page 121).

Malta

Our Lady of the Assumption.

St. Paul (see page 88).

Mexico

Our Lady of Guadalupe (see page 198).

Monaco

St. Devota (January 17). A Corsican Christian in the fourth century, Devota was martyred by being stretched on a rack. When she died, a white dove was seen hovering over her body. A priest and a nearby boatman placed her remains on a skiff, and it sailed along with the dove across the sea to Monaco, where she is interred.

Moravia

Sts. Cyril and Methodius (see Europe).

Netherlands	St. Plechelm (May 8). An eighth-century native of Ireland or Scotland, he was ordained and, with another priest and a deacon, did missionary work in the Netherlands, concentrating on the lower Meuse Valley. They also built churches. St. Willibrord.
New Zealand	Our Lady Help of Christians.
Nicaragua	St. James the Greater.
North America	**St. Isaac Jogues and companions (see page 186).**
Norway	St. Olaf (July 29). Norseman Olaf Haraldsson (995–1030) started out as a pirate, then was baptized and went to England to help King Ethelred in his battle with the Danes. Back in Norway, after a few more battles, Olaf became king. He tried to unify and Christianize his country but was eventually slain. Afterward miracles were attributed to him, and a chapel was built that became the Cathedral of Trondheim, a pilgrimage site.
Papua New Guinea	**St. Michael the Archangel (see page 256).**
Paraguay	Our Lady of the Assumption.
Peru	**St. Joseph (see page 8).**
Philippines	Sacred Heart of Mary.
Poland	**Our Lady of Czestochowa (see page 203).** St. Casimir (see Lithuania). **St. Florian (see page 256).** St. Hyacinth (September 11). Dominican priest born in Poland, he was sent to evangelize Silesia. He preached in Scandinavia and Lithuania as well, and is said to have performed many miracles. St. John Cantius (see Lithuania). St. Stanislaus of Cracow (April 11). A nobleman, Stanislaus (1030–1079) was born near Cracow, was ordained and became a successful spiritual adviser and reformer. When made bishop of Cracow, he incurred the wrath of King Boleslaus the Bold by denouncing the king's many injustices. When Stanislaus excommunicated the king and stopped saying mass when the king walked into the cathedral, Boleslaus killed him as the saint was saying mass in a small chapel outside the city. St. Stanislaus Kostka.
Portugal	Immaculate Conception. **St. Anthony of Padua (see page 14).** St. Francis Borgia (October 10). Member of the Spanish branch of the sixteenth-century Borgia family, Francis became a member of the court of Charles V. He was married and in 1539, appointed viceroy of Catalonia. He held a number of other important court posts, but when his wife died, leaving him with eight children, he elected to pursue the religious life he said he had always wanted. At age 41 he turned his inheritance over to his son and was ordained. He preached, founded numerous monasteries, and in 1565 was elected father general of the Jesuits. During his seven-year term he expanded the

society greatly, building colleges and revising the society's rules. He is often called their second founder.

St. Vincent of Saragossa (January 22). A fourth-century Spanish martyr, Vincent was educated and ordained by the bishop of Saragossa. Both were arrested during Emperor Maximian's persecution of Christians and imprisoned at Valencia. The bishop was sent into exile, but Vincent was tortured when he refused to sacrifice to pagan gods. He died dying in prison from the effects of those wounds.

Romania	St. Nicetas (June 22). Fourth-century bishop of Remesiana in Dacia, now Romania, he was noted for his missionary activities. He wrote a number of dissertations, and also liturgical songs. He is believed to be the author of the hymn, *Te Deum*.
Russia	**St. Andrew (see page 93).**
	St. Nicholas of Myra (see page 75).
	St. Vladimir I of Kiev (July 15). Illegitimate son (ca. 975–1015) of a grand duke, he spent much of his youth fleeing family problems, being quite cruel, and even killing along the way. Eventually he became ruler of Russia and married. He converted after becoming intrigued by the new (to him) Christianity. The conversion transformed him. He set aside his five former wives and concentrated on the current one, brought in missionaries, built schools and churches, and proved the adage there is no one stronger in faith than a convert. On his deathbed—he was only 35—he gave his possessions to the poor.
Scandinavia	St. Ansgar (see Denmark).
Scotland	**St. Andrew (see page 93).**
	St. Columba (see page 84).
	St. Margaret of Scotland (November 16). Queen to King Malcolm III (and cousin of William of Normandy) in the eleventh century, she was known for her pious life and charitable causes, and for raising eight children. However, unusual for a woman in this position, she was also known for her many works of charity. Bishop Turgot of St. Andrews, Margaret's biographer and confessor, wrote: "Not only would she have given to the poor all that she possessed; but if she could have done so she would have given away her very self. She was poorer than any of her paupers; for they, even when they had nothing, wished to have something; while all her anxiety was to strip herself of all she had."Her husband was crude and illiterate, but he adored her and she was good for him. He helped her in good works; sometimes the two of them would wash the feet of the poor before giving them alms.
Slovakia	Our Lady of Sorrows.
South America	**St. Rose of Lima (see page 256).**
Solomon Islands	Most Holy Name of Mary.
Spain	St. James the Greater.
	St. John of Ávila (May 10). Teresa wasn't the only saint to be produced by this walled city. John (1499–1569), born in New Castile to wealthy parents, was educated

accordingly—he studied law and philosophy and eventually was ordained. He served as a missionary in Andalusia and was popular as a preacher. Imprisoned by the Inquisition, his harsh treatment was due to sermons on the rich not reaching heaven. Upon his eventually release, he became even more popular, preached throughout Spain, and was a spiritual adviser to St. Teresa of Ávila—not to mention St. John of the Cross and St. Peter of Alcántara.

St. Teresa of Ávila (see page 97).

Catalonia   **St. Andrew (see page 93)**

Madrid   **St. Isidore the Farmer (see page 255).**

Seville   St. Ferdinand III of Castille.

Sts. Justa and Rufina (July 19). Two sisters who were potters in Seville in the third century during the Emperor Diocletian's persecution of Christians. They refused to sell their pottery for use in pagan rites, so their stock was destroyed. In retaliation they tore down the image of a pagan goddess. Retribution from the persecution squad followed, they were tortured and executed. Justa died on the rack; Rufina was strangled.

Sri Lanka	**St. Lawrence (see page 251).**
Sweden	St. Ansgar (see Scandinavia).

St. Bridget (July 23). A fourteenth-century mystic from a noble family and an important religious figure of the late Middle Ages. As a widow with eight children she founded the Brigittines, a religious order of both women and men, living in separate monasteries at Vadstena, which became the intellectual center of Sweden in the fifteenth century. Bridget (also known as Birgitta) worked in Rome for the return of the papacy from Avignon, and wrote *Revelations*, recording her temporal and spiritual lives. Her daughter was St. Katherine of Sweden.

St. Eric. Twelfth-century king of Sweden who is credited with supporting the spread of Christianity in that nation. He was killed by warring Swedish nobles in cahoots with Danish invaders. Though the traditional patron saint of Sweden, he was never formally canonized.

Switzerland	St. Gall.
Tanzania	**Immaculate Conception (see page 2).**
United States	**Immaculate Conception (see page 2).**
Uruguay	**Blessed Virgin Mary (see page 2).**
Venezuela	Our Lady of Coromoto.
Wales	**St. David (see page 259).**
West Indies	St. Gertrude the Great (November 10). For reasons unknown, when Gertrude was five years old she was left with nuns at a monastery at Helfta in Saxony. She was to spend her life (1252–1302) within those walls, being professed as a nun. She experienced visions and revelations, recording them in a book, *The Herald of Divine Love*, combining theology and mysticism. Although often in poor health, Gertrude rose to become her community's spiritual director.

Glossary

Abbess. Leader of a group of nuns in a convent. An *abbot* is head of a male monastic community.

Antioch. Until the rise of Constantinople, the third most important city in the Roman Empire, after Rome and Alexandria. It was situated on the Orontes River in Syria.

Antipope. Individual who says he is the pope, but whose claim is rejected by the church. Over the centuries just what constitutes an invalid claim has fluctuated. The third century's Hippolytus, for example, is considered the first antipope; yet he has been canonized. The last antipope was Felix V in the fifteenth century.

Apostle. In the context of Christianity, an individual or a group of people sent out by God to spread a message. A *disciple* is one who believes in, follows, and may even imitate a master. One can be both; the twelve Apostles were.

Apparition. The inexplicable appearance of a being, usually someone who is deceased.

Aramaic. Semitic language somewhat like Hebrew. A form of Aramaic is likely to have been the language of Jesus.

Archangel. Angel of the highest order. In the New Testament, they were named: Michael, Gabriel, Raphael.

Archdiocese. Term for a principal diocese composed of a regional group of dioceses known as a province. It is centered in the city that is of greatest importance—the Archdiocese of New York, for example, is headquartered in New York City—and is headed by an archbishop or a cardinal.

Arianism. Fourth-century movement, declared heresy by the church, that denies the divinity of Christ by saying that if both the Father and the Son are "unbegotten," then there must be two individual Gods. Arius, the priest who brought up the whole matter, held that therefore there was only one God unbegotten, and that was the Father, and He created the Son.

Ascetics. Those who strive to become more virtuous, while practicing extreme self-control and austerity.

Asia Minor. Land roughly equal to today's Turkey. Site of such early Christian communities as Smyrna and Ephesus.

Avignon. City in southeastern France that was the seat of the papacy from 1309 to 1377 and of rival popes during the Great Schism, 1378–1417. Pope Clement V started it all by moving the papal court to Avignon because of dangerous political and religious situations in both Italy and France.

Basilica. Certain type of church of historical significance, designated for specific ceremonies. There are *minor basilicas*, which are churches of particular artistic or historic relevance designated as such by the pope, and *major basilicas,* which are principal churches in Rome: for example, St. Peter's, St. John Latern, St. Paul's Outside the Walls, and St. Mary Major.

Beatification. The second step in the process of proclaiming a holy man or woman a saint. It follows the first step, in which the Congregation for the Causes of Saints in Rome has accepted all the documents pertaining to a candidate and has declared him or her "Venerable."

Bishopric. The office of bishop, or the diocese of a bishop.

Byzantine rite. May also be called the "Greek rite," a liturgical system of the Orthodox and Byzantine churches. Called Byzantine because it originated in Orthodox Constantinople (Byzantium, now Istanbul).

Calvinism. Religious orientation within Protestantism that originated with the reformer and theologian John Calvin in the sixteenth century.

Canon. Title referring to a diocesan priest who is attached to a cathedral, and to a member of certain religious orders.

Canonization. The procedure by the church leading to declaring a particular man or woman a saint and worthy of being venerated by the public.

Cathedral. Church where a bishop, archbishop, or cardinal presides; seat of that particular see. Usually but not always the most prominent religious edifice of that faith in a particular geographic area.

Chapel. Place of worship with a separate altar that can be in a cathedral, or, for that matter, any institution or, for the very wealthy, a private home.

Chaplain. A priest who counsels and sees to the spiritual welfare of a particular group: the U.S. armed forces, for example.

College of Cardinals. Body of all who hold the rank of cardinal in the church, meeting as a unit to discuss and/or vote in an election, such as for a pope. A cardinal must be under eighty years of age to participate in a papal election. Europe has the most members of the College of Cardinals—81 cardinals out of a total of 154.

Conclave. The meeting of cardinals held to elect a pope.

Concupiscence. Strong desire, especially sexual desire.

Confessor. In early Christianity, term for those who suffered for their faith but were not martyred.

Contemplative. Way of life characterized by solitude and prayer, practiced by some nuns and monks.

Convent. A congregation of a number of nuns; can also apply to the building in which they live.

Council of Trent. Meeting from 1545 to 1563 that was a Roman Catholic attempt to reform the church. Became known as the Counter-Reformation as the council issued decrees in opposition to what had become Protestantism.

Counter-Reformation. Some say this was a Roman Catholic response to the Protestant Reformation; others call it an intellectual and spiritual renewal at that time. Took place in the late fifteenth and early sixteenth centuries.

Crèche. Name for a manger, or Nativity, scene, displayed in churches and other places during the Christmas season. Instituted by St. Francis of Assisi in the thirteenth century, using live animals.

Crypt. Underground area or vault beneath the main area of a church. In the early days of Christianity, it was used for worship and as a burial place.

Cult. In the context of saints, a group of people in the early days of the church who strongly supported a particular saint.

Curia. Papal or diocesan governing agency. Common usage: Roman curia, which comprises the bureaucracy that assists the pope in his work.

Dauphin. The oldest son of a legitamate French king.

Diocese. District composed of several parishes, under the supervision of a bishop.

Discalced. Unshod, although sometimes wearing sandals. Used in reference to religious orders, some of whose members are discalced, others calced.

Disciple. A pupil who learns from, and even imitates, a master. Those who listened to and believed Jesus were disciples. Sometimes used interchangeably with apostle, but there are differences. See *Apostle*.

Doctors of the Church. Thirty-three saints—30 men and 3 women—who have been recognized by the church as pre-eminent theologians, those the faithful can learn from. A list of Doctors of the Church can be found in Appendix B.

Druids. Ancient Celtic priests, appearing in Irish literature and history as magicians.

Dualism. Doctrine stating that the universe is under the dominion of two opposing principles: one is good, the other evil.

Ecstasy. The suspension of all sensory reactions while in union with the divine. Some saints were said to have experienced this state of rapturous delight.

Ecumenical councils. Meeting of representatives from the church to discuss all manner of religious affairs. The most recent ecumenical council was Vatican Council II, held from 1962 to 1965, with the bishops of the world gathering at St. Peter's Basilica.

Evangelist. From the Greek meaning "proclaimer of good news." Evangelists disseminate the gospel and often try to convert others to Christianity.

Flagellation. The scourging, or beating, of another or oneself. The latter was seen in the Middle Ages as atonement for sins.

Friar. Title of those who belonged to the mendicant orders (combining monastery life with outside religious activity) in thirteenth-century Europe. Some major orders were the Dominicans, Franciscans, and Augustinians.

Gospel. Comes from the old English "godspel" meaning "good news." The four Gospels of the New Testament—by Matthew, Mark, Luke, and John—were derived from oral and written tradition about Christ's life, Passion, death, and Resurrection.

Gregorian Chant. Plainsong named after the seventh-century pope and saint Gregory the Great but not composed by him. Gregorian chant has no musical accompaniment.

Hagiography. Biography of saints.

Halo. Ring or circle of light around the head of a holy person in an artistic depiction. The Greeks and Romans used halos to depict association with the gods. Early Christians took up the practice, with the halo meaning light and used for Jesus. Around the fifth century, the halo's use in art extended to his mother, Mary, and to the angels and saints.

Hermitage. Habitat of a hermit.

Hyperdulia. Special reverence rendered to Mary, distinct from "worship" and veneration accorded to God and the other saints.

Jansenists. Believed God was a severe taskmaster and claimed believers were unworthy of frequently receiving the sacraments. They had a generally dark outlook on life and were pessimistic about salvation.

Marian devotion. Veneration of Mary, mother of Jesus, in the form of various special prayers, processions, and celebrations.

Martyr. A person who gives up his or her life for the faith.

Martyrology. A listing of saints' feast days that gives all of the saints' names for any given date. A martyrology also gives some biographical data about each saint.

Middle Ages. Historical period between the fifth-century fall of the Roman Empire and the beginning of the modern world, which some put at the end of the fifteenth century, others at the beginning of the twelfth.

Miracle. An extraordinary happening showing divine intervention in human affairs.

Monastery. Dwelling place of monks, sometimes used for nuns as well in early days of Christianity.

Monk. Member of a religious community who has taken vows to follow a monastic way of life.

Mortification. Deprivation of what is necessary for life, such as food or sleep, as well as illicit and even licit pleasures, all with the purpose of drawing closer to God.

Mysticism. The belief that personal communication, or union, with God is achieved through intuition, faith, or a sudden insight, rather than through rational thought or reasoning.

Novena. Series of prayers having a specific purpose and spread over nine days or once a week for nine weeks, or sometimes ongoing.

Novice. Person in the probationary stage of being fully admitted to a religious order.

Nuncio. Papal delegate of the highest rank, accredited to a civil government.

Oblates. Laypersons who choose to live in religious communities and do not take vows but live under modified regulations.

Order. Religious community of men or women who live according to a specific rule or rules laid out for that life.

Papal bull. A document of importance from the pope stamped with a lead seal.

Parish. A community of Christian faithful within geographically defined lines. A group of contiguous parishes constitutes a diocese, overseen by a bishop.

Pentecost. Comes from the Greek for "the fiftieth day," and is the liturgical feast held 50 days after Easter, commemorating the point from which the apostles began to carry the message of Christ to the world. Less commonly known as Whitsunday.

Pharisees. Jewish sect at the time of Jesus that extended Hebrew law for priests and the temple to all believers. Pharisees are often criticized in the New Testament for being hostile to Jesus, but there were some who were favorable to him.

Plaster saint. Person without human feelings or failings.

Pilgrimage is a journey to a shrine or other place of faith taken by a devotee.

Prior. The second in command in a monastery, just below the abbot; can also be the head of a priory, which is a subordinate unit of a monastery.

Prioress. A nun corresponding in rank to a prior.

Purgatory. A temporary state after death where souls go to be cleansed of past sins before becoming worthy to enter heaven.

Reformation, the. Religious and political event in the sixteenth century that split the Western Christian Church into Catholic and Protestant. Many factors contributed to the split, among them Martin Luther and his 95 theses in 1517, and King Henry VIII wanting to remarry after divorcing Catherine of Aragon, breaking with Rome, and declaring himself head of the Church of England.

Relics. Remains of the bodies of canonized saints and those on the road to canonization, but also used to refer to items that have touched those body parts.

Renaissance. Period of 1350–1550, bringing rebirth in the arts, most commonly used in reference to events in Italy.

Saints. Those recognized by the church for particular holiness and who now share in the presence of God and may be venerated by the public. However, any person who leads a good life may be presumed to go on to eternal life, and there are far more of them than there are of recognized saints. There is no particular model for sainthood. The word comes from the Latin *sanctus,* which means "holy." St. Paul of Tarsus first used the word to mean all of the Christian faithful.

See. The chair of a bishop. Symbolizes his presiding over a group of parishes within a particular geographic area. *See* comes from the Latin meaning "seat."

Seminary. The program for training men for the priesthood, as well as the building where that education is conducted.

Shrine. Several definitions: a pilgrimage destination—Lourdes, for example—where there may be several buildings, but the main focus is a cult figure, such as a saint (in the case of Lourdes, it is the Blessed Mother); also a church with a special artifact that people visit for purposes of veneration, or a separate building close to a church that contains a statue or other item of devotion.

Sisters of Charity. An umbrella term for nuns who engage in works of charity.

Stigmata. Appearance on a person of the wounds suffered by Christ on the cross: on the hands, feet, and side. Sometimes they can be seen by others, as with St. Francis of Assisi, sometimes not, as with St. Catherine of Siena. Occasionally the wounds vary in location and number of times they appear. Hundreds of instances of the appearance of stigmata have occurred over the years, but the church has recognized very few as authentic and does not offer an explanation for their origin.

Synoptic Gospels. Gospels of Matthew, Mark, and Luke, which have many similarities. The Gospel of John was written much later and has a style of its own. Still, the four hold to an overriding pattern of the gospel message.

Tertiary. A member of the Third Order, which is an association of lay men or women who follow the rules of a religious community, but usually without the vows, and continue to live secular (worldly) lives. Tertiaries were formalized by St. Francis of Assisi.

Venerate. How the faithful are to pay homage to the saints. *Worship* and *adore* are reserved for God.

Vicar. One who has the authority to act in the place of another, authority that comes with the nature of that office, not delegated to that individual. For example, the pope has been called the vicar of Christ on earth.

A

Adversum Helvidium (Jerome), 174
Agnes, Saint, 164–165
AIDS, 102
Albert the Great, Saint (Albertus Magnus), 109
All Saints Day, 168–169
Alphonsus Liguori, Saint, 186–188
Ambrose, Saint, 20–21
André, Saint, 197
Andrew, Saint, 93
animals, blessing of, 36
Anne, Saint, 12–13
    basilica of, 197–198
Anthony of Egypt, Saint, xiii
Anthony of Padua, Saint, 14–17
apostle, 29
apparition, defined, 6. *See also* Mary, Mother of Jesus
arianism, 76
ascetics, 167
Asia Minor, 76
Augustine of Canterbury, Saint, 177, 180
Augustine of Hippo, Saint, 18–26
Auriesville, New York, 186, 198

B

Baltimore, Maryland, 192
baptism, 66–67
Barnabas, Saint, 160
basilica, 190–191
Basilica of Saint Francis, 38
Basilique Ste-Anne-de-Beaupré, 197–198
Belleville, Illinois, 192
Benedict, Saint, xiii
Bernadette of Lourdes, Saint, 200–201
Bernanos, George, quoted, 4

Bible, Saint Jerome's translation of, 174, 175
bishops, 96
Bl (Blessed), xviii
Boniface Dryda, Sister, 150
Book of Kells, 47
Book of Saints, A (Gordon), 69
Brébeuf, John de, 186
Brendan of Clonfert, Saint, 84
Bridget of Sweden, Saint, xiii
Brigid of Kildare, Saint, 84
Brooks, Phillips, quoted, 196
Brown, Thomas, quoted, 170
Bury, J.B., 85

C

Cahill, Thomas, 47
Caldey Island, 167
California missions, 151
Calvinism, 183
Camillus de Lellis, Saint, xv
canonization, 171, 208–231
Canterbury, England, 179–180
"Canticle of the Sun" (Saint Francis), 37
Carmelite order, 64–65, 198–199
Cathedral of Saint Augustine, 191
Catherine of Siena, Saint, xv, 27–31, 95, 97
Cauchon, Bishop Pierre, 61
Chabanel, Noël, 186
Charles Borromeo, Saint, xiv
Charles VII, King of France, 60–61
Chaucer, Geoffrey, 179
Christmas, 36, 77–78
Church of Saint Enda, 85
Cistercian monks, 167
Clare, Saint, 35
College of Cardinals, 30
Columba of Iona, Saint, 84

concupiscence, 23
Confessions of Saint Augustine, The (Augustine of Hippo), 24
confessors, 166, 169
Copts, 45
Council of Trent, 175
crèche, 36
Croagh Patrick (mountain), 199–200
cults, 170
Cyprian, Saint, 162–163
Czestochowa, Poland, 203–204

D

Damien of Molokai, Saint, 145–149
Daniel, Anthony, 186
Darien, Illinois, 194
Daughters of Charity, 123–124
Dialogue, The (Catherine of Siena), 31
Diana, Princess of Wales, 104
Diary of a Soul, The (Thérèse of Lisieux), 104
Di Boudricourt, Robert, 59
Diego, Juan, 198–199
Discalced Carmelites, 99, 101
disciple, 29
Doctor(s) of the Church, xii
    list of, 246
Donne, John, quoted, 118, 146, 193
Dorothy, Saint, 164
Dostoyevsky, Fyodor, quoted, 161
Doylestown, Pennsylvania, 204
Drexel University, 141
Drinking from the Sacred Well (Matthews), 80–81
dualism, 20
Du Pithon, John Berard, 214

E

ecstasy, xvii
Elizabeth Ann Seton, Saint, xiii, 126–131
  shrine to, 192–193
Elizabeth of Hungary, Saint, 181–182
Emmitsburg, Maryland, 192–193
Erasmus, 114
Eustochium, Saint, 174

F

Farmer, William R., 44
Fatima, Portugal, 6, 201–202
Felicitas, Saint, 160, 161–162
Filicchi, Antonio, 128
Frances Xavier Cabrini, Saint, 132, 135–137, 144
  shrine to, 195–196
Francis Borgia, Saint, 52
Franciscans, 16–17
Francis de Sales, Saint, 11, 182–184
Francis of Assisi, Saint, xiv, xv, 32–38
Francis Xavier, Saint, xiv, 39–42
Francis Xavier Seelos, Saint, 134
Franco, Francisco, 101
funerals, 158
FutureChurch, 74

G

Gabriel (archangel), 3
Gajowniczek, Francis, 195
Garnier, Charles, 186
gift giving, 78–79
Golden, Colorado, 195–196
Goodman, Ellen, 179
Gordon, Anne, 69
Gospels, 43–44

grandparents' garden, 12–13
Gregory I, Saint (the Great), 177
Gregory IX, 53
Gregory XI, 30
Gregory XIII, 101
Grotto of Lourdes, 193
Guadalupe, 198–199

H

hagiography, xiv
halo, xvii
Henry, O., quoted, 164
Henry II, King of England, 179–180
Henry VIII, King of England, 112, 113, 115
hermitage, 167
Hildegard of Bingen, Saint, xvii, 178–179
How the Irish Saved Civilization (Cahill), 47
Hyde, Charles McEwen, 148
hyperdulia, 7

I

Ignatius of Loyola, Saint, xiii, xv, 49–55
Inquisition, 53
Institute of the Missionary Sisters of the Sacred Heart, 135
intercession, xi
International Bible Commentary (Farmer), 44
Internet, patron saint of, xi–xii
Introduction to the Devout Life (Francis de Sales), 184
Ireland, 80–81, 84, 87
Irish toast, 87
Isaac Jogues, Saint, xiv, 185–186
Isidor of Seville, Saint, xii

J

Jansenists, 187
Japan, 40–41, 42
Jasna Gora shrine, 203–204
Jeanne de Chantal, Saint, 184
Jerome, Saint, xiv, 173–176
Jesuits. See Society of Jesus
Joachim, Saint, 12–13, 167
Joan of Arc, Saint, xiv, 56–62
John, Saint, 47–48
John Bosco, Saint, xiv
John Fisher, Saint, 116
John Nepomucene Neumann, Saint, 132–134
John of the Cross, Saint, xiii, xvii, 63–65, 100, 101
John Paul II, 208, 209, 210
John the Baptist, Saint, 66–67
John XXIII, 109
  quoted, 142, 168
Joseph, Saint, 8–11
Josepha Sancho de Buerra, Saint, 144
Josephine Bakhita, Saint, 144
Joseph of Arimathea, Saint, 73
Jude, Saint, 68–71
  shrine to, 192
Junipero Serra, Bl., 150–152, 191
Jutta, Bl., 178

K

Kateri Tekakwitha, Bl., 153, 211
  shrines to, 198
Katharine Drexel, Saint, 139–144
Kevin of Glendalough, Saint, 84
Knights of Mary Immaculate, 195
Knock, Ireland, 199–200

L

Lake Zurich, Illinois, 194

Lalemant, Gabriel, 186
Lande, Jean de la, 186
Latin mass, 194
laypeople, as saints, 211, 213–214
Leo XIII, 141
leprosy, 146, 149
Lewis, C. S., quoted, xi
Libertyville, Illinois, 194
*Life of Saint Patrick and His
    Place in History, The* (Bury), 85
lost objects, 14–16
Louise de Marillac, Saint, 123–124
Lourdes, France, 200
Lucy, Saint, 165
Ludwig IV, King of Thuringa,
    181–182
Luke, Saint, 46–47, 89

M

"Magnificat," 3
Marian, 5
Mark, Saint, 45
Martin, Leonie, 105–106
Martin, Zélie, 103, 105
Marto, Francesco, 201–202
Marto, Jacinta, 201–202
martyrology, 159
martyrs, 156–165, 168–169, 186
Mary, Mother of Jesus, 2–7
    apparitions of, 6–7, 198–202,
        204–205
    church doctrine about, 5
Maryland, 129, 134, 172, 192–193
Mary Magdalene, Saint, 72–74,
    94–95
Mary McKillop, Saint, 209
Matthew, Saint, 44
Matthews, John, 80–81
Maximilian Kolbe, Saint, 195
    shrine to, 194
Medjugorje, Herzegovina, 204–205

Middle Ages, 170
miracles, required for sainthood,
    212
Missionary Sisters of the Sacred
    Heart of Jesus, 196
Mission Dolores, 191
Mission of Nombre de Diós, 193
Monica, Saint, 19, 20, 22, 25
Montreal, Quebec, 196
Morand, Saint, xiv
mysticism, xvii

N

National Shrine of Our Lady of
    the Snows, 192
National Shrine of Saint Elizabeth
    Ann Seton, 192–193
National Shrine of Saint Thérèse,
    194
National Shrine of the
    Immaculate Conception,
    191–192
Newman, John Henry, 133
Nicholas of Myra, Saint, 75–79
novena, 71
novice, 16
nuncio, 40

O

Order of the Visitation, 184
Our Lady of Czestochowa
    shrines, 203–204
Our Lady of Guadalupe, 198–199

P

Padre Pio, xvii–xviii
papal bull, 213
Patmore, Coventry, quoted, 171
Patrick, Saint, 80–87
    pilgrimage to statue of, 199–200

patron saint, 171–172
Paula, Saint, 174, 175
Paul III, 54
Paul of Tarsus, Saint, x, xv, 88–91
Pentecost, 46
Perpetua, Saint, 160–162
Peter, Saint, 89, 92–96
    basilica of, 203
Peter Canisius, Saint, 52
Peter Favre, Bl., 52
pilgrimage, 190
Pius V Traditional Roman
    Catholic Shrine, 194
plaster saint, xiii
Polycarp, Saint, 159
Portolá, Gaspar de, 151
postulator of the faith, 210
prayer(s)
    of Saint Anthony, 15
    to Saint Joseph, 9
    of Saint Frances Xavier Cabrini,
        136
    of Saint Ignatius of Loyola, 55
    to Saint Jude, 70
    of Saint Thomas Aquinas, 110
promoter of the faith, 210
Protestant Reformation, 182,
    183–184
Purgatory, 98

Q

Quebec City, Canada, 197–198
Quicherat, Jules, 62

R

Raymond of Capua, Bl, 28
Redeptorist order, 187, 188
Reformation, 182, 183–184
relics, 170, 171
René Goupil, Saint, 185, 186

Rome, Italy, 203
Rose Philippine Duchesne, Saint, 132, 138

S

Sacred Heart Basilica, 191
Saint Augustine (Wills), 25
saints
    canonization of, 171, 208–231
defined, x, xi
    feast days of, 247–250
    in historical context, 239–245
    listed by occupation, 251–263
    of nations, cities, regions, 264–271
    relevance of, today, x–xi
    veneration of, 166–172, 209
    who worked together, 176
Santa Claus, 77–78
Santayana, George, quoted, xiii
Santos, Lucia dos, 201–202
Scivias (Know the Way) (Hildegard of Bingen), 179
Sebastian, Saint, 163–164
"see," 162
Sepphoris, 10
Seton, Anna Maria, 127, 128, 130–131
Seton Hall University, 131
Shakespeare, William, quoted, 120
shrine(s)
    in Canada, 196–198
    defined, 190
    in Europe, 199–205
    in Mexico, 198–199
    in United States, 191–196
Simeon Stylites, Saint, xiv, 176–177
Sisters of Charity of Saint Joseph, 129–130
Sisters of the Blessed Sacrament, 141–142

Sixtus V, 208
Society of Jesus, 40, 50, 54
    colleges of, 54
Sontag, Susan, quoted, 147
Spiritual Exercises (Ignatius of Loyola), 51–53, 55
Saint Anthony's bread, 17
Saint Anthony Messenger, 16
Saint Augustine, Florida, 26, 193
Saint Joseph's Oratory, 196
Saint Peter's Basilica, 203
Saint Vincent De Paul Society, 121, 123
statues, burying of, 11
Stephanopoulos, George, quoted, 20
Stephen, Saint, 157
Stevenson, Robert Louis, 148
stigmata, xvii–xviii
Stritch, Cardinal Samuel, quoted, 137
Summa Theologica (Thomas Aquinas), 108–109, 111
synoptic Gospels, 48

T

tekton, 10
Teresa of Ávila, Saint, xiii, xiv, xvi, 9, 11, 64, 97–102
Teresa of Calcutta, Mother, 104, 210
tertiary, 28
Theodore Guerin, Bl., 154
Theologia Moralis (Alphonsus Liguori), 187
Theophilus, 164
Thérèse of Lisieux, Saint, xv, 103–106
    quoted, 45
    shrine to, 194
Thomas, Danny, 69

Thomas à Becket, Saint, 179–181
Thomas Aquinas, Saint, xiv, 107–111
Thomas More, Saint, xvii, 112–117
Tolton, Augustus, 143
Toussaint, Pierre, 211, 214
Tugwell, Simon, quoted, xvi

U

Ulrich of Augsburg, Saint, 170
Urban VI, 30
Utopia (More), 114

V

Valentine, Saint, 118–120
Vandals, 82
Vatican Council II, xi, 109
Venerable Bede, xv
veneration, 166–172, 209
Vincent De Paul, Saint, xiv, xv, 121–124
virgins, 166–167
Vulgate Bible, 175

W

Washington, D.C., 191–192
Wills, Gary, 25
Woodward, Kenneth L., 133

X

Xavier University, 142, 143

We Have EVERYTHING!

Everything® **After College Book**
$12.95, 1-55850-847-3

Everything® **American History Book**
$12.95, 1-58062-531-2

Everything® **Angels Book**
$12.95, 1-58062-398-0

Everything® **Anti-Aging Book**
$12.95, 1-58062-565-7

Everything® **Astrology Book**
$12.95, 1-58062-062-0

Everything® **Baby Names Book**
$12.95, 1-55850-655-1

Everything® **Baby Shower Book**
$12.95, 1-58062-305-0

Everything® **Baby's First Food Book**
$12.95, 1-58062-512-6

Everything® **Baby's First Year Book**
$12.95, 1-58062-581-9

Everything® **Barbeque Cookbook**
$12.95, 1-58062-316-6

Everything® **Bartender's Book**
$9.95, 1-55850-536-9

Everything® **Bedtime Story Book**
$12.95, 1-58062-147-3

Everything® **Bicycle Book**
$12.00, 1-55850-706-X

Everything® **Build Your Own Home Page**
$12.95, 1-58062-339-5

Everything® **Business Planning Book**
$12.95, 1-58062-491-X

Everything® **Casino Gambling Book**
$12.95, 1-55850-762-0

Everything® **Cat Book**
$12.95, 1-55850-710-8

Everything® **Chocolate Cookbook**
$12.95, 1-58062-405-7

Everything® **Christmas Book**
$15.00, 1-55850-697-7

Everything® **Civil War Book**
$12.95, 1-58062-366-2

Everything® **College Survival Book**
$12.95, 1-55850-720-5

Everything® **Computer Book**
$12.95, 1-58062-401-4

Everything® **Cookbook**
$14.95, 1-58062-400-6

Everything® **Cover Letter Book**
$12.95, 1-58062-312-3

Everything® **Crossword and Puzzle Book**
$12.95, 1-55850-764-7

Everything® **Dating Book**
$12.95, 1-58062-185-6

Everything® **Dessert Book**
$12.95, 1-55850-717-5

Everything® **Digital Photography Book**
$12.95, 1-58062-574-6

Everything® **Dog Book**
$12.95, 1-58062-144-9

Everything® **Dreams Book**
$12.95, 1-55850-806-6

Everything® **Etiquette Book**
$12.95, 1-55850-807-4

Everything® **Fairy Tales Book**
$12.95, 1-58062-546-0

Everything® **Family Tree Book**
$12.95, 1-55850-763-9

Everything® **Fly-Fishing Book**
$12.95, 1-58062-148-1

Everything® **Games Book**
$12.95, 1-55850-643-8

Everything® **Get-A-Job Book**
$12.95, 1-58062-223-2

Everything® **Get Published Book**
$12.95, 1-58062-315-8

Everything® **Get Ready for Baby Book**
$12.95, 1-55850-844-9

Everything® **Ghost Book**
$12.95, 1-58062-533-9

Everything® **Golf Book**
$12.95, 1-55850-814-7

Everything® **Grammar and Style Book**
$12.95, 1-58062-573-8

Everything® **Guide to Las Vegas**
$12.95, 1-58062-438-3

Everything® **Guide to New York City**
$12.95, 1-58062-314-X

Everything® **Guide to Walt Disney World®, Universal Studios®, and Greater Orlando, 2nd Edition**
$12.95, 1-58062-404-9

Everything® **Guide to Washington, D.C.**
$12.95, 1-58062-313-1

Everything® **Guitar Book**
$12.95, 1-58062-555-X

Everything® **Herbal Remedies Book**
$12.95, 1-58062-331-X

Everything® **Home-Based Business Book**
$12.95, 1-58062-364-6

Everything® **Homebuying Book**
$12.95, 1-58062-074-4

Everything® **Homeselling Book**
$12.95, 1-58062-304-2

**For more information, or to order, call 800-872-5627
or visit everything.com**

Adams Media Corporation, 57 Littlefield Street, Avon, MA 02322